THE ELECTION OF 1996

THE ELECTION OF 1996
Reports and Interpretations

GERALD M. POMPER

WALTER DEAN BURNHAM

ANTHONY CORRADO

MARJORIE RANDON HERSHEY

MARION R. JUST

SCOTT KEETER

WILSON CAREY MCWILLIAMS

WILLIAM G. MAYER

Chatham House Publishers, Inc.
Chatham, New Jersey

THE ELECTION OF 1996
Reports and Interpretations

Chatham House Publishers, Inc. / Post Office Box One / Chatham,
   New Jersey 07928

Publisher: Edward Artinian
Production editor: Katharine Miller
Jacket and cover design: Lawrence Ratzkin
Composition: Bang, Motley, Olufsen
Printing and binding: R.R. Donnelley and Sons Company

LIBRARY OF CONGRESS CATALOGING-IN-PUBLICATION DATA

The election of 1996 : reports and interpretations / Gerald M. Pomper
   ... [et al.].
         p. cm.
      Includes bibliographical references and index.
      ISBN 1-56643-056-9. — ISBN 1-56643-055-0 (pbk.)
      1. Presidents—United States—Election—1996. 2. United States.
   Congress—Elections, 1996. 3. Elections—United States.
   I. Pomper, Gerald M.
   JK526   1996b
   324.973'0929—dc21   97-4618
                                                           CIP

Manufactured in the United States of America
10 9 8 7 6 5 4 3 2 1

Contents

Figures and Tables

Figures

Tables

Preface and Acknowledgments

The Election of 1996 is the sixth volume in a series on U.S. elections since 1976. In this lengthening perspective, the latest national contest seemingly combined experiences of the past two decades. As in 1976, a southern Democrat was elected president amid concerns over campaign financing. As in 1980, Republicans scored well in congressional races. As in 1984, the incumbent president was returned to office in a time of prosperity and good feeling. As in 1988, the quality of the nation's decisions was diminished by advertising and reporting in the mass media. And, as in 1992, William Jefferson Clinton won the White House.

Yet, change is also evident. The 1996 election evokes speculation about the future of American politics as well as reminiscence about its past. The nomination process now strongly advantages candidates of wide reputation and deep pockets, dispatching dark horses to history books. The gender gap, differences in preferences between women and men, now emulates established divisions of class, race, and region. Candidates and parties have found new ways to spend vastly larger funds. Novel political coalitions have appeared, even as a Democratic president has won reelection for the first time in half a century, and Republicans have held control of Congress for the first time in over six decades. The nation seeks a new public philosophy as it realizes the frailties of both governmental liberalism and free-market conservatism.

America is always a history in the making, its politics an enduring parable. At this writing, we find it difficult to define the deeper significance of the election of 1996. In our analyses, we can more easily understand what did *not* happen: the government did not shut down permanently, President Clinton and most incumbent legislators were not defeated, the course of public policy was not shifted in revolutionary directions. But, despite our presumed expertise, we frankly have only a dim view of what *will* happen in the coming years. Perhaps that is the most appropriate stance as we approach the end of the decade, century, and millennium.

The contributors to this book are:

WALTER DEAN BURNHAM, Frank C. Erwin Jr. Centennial Professor at the University of Texas at Austin and author of *Critical Elections*

ANTHONY CORRADO, Associate Professor at Colby College and author of *Paying for Presidents*

MARJORIE RANDON HERSHEY, Professor at Indiana University and author of *Running for Office*

MARION R. JUST, Professor at Wellesley College and co-author of *Crosstalk: Citizens, Candidates and the Media in a Presidential Campaign*

SCOTT KEETER, Professor and Chair of the Department of Political Science and Public Administration at Virginia Commonwealth University and co-author of *What Americans Know about Politics and Why It Matters*

WILSON CAREY MCWILLIAMS, Professor at Rutgers University and author of *The Politics of Disappointment*

WILLIAM G. MAYER, Assistant Professor at Northeastern University and author of *In Pursuit of the White House*

GERALD M. POMPER, Board of Governors Professor at Rutgers University and author of *Passions and Interests*

Inevitably, we have relied on many friends and colleagues to help our work. The individual authors acknowledge particular persons in their chapters. For all of us, Kathleen Frankovic, Director of Surveys, has been especially helpful in providing access and analyses of the excellent CBS News poll. Ross K. Baker, a former contributor to this series, continues to provide sound judgment and good humor. Chatham House, now a major publisher, still provides the warmth and individual attention of devoted booklovers; we appreciate the care of Edward Artinian, Irene Glynn, and Katharine Miller. I am personally thankful to Larry and Sherry Delsen for their hospitality at the Republican convention; to Ken Dautrich, Kim Downing, John Hart, Stanley Kelley, Andrea Lubin, Sandy Maisel, and Maureen Moakley for professional advice; and to Joanne Pfeiffer for secretarial assistance. I am even more grateful to my family, especially for the wonder of two future voters, Aidan and Jacob Pomper.

As we travel toward the future, we are particularly thankful to those who share the journey, our spouses and lovers. We dedicate this book to them, specifically Tish Burnham, Howard V. Hershey, Rosemary Jann, Hal Just, Susan Kenney, Amy Logan, Nancy Riley McWilliams, and Marlene Pomper.

— Gerald M. Pomper

INTRODUCTION

Bill Clinton: Riding the Tiger

W ALTER D EAN B URNHAM

All other doubts, by time let them be clear'd,
Fortune brings in some boats that are not stear'd.
— *Cymbeline* (IV, iii)

The Triumph of Luck, Skill, and Adaptability

When considering candidates among his generals for promotion to the supreme rank of marshal, Napoleon was thoroughly briefed about their abilities in the field. But then he asked the decisive question: "Yes, yes, but is he lucky?" And he would appoint no one, however distinguished his credentials, if he was not. In social science we tend to transmute the term into the concept of contingency, perhaps in the hope of taming its always lively potential for disorder. Contingency is a more systemic term, luck a more personal one: a "wild card," perhaps, in any analytic scheme. This chapter seeks to put in a good word for luck as at least a descriptive reality, and to view Bill Clinton accordingly.

This introduction should by no means be thought to deprecate or underestimate Clinton's skills, determination, and on-the-job achievements as president. But something we sometimes also call "destiny" does take a hand in politics—not least in the shaping of opportunities for and constraints on presidential ambitions to make a mark on American politics. Thus, Bill Clinton's first election required the opening of a huge power deflation affecting the Republican incumbent, George Bush; candidates of Bush's party had largely dominated presidential elections for the preceding generation. Beyond such elemental strikes of fortune comes the question of what happens after a given individual takes the oath of office. Quite apart from his own gifts and professional ambitions, the moment in political time when he takes the oath is crucial in defining the opportunity available to an incoming president for action and for achieving "greatness" in office. Both Theodore Roosevelt and John F. Kennedy were keenly aware of the limitations imposed upon them by the times in which they lived. Each of them, TR in particular, chafed at not having a context in which he could be as big as he might be under better circumstances. This is hardly surprising. Presidents may be routinely order disrupters, as Stephen Skowronek has claimed.[1] But the presidency as an office thrives on crisis. No "great times," no great presidents: such has been the rule.

Let us turn first to a very brief review of Bill Clinton's ascent to power. The biographical data about William Jefferson (Blythe) Clinton are too well known to acquire elaborate discussion here. Born in Hope, Arkansas, in August 1946, Clinton seems to have had a passion for politics from his earliest days. This passion was linked to high intelligence and abounding energy. Graduating from Yale Law School, where he met his future wife, Hillary Rodham, he was elected at age thirty-two to the governorship of his home state in 1978. Defeated for reelection two years later, he came back in 1982 and remained in the governorship until his election to the presidency a decade later. As he had been one of the youngest incoming governors in Arkansas history, on inauguration day Bill Clinton became the third youngest of incoming American presidents, after Theodore Roosevelt and John F. Kennedy. Since Arkansas pays its governors only $35,000 a year, Hillary Rodham Clinton was the chief breadwinner of the family as a practicing attorney during this period, from which the murky Whitewater affair stems.

In his prepresidential public life, Bill Clinton proved so effective a chief executive that he won acclaim from his fellows as the "best governor" of the lot. He was also a leader of the moderate-to-conservative Democratic Party group, the Democratic Leadership Council. In view of subsequent developments, it is worthy of note early in our discussion that in 1992 Clinton ran explicitly as a "new Democrat," in no way identified with the liberal core of the national party or its unsuccessful presidential nominees. You can take the man out of Arkansas, but you cannot take Arkansas out of the man, and Arkansas is a southern state.

There was a critical realignment in the late 1960s, out of which grew a sixth electoral system that lasted until 1994.[2] Institutionally, this system was particularly marked by divided government as a normal state of affairs. The presidency then was normally Republican, the House of Representatives always Democratic, and the Senate more often Democratic than Republican. In the formulation provided by Byron E. Shafer in 1991—just as this system was about to come to an abrupt end—the presidency was normally Republican because it was the focus of public concern about foreign policy and social values, a concern that was conservative.[3] The House remained Democratic even in the face of Republican presidential landslides in 1972 and 1984 because it was centered on social welfare and service provision. Here the position of the "median voter" was liberal. The Senate, amenable to both sets of concerns, oscillated in its partisan control during this period.

Given this conjuncture, any Democratic presidential candidate has obviously had a great deal to overcome. Victories, when they occurred, were not overwhelming. Jimmy Carter in 1976 received 50.1 percent of the total vote. And Bill Clinton, in his two three-man races of 1992 and 1996, garnered only 43 percent on the first occasion and 49.2 percent on the second. Carter and Clinton were both southern governors relatively removed from the "liberal" taint. But another condition also had to be satisfied: for different reasons in each case, the incumbent Republican opponents had to be highly vulnerable.

In 1992 the dominant issue was "the economy, stupid." The first half of this decade was marked by an outpouring of public rage and anxiety directed against established politicians. In 1992 (and again in 1994) the public was in a china-smashing mood. George Bush's primary background and interests lay in the realms of foreign and defense policy. At a time when the abrupt implosion of the USSR had suddenly revolutionized geopolitics and eliminated a Manichean threat to the American way of life, these assets suddenly traded at a 90 percent discount. The domestic impact of corporate downsizing and the ever fuller integration of the United States into the disciplines of a global economic order based on free trade interacted with a pervasive public sense of malaise. The perception grew that the president was out of touch with America on economic issues of vital concern to Americans' well-being.

As so often in the past, malaise and alienation gave ample scope for the emergence of a significant third candidacy, that of Texas billionaire Ross Perot. With 18.9 percent of the total vote in 1992, Perot received the third-largest vote share of all time for any third candidate and the highest share in history for a candidate with no prior career as a leading figure in the politics of a major party. This vote was mostly siphoned off from previously Republican voting streams. While it is possible that Clinton would have defeated Bush in a two-man contest, there is little doubt that Perot's entry made his task considerably easier.

Bill Clinton's tenure in office has been noteworthy for a number of major shifts in policy direction, and to an extent for which little parallel exists in modern presidential history. One is at times reminded of an earlier process of change in Italian politics called *trasformismo* ("transformism"). Such a process dominated the politics of the liberal Italian state before World War I. Politicians would make and remake coalitions and policies as opportunity indicated or exigencies required: great premium was placed on simply staying on top of the situation, whatever that might require. Some of these politicians, notably one long-term prime minister, Giovanni Giolitti, became internationally recognized virtuosi of this particular art form. Something quite similar also developed in the interwar history of the French Third Republic.

Of course, a certain opportunism verging on lack of integrity pervaded the political scene and contributed to growing public cynicism about politics. This was the price to be paid for such dexterity. In today's America—to the fury of conservative Republicans and liberal Democrats alike—Bill Clinton has emerged as a one-man incarnation of *trasformismo,* (American-style, of course). But it must be said that he has had to deal with two radically different political environments in his first term in office. These were separated by the earthquake election of 1994 and the huge power shift in Congress it produced. Getting on the tiger is one thing; staying on top of it for the whole ride is something else again. Clinton thus, and uniquely in modern times, has had in effect two administrations within a single term, those of 1993–94 and 1995–96.

The new administration got off to an unpropitious if not chaotic start, beginning with a fateful symbolic misstep, the emergence in the earliest days of the issue of gays in the military. Clinton's credibility also was jeopardized almost at once by his abandoning the middle-class tax cut he had promised in 1992. The difficulties that Clinton had in organizing his administration bespoke not only his personal lack of interest in nuts-and-bolts administrative questions but also two other major weaknesses. The first of these, which has tended to disappear with time and with experience, was the distance in political fact, one better measured in light-years than in miles, between politics and government in Little Rock and in Washington. The second weakness in part grew out of his pledge to form an administration that "looked like America." One price to be paid for this effort was the making of certain unfortunate nominations and the withdrawal of others, in a highly visible response to the pressures generated by the dense network of claimant constituency groups within the Democratic Party's coalition. This, along with a distinctly liberal policy thrust reflected, for example, in the sponsorship and enactment of the Brady bill and the "motor-voter" act, conveyed a message to Middle America that Clinton may have run as a "new Democrat" in 1992 but was governing as a liberal one in 1993–94.

Three major initiatives dominated the policy scene during the first half of the Clinton administration. By far the most spectacular and comprehensive was a highly complex national health-care plan in which Hillary Clinton as quasi "co-president" played a key role. The second of these initiatives was an increase in taxes falling mostly on the top 1.5 percent of income receivers and called ever since by the Republican opposition "the biggest tax increase in the history of the world." This measure passed through Congress without a single Republican vote in either house. The third initiative, abundantly displaying the president's devotion to free trade, was the North American Free Trade Agreement (NAFTA). In sharp contrast to the tax measure, this was enacted with predominantly Republican support in Congress over the bitter protests of core Democrats and the organized labor movement.

Without going into great detail over these policies, some general themes emerge when they are considered as a whole. Liberals had tended to support a single-payer system for delivering medical care, that is, one that would essentially cut out the private insurance companies and create government-based funding for the program. In truth, at the end of the day the president could have hardly done worse by adopting something resembling the Hawaii-Rochester-Canadian model for reform. The administration plan as unveiled could too easily be attacked by the insurance industry and congressional Republicans as a Rube Goldberg contraption, a textbook case of Big Government run amok in an area that constitutes one-seventh of the national economy. We all remember "Harry and Louise," actors in an industry television commercial, for who could turn on a television set in 1993–94 without seeing them and hearing their complaints? The failure of the Clinton health-care plan even to come to a vote in Congress controlled by his own party disclosed the political effectiveness of attacks on Big Government as the way to define, and thus settle, the issue. It also played into opposition claims that in addition to being a tax-and-spend liberal, President Clinton was an ineffective leader.

Another major policy item was the 1993 tax increase. This has ever since been mischaracterized by Republican campaigners as having an impact on Middle America when, except for a gasoline-tax increase included in its provisions, it did nothing of the sort. But no matter: this was, it was argued, the initiative of a president who, having promised to "govern from the center," was now "governing from the left." Much of the Republican campaign effort in 1996 to paint Bill Clinton as a conventional tax-and-spend Democrat stemmed from this tax increase. But, very characteristically, the president undercut such efforts early in his second (half) term when he cheerfully announced to an audience of corporate executives that he agreed with them: he had raised their taxes too much.

As for the NAFTA struggle, this was an early warning that Clinton has some principles that liberals and labor do not like. Paradoxically, those who might argue that Clinton is a pure *trasformismo* politician would have heavy weather trying to fit his actions in this case into their model. For he sometimes reveals ironclad, even passionate conviction and a willingness to run political risks on its behalf. Whatever the negative implications may be for jobs and wages in certain sectors of the economy, NAFTA revealed Clinton to be a true believer in free trade. Perhaps both of these signals may account in part for the 1996 endorsement of his candidacy by hundreds of corporate CEOs.

The *"Comeback Kid"* Comes Back Again

The 1994 election has already attracted a considerable literature, and it deserves still more.[4] My own treatment of the subject places it in historical context. In such extended perspective, the abrupt break with a previously stable political equilibrium governing congressional elections was (in relative terms) one of the largest recorded in two centuries.[5] Since one could not know the outcome of subsequent elections at the time of writing in 1995, analysis had to be content with measuring the deviation in a sixth election from the mean two-party percentages of votes and seats for the preceding five elections and then dividing this deviation by the standard deviation centered on that mean.

The d/s.d. measure of relative displacement from previous "expectations" will of course be determined by both the numerator and the denominator. The latter, the standard deviation, has systematically shrunk as we approach the present, and especially so since the early 1980s. This reflects the fact that the equilibrium on which continuous Democratic control of the House had rested before 1994 had become not only stable but metastable. By 1988, for example, more than nine-tenths of all seats were contested by incumbents (exactly three-fifths of whom were Democrats), and of these, 98.5 percent were reelected. The stage was being set for the term-limits movement.

Thus the 1994 displacement, while involving a net loss of fifty-two seats by the previously hegemonic Democrats, was rather smaller than in some notable earlier punctuated-change upheavals. For the nonsouthern states, a pro-Republican shift of 5.6 percent of the two-party vote and 11.5 percent of the two-party seats was less than one-half the absolute magnitude of the 1932 upheaval in the former, and less than one-third in the latter. Despite this, the famous "stickiness" of congressional-outcome elections in the late-sixth-electoral-system era produced standard deviations such that the d/s.d. "discontinuity" value was actually larger in 1994 than in 1932, −5.877 in terms of votes, and −8.219 in terms of seats.

But in a real sense, the comparative size of extreme values of this measure is less to the point than the fact of their very existence and timing. *Any* such values are rare occurrences in the sweep of American political history. Viewing the northern and western states for ninety-nine observations across two centuries, we find only four cases of displacement values of 3.5 or greater as far as the two-party congressional vote is concerned, and only five such cases involving the two-party share of seats. Similarly, when the nonsouthern states and the United States as a whole are evaluated for state legislature partisan outcomes since 1834 (seventy-six cases are involved), only four of these cases show values of 3.5 or greater for the non-South, and only three for the United States as a whole. In short, on this dimension of analysis, 1994 keeps company with a select group of past upheaval events such as 1800, 1854, 1860, 1894, and 1932. And the state legislature data remind us that 1994 was a Republican *partisan* victory that extended to all levels of election.

This book is about the 1996 election, and its features are covered in detail by other contributions to it. But it seems appropriate to note that at all levels except the presidential contest, the 1996 election was basically a reiteration of the 1994 outcome; and this despite a huge countermobilization effort on the part of Democrats and organized labor, and despite the participation of at least 17 million more citizens in the process of choice than came to the polls at this level of contestation in 1994.

Suffice it to say—very significantly, in my view—that in 1996 Republicans won two congressional elections in a row for the first time since the 1926–28 sequence. Accordingly, Newt Gingrich will be the first consecutively elected Republican House Speaker since the days of Nicholas Longworth (R-Ohio, Speaker 1925–31). Nor, for many reasons—including the fact that it will be the sixth year of an incumbent administration, a year when the congressional troops of a president's party fare badly—does it seem very likely even this soon before the fact that 1998 will show any great countermovement toward the Democrats. The 1996 election is thus to be regarded as a confirming event following a historically rare level of upheaval; it looks to be the second event in a new equilibrium sequence very different indeed from the old. This is not partisan realignment old-style, since Robert Dole is not president-elect. It is, however, its functional equivalent given the current organization of the electoral market. President Clinton's rapid shift toward a newly defined center point considerably to the right of the earlier one permits House Speaker Gingrich to talk of the 105th Congress in terms of an "implementation Congress" to replace the "confrontation Congress" of the 104th. Precisely to the extent that the president's move toward the right takes concrete form, Gingrich can rightly claim victory, even if not precisely the victory he wanted.

Let us now return to the "confrontation Congress" elected in 1994. As is well known, the victorious Republicans had a combined policy/constitutional agenda of such sweeping range that they routinely referred to it as a "revolution." In the immediate aftermath of the election, Democrats were demoralized and President Clinton felt it necessary to assert that he was still "relevant" to the political process. Moreover, this proposed "revolution" was led with great élan and zeal by the new leadership not of the Senate but of the House of Representatives. In institutional terms, one can find no parallel to this abrupt transformation in the twentieth century.

Very remarkable things materialized under this leadership. The 1994 Contract with America on which the Republicans had run was in large part enacted, with some important exceptions such as proposed amendments to establish term limits and mandate a balanced budget. A budget was prepared whose objectives were to reduce drastically the role and salience of the federal government. This was to be accomplished in part by abolishing or sharply curtailing programmatic functions and agencies and in part by resurrecting the state governments as autonomous actors, shipping other functions to them via block grants.

Moreover, 1995 capped a longer-term trend toward ever greater partisan polarization in Congress. This polarization now reached levels not seen since before World War I; the majority was so cohesive as to occasion comment about the "parliamentarization" of American legislative politics. All the while, Speaker Newt Gingrich and House Majority Leader Dick Armey (R-Tex.) made themselves extremely visible in the media, a fact that in the end was not to work overwhelmingly to their or their party's advantage in the struggle to shape public opinion for the 1996 elections.

Easy come, easy go. The classic partisan realignment recipe called for Republican victory in the presidential election. The "revolution" and its proponents looked all-powerful in 1995. But within little more than a year, Bill Clinton had conclusively shown how relevant he continued to be, using the veto power to defeat the Republican budget and other policy initiatives sent up by the new congressional majority. Still more remarkably, he achieved the most spectacular of all his comebacks by handily defeating Republican nominee Robert J. Dole. Unfortunately for Clinton's "team," this was a personal victory. If euphoric leaders of the Republican campaign committees had in 1995 insisted that the party was on the way to gaining twenty or even thirty seats in the House and a filibuster-proof sixty seats in the Senate, they were to be disappointed—but not very disappointed, since the party retained control of both chambers.

Still, Bill Clinton had been resurrected from the political dead. What happened? Three intervening vectors of change crystallized very rapidly; and on one other dimension, no change at all seems to have occurred from pre-1994 days. The three elements of change were linked to what the Republicans did, what Clinton did, and what the economy did. Republicans had clearly hoped after 1994 that a coherent conservative majority had at last materialized in public opinion. Instead, what seemingly failed to change was the electorate's long-standing, simultaneously held aggregate preference for ideological conservatism and operational liberalism concerning government.

Let us consider first what the Republicans did. One could put it most simply by saying that congressional party leaders vastly overinterpreted their mandate. But this needs some unpacking. In many respects, Republican analysis had been quite correct back in 1994. Conservatives had the bold, innovative ideas and the moral energy (and physical stamina) to carry them out if given the opportunity. Liberals and Democrats, in contrast, were largely on the run across a wide front, not least in the ongoing struggle to define what politics and government should be all about. The old Democratic congressional leadership had become sclerotic with age, and an atmosphere of penny-ante corruption had been allowed to drift in like a miasma, especially in the House. Public reaction against invincible, mostly Democratic, incumbents had waxed and given rise to a vigorous term-limits movement.

With little serious ideological opposition, Republicans in 1994 effectively portrayed their opponents—the president and his first lady chief among them—as liberals promoting a Big Government that by the mid-1990s had become discredited and widely rejected. Thus defined, Clinton and the Democrats rode to their epic fall, and Clinton's days in office seemed to be numbered. But then, in 1995–96, the popularity of Congress and the Republicans plummeted, with Speaker Gingrich's approval ratings falling to particularly abysmal depths (see chapter 6). Gingrich himself contributed to this process by talking too much, even being caught on record with a throwaway remark about dealing with Medicare by letting it "wither on the vine."

Accounting for this reversal makes it necessary to review how what the Republicans did intersected with a substantial dimension of nonchange in public attitudes toward government. Coupled with this is another fact of political life: the public is much more centrist than political activists of either of today's political parties. Back in 1967, Lloyd A. Free and Hadley Cantril first clearly documented the existence of two dimensions, not just one, in these public attitudes.[6] One of these is ideological, the other more concrete and operational. Asked about Big Government in general, respondents' modal answers are conservative and hostile. For more than a century and a half, observers of the American scene have repeatedly identified this potent antigovernmentalism as a singular feature of American political culture. But when the same respondents are asked about programs and entitlements that Big Government has created (and that only such government can create and maintain), the opinion mode becomes liberal and supportive. In the main, the citizenry likes these programs and tends to be highly resistant to proposals to scale them back, much less eliminate them.

Such an opinion configuration is deeply frustrating to tidy-minded intellectuals and political activists of left or right. And there are good reasons for this. For as long as this opinion bimodality endures, it not only greatly complicates politicians' efforts to find and win the "median voter"; it also lends itself to public rejection of all serious policy initiatives from either the liberal or the conservative side. The political integration problem posed here is further complicated by the steep increase over the past two decades in the level of ideological polarization between the two partisan activist teams. The consequence, on this dimension at least, has been an increasingly serious gap between public and elite politics. Some, indeed, have argued that this widening gap had been a prime mover in promoting the public's alienation from politics and politicians.[7]

It is time to suggest some reasons for these developments. As John Aldrich has recently pointed out, the old "mass parties" did not survive the realignment of the late 1960s.[8] The new "parties-in-service" (to candidates) have quite different activist cadres and supporters from the older ones. These earlier activists were often attracted to party work for a combination of available expressive, solidary, and divisible personal benefits (patronage, jobs, and the like) that tended to keep ideological temperatures low. The newer variety are much more upscale and better educated than their predecessors. They also tend to be driven toward activism by commitment to causes about which they care deeply. Moreover, their support for a party is more likely to be contingent: the price for their wholehearted support is that the party must be willing to embrace their issues.

The issue of gays in the military reflected some of this "new" issue emphasis in the early days of the "first" Clinton administration. But such emphasis has its perfectly symmetrical counterpart on the Republican side, with its cluster of high-profile conservative issue activists. One need think here merely of the Christian Coalition and its numerous successes in the party's nomination politics at state and congressional levels, in both 1994 and 1996. Such new activist configurations generate a very powerful push toward the poles in both major parties. They have been a major force behind the persistent climb in interparty polarization on congressional roll calls over the past generation. One way to measure this is by deriving a mean support score among the party delegations for, say, the policy positions of the liberal group Americans for Democratic Action, with a theoretical maximum of 100 (Democrats' mean support = 100, Republicans' zero). In 1970, during the early period of the Nixon administration, this score was 29. Climbing steadily since, especially from 1982 on, it dramatically surged forward under the 104th "confrontation Congress" to a modern record of 76 in 1995.[9]

The post-1994 Republican congressional majority is the institutional vehicle for the ideologically conservative opinion dimension, as its Democratic counterparts have ever more clearly become the vehicle for operational liberalism. The Republican majority did what came naturally to it: proposals for tax cuts for the wealthy, and in the 1996 campaign for much of Middle America as well; measures to repeal the Brady bill and the ban on AK-47 automatic weapons; drastic relaxation of environmental pollution (and other) regulations; a balanced-budget amendment with provisions for an extraordinary congressional majority required to enact any future increases in income tax; proposals for constitutional amendments to outlaw burning the American flag and to overturn *Roe* v. *Wade*'s legalization of abortion; and the elimination of a sixty-year-old federal guarantee of an income "floor" for welfare recipients. The list goes on and on, all elements in it parts of an internally consistent right-wing ideological program aimed at dismantling the post-1933 federal government.

These preferences now fully revealed, they were often enough presented through the media by Speaker Gingrich and his associates in a hard-edged ideological mode. Many of these issue stands lent themselves admirably to campaign attack from the Democrats couched in operational liberal terms. At the margins, at least, some 1994 voters might be made willing to consider the possibility that while they had voted *against* an established order they disliked, this package was not after what they had voted *for*.

The Republican congressional leadership then made a serious strategic blunder. In quite a few ways, Bill Clinton might be plausibly regarded as not far removed from the liberal Republicanism of yesteryear. But he does not remotely inhabit the conceptual or policy world of the Republican "mountain" of 1995–96. Accordingly, in late 1995 he began vetoing the new majority's enactments—most significantly, its comprehensive budget plan. The new Republican majority, while an impressive and novel fact in its own right, was nowhere near large enough to override these vetoes. Newt Gingrich and his associates then tried to coerce Clinton into compliance with their objectives by twice shutting down the government in the winter of 1995–96, refusing to permit operations to carry on through the device of continuing resolutions that had been customary in the past.

As Senator Dole suggested might happen, these actions evoked a strongly negative public reaction. They played into the hands of a canny president, who could credibly claim that Congress was in the grip of right-wing extremists who seemed prepared to rule or ruin. One wonders in retrospect what was on the congressional Republicans' minds. "Dizzy with success" might be one explanation. If they considered the public's two opinion modes or its distaste for ideological politics at all, they may have bet that 1994 had given them the equivalent of the philosopher's stone: at long last, an unequivocal conservative majority. But, more likely, the government shutdown was the artifact of ideologically driven activists who tend to talk only to each other and to live in their own worlds. The heavy erosion of public support for their endeavors following the government closing fiasco proved a mighty reality check. It underscored a set of reasons why it is so difficult to carry out a principled, ideologically consistent "revolution" in today's America. And government closing was an extremely important factor in opening the way not only for Bill Clinton's political rehabilitation but for his victory in the 1996 presidential election.[10]

We must now consider what President Clinton did in response to the message of 1994. Here we should probably pause long enough to put in a good word for *trasformismo* as he practices it. After all, in the classic European cases as in today's America, it comes into being as a by-product of the profound contradictions embedded in middle-class politics. In today's

America, these contradictions certainly include but extend beyond the discrepant bimodality in public opinion that we have discussed. The general atmosphere of the mid-1990s is notably more conservative than it was even in the recent past. The right dominates much of the ideological and media-disseminated high ground of political discourse today. There is no reason to suppose that any outspoken Democratic liberal could achieve election, not to mention reelection, to the presidency. Nor did Bill Clinton ever mislabel himself as such. The two-year experiment in quasi-liberal government had gone down to shattering defeat in 1994. The Republican opposition, were it also to capture the presidency in 1996, would have a clear road before it to carry out the full sweep of its revolution. This would be achieved not only through legislative action and constitutional amendments but also through the president's judicial appointments over the next four years.

Not having access to the president's innermost thoughts, this writer can hardly be sure that Bill Clinton saw things in just this way. But his 1995–96 shift toward a "second" administration marked by a Dick Morris–inspired strategy of "triangulation" might render such an account plausible. Consummate campaigner that he is, Clinton sought to position himself toward the pragmatic center under conditions in which this center had apparently shifted abruptly to the right. Not for him the go-down-with-the-ship attitude of, say, James Buchanan in 1860, Grover Cleveland in 1894–96, Woodrow Wilson in 1919, or Herbert Hoover in 1932. And if this contributed to doubts about Clinton's integrity, this price might have to be paid for his electoral survival in a conservative country that was at a conservative moment in its history. Considering the alternative, one supposes, the price seemed well worth paying. A successful campaign formula stressing the president's reassuring qualities somewhere in the vicinity of the center, laced with appeals to the fear among many citizens of what a thorough right-wing ideological revolution might do to them concretely, might so marginalize the Republican candidate as to achieve victory. So it proved in the end.

Thus, in his 23 January 1996 State of the Union message, President Clinton proclaimed the doctrine that evidently informed his subsequent campaign: "The age of big government is over." Likewise, the following August he demonstrated his willingness to accept a solution to the welfare issue that was very close to the original Republican objectives. This area had long been the weakest link in the network of federal programs generated since the New Deal. Public support for it was minimal and, indeed, back in 1992 Clinton had pledged to "end welfare as we know it." Ceding to the Republicans on this issue served to neutralize their efforts to portray the president as just another liberal politician. His signature drew heavy fire

from important constituent groups in his own party and prompted that
Washington rarity, resignation on principle by two key administration
aides. But here too, Clinton was the beneficiary of good fortune, and for the
same reason that led to absolutely no challenge to his renomination. At
least through 5 November 1996, the Democratic Party remained united behind him by its mortal fear of an across-the-board Republican electoral victory.

Nor was this the end of Bill Clinton's string of lucky breaks in 1996.
Perhaps the most important of them was provided by the Republicans when
their selection process resulted in the nomination of Senator Robert J. Dole.
This gets us close enough to the campaign itself to defer comment to other
contributions to this volume (see chapter 1). Let us simply remark here that
it was already clear early on that Dole, with most respectable credentials as
an experienced master of the legislative process, had significant issue and
image problems in appealing to a mass electorate. Two adjectives perhaps
best convey that image: dour and saturnine, with an element of the hard-
bitten thrown in. He has had a difficult life in many well-known respects;
unfortunately, this shows. Given the specific field of Republican contenders
in 1996, Dole was probably in the strongest of the lot. But he nevertheless
persistently trailed Clinton by a wide margin in the polls, even if at the end
he lost by a much narrower margin than virtually all of them had projected.
One wonders whether someone not in that field could have made a crucial
difference—someone, perhaps, like General Colin Powell, who could capitalize by his very candidacy on Bill Clinton's weaknesses. Such musings underscore a central reality of American politics: particularly where the presidency is concerned, the importance of individual leaders and the decisions
they make in shaping the ultimate outcome is in the end decisive. On this
dimension, Clinton was dealt a very good hand in 1996 when it might have
been otherwise.

The third set of events that immeasurably brightened Clinton's reelection prospects lay in the fact that several years of improved economic performance had at last produced a positive public response. Naturally, the
Clinton campaign pointed to the administration's and the president's activities in contributing to this happy state of affairs. But in a private-enterprise
economy, economic "times" in election years, whether good or bad, have a
significant element of external contingency about them. Between 1952 and
1992 seven incumbents—including two originally elected to the vice-presi-
dency—had run for election or reelection. Three were defeated (Ford in
1976, Carter in 1980, and Bush in 1992), and four were reelected, in all
cases by landslide margins (Eisenhower in 1956, Johnson in 1964, Nixon in

1972, and Reagan in 1984). Of course, many factors shape a final presidential election result, but the state of the economy under the incumbent's watch has long been recognized to be of cardinal importance.

We present here findings from an economics-and-politics model which, unlike many more complex ones, at least got the 1992 result right. It includes an average of both the election-year growth rate in disposable personal income over the preceding year and the growth rate in this measure across the entire presidential term. For 1992 had made clear, if nothing else had, that this latter variable is also of importance to economics-and-politics predictions. First, we note the average growth rates for the successful and unsuccessful incumbents.

GROWTH RATE IN PER CAPITA DISPOSABLE INCOME,
1956–92; MEANS BY CATEGORY OF INCUMBENTS

	Election year	Presidential term	Composite
Winners (4)	+4.3	+8.2	+6.2
Losers (3)	+1.3	+2.9	+2.1

Using the composite figure, the overall 1945–92 equation is

$$Y = 41.748 + 2.835X,$$

with $r = +.927$, $r^2 = .857$, and a standard error of ±2.1 percent. As we noted earlier and as irritated Republicans have insisted ever since, George Bush did preside over disposable-income growth in 1991–92, but the presidential term rate was a paltry +1.5 percent. Fatally for him, this was the lowest such rate in the whole postwar period. A slightly different equation covering the period 1952–84 resulted, as it happened, with a prediction identical to the final result: Bush lost with 46.5 percent of the two-party vote. The economic numbers used for 1996 are of course preliminary figures through the end of the second quarter (election-year growth in per capita disposable income = 2.9 percent; presidential term growth rate, +7 percent; composite, +4.95 percent), but they are clearly closer to those registered among the first group of incumbents than those of the second. They projected a solid, though not overwhelming, Clinton victory.[11]

One remarkable aspect of the 1996 year that is almost certainly linked to improved economic performance, and its translation recently into real family income growth for the first time this decade, was a remarkably swift atmospheric transition from the *Sturm und Drang* of 1992 and 1994 to something not far removed from a flat calm. Revolutions are driven by intense bursts of moral energy, in which public anger, anxiety, and fear are major components. Without such exigent drivers, the revolution wanes. Incumbents normally profit from such calm political seas. In 1996 this abrupt reduction in tension appears to have favored both President Clinton and Republican as well as Democratic incumbents in the congressional and senatorial races. From Clinton's point of view, it would have been hard to improve on either the positive economic picture or the atmosphere linked to it. And whatever his own contributions may have been, there was a powerful element of good fortune in this timing of the business cycle. Robert Dole, his Republican challenger, had to take the difficult course of arguing that the economy could do ever so much better if only he were elected. In modern times, pursuit of such a course has never been successful. 1996 proved no exception to this rule.

An Age of Diminished Expectations and a Diminishing Presidency

Finally, where overall does Bill Clinton fit into the ongoing history of the country? Even after his reelection, we cannot of course gain a full or perhaps even accurate answer to this question for another four years. The president is a work in progress. Yet there is already enough of a record at hand to permit a preliminary casting of accounts.

One major element in Bill Clinton's good fortune is that his own shortcomings, while generally known to the public, have been generally ignored or downplayed by it. "Where's the outrage?" asked GOP candidate Dole. The short answer, given the specifics of the 1996 campaign year, was nowhere. But these shortcomings loom rather larger in a review of his legacy, and their concrete implications hang like storm clouds over his second term. "Affairs" such as "Travelgate" and the 900 or so FBI files that ended up in the White House suggest a combination of administrative ineptitude and laxity in its standards of official conduct. Moreover, not a few administration officials have resigned under a legal cloud or have become objects of investigations by special prosecutors. The Republicans have naturally seized on all this, but, after all, they did not create the occasions for them. Some earlier administrations were notable for a "low moral tone," notably those of James Buchanan, Ulysses S. Grant, and Warren G. Harding. The associated scandal formed a distinct contribution to historians' negative judgments of these three presidents.

We suggest nothing so odoriferous as far as Bill Clinton is concerned, but odor there certainly is. Franklin Roosevelt had it right when he said of the presidency that it is "pre-eminently a place for moral leadership." We live under an elective monarchy. Even in jaded late-twentieth-century America the presidency as an office has a regal aspect, including a touch of "the divinity that doth hedge a king." More than that, presidents are called on to be in a sense high priests of the American civil religion; most visible in inaugural ceremonies, this liturgical function extends far beyond them. Performance of any such function is impaired to the degree that the whiff of scandal becomes noticeable. When it does, public morale also suffers.

Perhaps the most consequential development of the Clinton years has been a sea change in world affairs that abruptly materialized during George Bush's presidency and continues to unfold today, with important implications for the American presidency. In political terms, centuries can be not only of usual chronological length, but "long" or "short"; the twentieth century has turned out to be a fine example of the latter. This "short" century may be said to have extended from the outbreak of World War I in 1914 to the disappearance of the Soviet Union on New Year's Day, 1992. This century was dominated by economic turbulence and above all by wars, hot and cold. The modern activist federal government came into being from 1933 onward to cope with both challenges. Not coincidentally, in this modern government something we call "the modern presidency" emerged as its pivot and linchpin. The liquidation of the Cold War and of the USSR itself brought us into the twenty-first century nearly a decade early. This global revolution, the third in little more than seventy-five years, is not merely of cardinal importance geopolitically. It is of equal importance to the future evolution of American domestic political institutions and processes.

For between the 1930s and the 1990s, Big Government in the United States was probably sustained more by nuclear terror in a bipolar world than by domestic social or economic considerations. Disappearance of this global threat has contributed to the opportunity space for a conservative deconstruction of the federal government that, given the extent to which it has cut across the grain of our political culture, may well have been overdue. By the same token, the "modern presidency" is rapidly being replaced by an institution of smaller and more nearly traditional range and impact on the political process, while a resurgent Congress grows in the overall ordering of things in Washington. Not even the impending addition of the line-item veto to the array of presidential powers can quite conceal this structurally induced decline of the office itself. If the age of Big Government is over, as Bill Clinton has proclaimed, then the age of the modern presidency is probably over too.

Bill Clinton has demonstrated an astonishing ability to adapt to changed circumstances; he has been deftly adapting to this sea change too. He had aspired to lead a government that could make a positive difference in crucial areas of public need and concern. At the end of the day, he is a decent and very intelligent man who, like many presidents with high activity levels, would like to be greater than times and opportunity will allow. But, in the words of the *Threepenny Opera* song, "circumstance won't have it so." So Clinton has made it clear that he is willing to settle for less. Nor, one supposes, would a President Dole have had greater scope for order-changing action.

Well before the election, the absence of any overarching vision of any kind in either major contender's camp had already occasioned considerable and negative notice. But here we come again to some of our major themes. The median voter—most likely, the suburban soccer mom, say—distrusts large-scale policy initiatives coming from either major party. The immediate past has been disagreeable, what with layoffs and stagnant family incomes, trash on television, and many other things to consider. The future looks scary to the soccer mom, for she is quite capable of perceiving that Medicare and Social Security sacrifices lie just over the horizon, and stock markets do not climb vertically forever. And she wonders just where the money is going to come from so that her children can get the education they need to get off the treadmill leading nowhere and, at the same time, avoid deadly encounters with guns or drugs at school.

But for now, the country enjoys peace and a measure of prosperity. Bill Clinton hasn't done a half-bad job of it, and he can be depended on to prevent Republicans in Congress from going too far too fast in cutting back the government's programs or its regulations, such as those designed to protect the environment. Our soccer mom doesn't care for Big Government, but neither does she welcome the prospect of its wholesale demolition. If she is unusually reflective or politically educated, she may have noted that there is no clear majority for doing much of consequence with political power today. So we will drift, if cumulatively in a rightward direction. But at the moment, that seems a much more pleasing prospect than Democratic activism on one side and Republican demolition on the other.

Such might be one imaginary account of the 1996 election from the median voter's vantage point. Moving beyond that account, we need only repeat that presidential *trasformismo* is superbly adapted to such a setting.

Moreover, there is much to be said for it, considering the likely alternatives. Adaptation in this case means that Bill Clinton will have to settle for what he can get, which is considerably less than he had hoped when he took office in 1993. But withal, it's better to ride the tiger than end up inside him. With both his adroitness and his remarkable luck working overtime for him, the president has thus far been able to do just that.

Let us conclude by turning once more to Napoleon and his marshals. Around 1810, the latter could look forward to becoming leaders of the first rank in a mighty European empire. By 1815, the emperor's bid for empire failed, and he disappeared into the mists of the South Atlantic Ocean. But some of his marshals, the really skilled and lucky ones, managed the transition to a new order of things very well. One of them, Jean-Baptiste Bernadotte, even became king of Sweden, founding a dynasty that rules there to this day.[12]

Notes

1. Stephen Skowronek, *The Politics Presidents Make* (Cambridge: Harvard University Press, 1993).

2. The fact of this realignment, long in controversy, has in my view been conclusively demonstrated in John Aldrich and Richard G. Niemi, "The Sixth American Party System: The 1960s and the Candidate-Centered Parties," Working paper 107, Duke University Program in Political Economy, 1990. A somewhat revised and updated version is found in Stephen C. Craig, ed., *Broken Contract: Changing Relationships between Americans and Their Government* (Boulder, Colo.: Westview Press, 1995), under the title "The Sixth American Party System: Electoral Change, 1952–1992," chap. 8 of that volume.

3. Byron E. Shafer, "The Notion of an Electoral Order: The Structure of Electoral Politics at the Accession of George Bush," in *The End of Realignment? Interpreting American Electoral Eras,* ed. B.E. Shafer (Madison: University of Wisconsin Press, 1991), 37–84, at 72.

4. See, for example, Gerald M. Pomper, ed., *The Election of 1992: Reports and Interpretations* (Chatham, N.J.: Chatham House, 1993), including my essay, "The Legacy of George Bush: Travails of an Understudy," 1–38; Harold W. Stanley, "The Parties, the President, and the 1994 Midterm Elections," in *The Clinton Presidency: First Appraisals,* ed. Colin Campbell and Bert A. Rockman (Chatham, N.J.: Chatham House, 1996), 188–211; and Gary C. Jacobson, *The Politics of Congressional Elections,* 4th ed. (New York: Longman, 1997), passim.

5. Walter Dean Burnham, "Realignment Lives: The 1994 Earthquake and Its Implications," in Campbell and Rockman, *Clinton Presidency,* 363–95.

6. Lloyd A. Free and Hadley Cantril, *The Political Beliefs of Americans* (New Brunswick, N.J.: Rutgers University Press, 1967).

7. E.J. Dionne Jr., *Why Americans Hate Politics* (New York: Touchstone, 1992).

8. John Aldrich Jr., *Why Parties?* (Chicago: University of Chicago Press, 1995), pt. 3, pp. 159–296. See also the vivid narrative account in Alan Ehrenhalt, *The United States of Ambition* (New York: Random House, 1992).

9. The 1995 ADA scores showed an average of 83 among House Democrats and 7 among House Republicans, a spread of 76 points. Back in 1970, the scores were 52 and 23 respectively. See Norman Ornstein, "Control of Congress Looks Like Election Nail-Biter," *USA Today,* 30 September 1996, 25A.

10. And yet, despite all this negativity surrounding the Speaker and congressional Republicans, they won at least 228 seats in the House in 1996, and will have 55 seats in the Senate of the 105th Congress. Moreover, some 17 million more Americans voted in the congressional election of 1996 than had done so two years earlier. In view of all this, the case for interpreting 1994 as inaugurating a new political equilibrium with some claim to durability becomes particularly compelling.

11. With these preliminary economic figures plugged into the 1956–92 equation, it projected a Clinton victory with 55.9 percent of the two-party vote, while he actually received 54.7 percent. While slightly on the high side, it certainly did better than almost all of the polls, where projected Clinton margins of 18–22 percent were commonplace.

12. Bernadotte reigned over Sweden (and Norway) under the name Karl XIV Johan from 1818 to 1844.

I

The Presidential Nominations

WILLIAM G. MAYER

> O heavens!
> If you do love old men, if your sweet sway
> Allow obedience, if you yourselves are old,
> Make it your cause. Send down, and take my part.
> — *King Lear* (II, iv)

In a curious way, the presidential nominations of 1996 look more interesting in retrospect than they did while they were being decided. Through 1995 and the first half of 1996, the most conspicuous source of energy and upheaval in American politics was the newly Republican Congress. The presidential election seemed, by comparison, rather staid and predictable. On the Republican side, a veteran party war-horse started out the race far ahead of all his rivals and then went on to victory, albeit with a few mishaps along the way. In the Democratic Party, an incumbent president was renominated without any organized opposition. To say the least, neither "contest" seemed like promising source material for a good novel.

But several months later, with the fall campaign and the November voting behind us, one cannot help but feel that there is more to the story than this. In particular, there is the puzzling matter of Robert Dole. How was it, one wonders, that a candidate so apparently ill suited to a contemporary national campaign nevertheless became the standard-bearer for a party that had just won control of both houses of Congress and most state governments? And how did Bill Clinton, who in early 1995 had to explain to a skeptical national press corps that he was still "relevant," reassemble the pieces of a diverse and fractious party?

The Nomination Process

Our inquiry starts, not unexpectedly, with a look at the process: the complex set of guidelines, deadlines, regulations, and expectations that all candidates and campaigns must come to terms with if they hope to win their party's nomination. In 1996, most aspects of this procedural environment had a familiar feel to them. The national party rules, in particular, displayed an unaccustomed continuity. Shortly after the 1968 election, the Democratic Party had created a Commission on Party Structure and Delegate Selection that had completely rewritten the party's presidential nomination rules.[1] And every four years thereafter, for the next two decades, a new commission was created to revise, reform, or reaffirm the work of its predecessor(s). But the last of these commissions completed its business in 1986; and though the Democratic National Committee can also tinker with the delegate selection rules, this time around it declined to do so. The Republican Party has never shown much interest in centrally directed rules reform and in the lead-up to 1996 it kept its record intact. As the 1996 nominations got under way, then, both parties could claim, for the first time in three decades, that the rules for this year's contest were essentially the same as those from four years earlier.

Much the same can be said about campaign finance laws. These laws had also undergone a series of dramatic changes in the 1970s, with the most important single piece of legislation coming in 1974 (see chap. 4). The system that emerged has been much criticized, especially over the past several years, but nothing new has been enacted to take its place.

What was different about the 1996 nomination process, then, was almost entirely the product of decisions made by state legislatures. In a word, a substantial number of states changed the scheduling of their primaries and caucuses so as to make the delegate selection calendar vastly more "frontloaded."

As the data in table 1.1 demonstrate, it was once the case that the delegate selection calendar started up rather slowly. Most primaries took place near the *end* of the process, in May and June. In 1968, for example, the first primary was held (as it still is) in New Hampshire, on 12 March. The second primary (in Wisconsin) did not occur until three weeks later, and only two more primaries were held in the four weeks after that. Not until week 9

TABLE I.I

THE RISE OF FRONT-LOADING, 1960–96

Figures are the cumulative percentage of delegates chosen via primary
that had been selected by the end of each week in the primary season.

_____ Republican Party _____

		1960	*1964*	*1968*	*1972*	*1976*	*1980*	*1984*	*1988*	*1992*	*1996*
Week	1	2%	2%	1%	2%	1%	1%	2%	1%	1%	1%
	2	2	2	1	7	4	4	2	3	2	7
	3	2	2	1	14	9	14	18	3	10	22
	4	2	2	7	14	15	20	24	49	36	51
	5	8	7	7	17	19	30	26	54	44	65
	6	16	15	7	17	19	35	37	54	46	77
	7	23	22	16	17	30	37	43	56	46	77
	8	40	36	22	28	30	37	43	59	56	77
	9	56	53	38	42	30	42	43	59	56	77
	10	63	58	44	55	35	42	47	65	56	81
	11	63	64	44	64	52	57	72	70	60	81
	12	71	70	53	68	55	61	75	78	66	88
	13	71	100	77	68	64	68	77	80	67	89
	14	100		86	90	75	72	77	82	71	91
	15			100	90	78	100	99	83	75	93
	16				100	100		100	83	99	100
	17								99	100	
	18								100		

Continued ...

was more than one primary held on the same day, and not until week 12
were a majority of the primary delegates selected.

Beginning in the 1970s, however, a different pattern started to emerge:
more and more primaries were being scheduled during the early weeks of
the delegate selection season. Several different features of contemporary
nomination politics are responsible for this trend. In the first place, as primaries came to play a more important role in presidential politics generally,
it soon became obvious that not all primaries were created equal: those held
early, especially the first-in-the-nation New Hampshire primary, got a great
deal more attention from the candidates and the national media.[2] The extraordinary focus on New Hampshire (and later, the Iowa caucuses), along
with the new campaign finance regimen, led to another important feature of
the contemporary nomination system, a phenomenon often called "winnowing." In the nomination contests of the 1950s and 1960s, presidential

TABLE 1.1 — *Continued*

_____ Democratic Party _____

		1960	1964	1968	1972	1976	1980	1984	1988	1992	1996
Week	1	2%	1%	2%	1%	1%	1%	1%	1%	1%	1%
	2	2	1	2	5	5	6	1	1	1	1
	3	2	1	2	13	9	14	18	1	8	15
	4	2	1	8	13	17	22	27	42	31	44
	5	6	6	8	17	19	36	29	49	41	59
	6	14	11	8	17	19	41	41	49	43	73
	7	20	18	15	17	35	43	49	51	43	73
	8	36	33	22	29	35	43	49	54	56	73
	9	56	53	43	43	35	51	49	54	56	73
	10	62	59	49	51	43	51	53	63	56	80
	11	66	66	49	61	54	61	74	70	62	80
	12	73	71	58	64	57	64	77	79	68	86
	13	73	100	84	64	65	66	77	81	70	88
	14	100		88	85	73	70	77	83	72	90
	15			100	85	76	100	100	83	75	92
	16				100	100			83	100	100
	17								100		

SOURCE: Computed by the author.
NOTE: Figures include all delegates selected or bound by primary vote.

candidates who chose to contest the primaries generally stayed in the race
to the end of the primary season—usually, indeed, all the way to the actual
convention balloting. Beginning in about 1976, however, candidates who
did poorly in one or two early caucuses and primaries were withdrawing
from the field just days after the delegate selection process had formally
commenced. In 1984, for example, five of the eight announced Democratic
candidates had withdrawn within just twenty-five days of the Iowa caucuses. In 1992, three of five Democratic aspirants were out by the third
week of March.[3]

All of which, in turn, soon led to feelings of great disappointment and
resentment among states holding late primaries. Even though such states
typically had populations many times larger than that of New Hampshire,
they seemed to have considerably less influence on presidential nominations. By the time these states voted, most contenders had long since
dropped out of the race, and one candidate had usually emerged as the all-
but-certain nominee. Hence, late primary states also received far less than a

proportionate share of campaign spending, candidate visits, and media attention.

States responded to these general patterns in an entirely predictable manner. Why schedule a primary in May or June, when it would have little or no effect on the final outcome? It was far more sensible to move a primary to a much earlier date, a few weeks after the Iowa–New Hampshire kickoff, and get at least a somewhat larger share of influence and attention. To judge from both contemporary press reports and the figures in table 1.1, states have recognized the advantages of holding early primaries and caucuses since at least 1976, and front-loading has been going on almost continuously ever since. But front-loading took a quantum leap forward in 1988 and then, after receding somewhat in 1992, took another giant step in 1996.

The most publicized single change since 1992 was the timing of the California primary. Under the old, "prereform" nomination rules, the California presidential primary, traditionally held on the first Tuesday in June, had been a major event in American politics. Since 1976, however, California has generally been an irrelevant final scene tacked on to the end of a drama that has already been resolved. Over the last six election cycles, there is not a single presidential nominee—in either party—of whom it can reasonably be said that a win in the California primary was a decisive step on his road to victory. Finally, in the fall of 1993, after years of fruitless complaining, California made the big leap forward: from the first Tuesday in June to the fourth Tuesday in March.[4]

And California was not alone. All told, 29 state primaries were crammed into the six-week period between 20 February and 26 March. By the end of March 1996, more than three-fourths of the Republican primary delegates would already be chosen.

What effect would front-loading have on the dynamics of the 1996 nomination races? Before those races began, there were two dominant lines of speculation. Many observers felt that front-loading would be a major boon to candidates who were already nationally known and who could raise a great deal of campaign money during the preprimary period. Only candidates with these advantages, it was argued, would be able to campaign effectively in so many states in such a short time. But other commentators felt that a front-loaded system could also provide a golden opportunity to a comparatively unknown, long-shot candidate who achieved a sudden breakthrough by winning (or doing "better than expected") in Iowa and New Hampshire. In a less compressed primary schedule, a front-runner who stumbled early (as nearly all front-runners do) had a chance to recover his footing, mount an effective counterattack, and regain the lead. Under front-loading, by contrast, a candidate might be able to slingshot out of Iowa and New Hampshire and then quickly lock up the nomination before anyone could put a brake to his momentum.

The Republican Nomination Race

According to some accounts, a new presidential campaign begins as soon as the previous one ends. Within days after the general election voting, various would-be presidents are already starting to assess their prospects, contact potential supporters, and make themselves more widely available for speeches and media appearances, especially in Iowa and New Hampshire.[5] In the beginning, however, most of this activity is carried out behind the scenes or at least outside the glare of the national media's spotlight.

DEFINING THE FIELD

The first *public* phase of a contemporary presidential nomination race generally does not occur until after the midterm election is over. After those votes have been counted and digested, the nomination race enters a stage that might be called *defining the field,* for it is during this period that the presidential prospects decide and then publicly announce whether or not they will be active candidates for their party's nomination.

To some extent, these decisions are based on a number of extremely personal considerations: the candidate's individual strengths and weaknesses, his health and family situation, the office he currently holds and the sorts of responsibilities and commitments it entails, his personal drive and ambition, and so forth. But the decision to become a presidential candidate also reflects the common political context that all candidates face; and in 1996 that context was dominated by two major factors that seemed to point in quite different directions.

The first factor was the remarkable outcome of the 1994 midterm elections, which brought Republican majorities to power in both houses of Congress for the first time in forty years. Even the most determined Democratic spin doctor found it difficult to place a favorable gloss on the 1994 results. Along with Clinton's comparatively low approval ratings through most of his first two years in office, the 1994 elections suggested—misleadingly, as it turned out—that the incumbent president would be a relatively easy opponent to contend with, thus prompting lots of Republicans at least to consider joining the race.[6]

But a second important feature of the political landscape, the frontloaded caucus and primary calendar, was distinctly less encouraging. Whatever its other effects, the front-loaded system in 1996 seems to have played a major role in scaring off potential candidates. Under the sort of primary calendar that had existed in the 1960s and 1970s, candidates who were not initially prodigious fund raisers could reasonably hope to overcome this disadvantage as the race progressed. Since the process started up slowly, a candidate who did well in a few early primaries and caucuses had an opportunity to raise more money for the next round of primaries, where further success might yield even more contributions, and so on, in a continuing cycle of upward momentum. As the process has become more front-loaded, however, it has become progressively more difficult to reap the financial benefits of momentum. With twenty-nine primaries in just six weeks, there would be much less time to convert a strong showing in Iowa and New Hampshire into a new surge of campaign contributions, which could then be used for advertising and organization in future primaries. Front-loading, it was widely believed, required a candidate to have a great deal of money up-front, *before* the caucuses and primaries began.[7]

And just in case there were candidates or commentators who did not understand the new dynamic, Senator Phil Gramm of Texas went out of his way to make the point clear. Whatever his other potential weaknesses as a presidential candidate, Gramm looked to be an enormously successful fund raiser. To begin with, federal election law permitted him to transfer $5 million from his last Senate campaign to his presidential bid. And then, on 23 February 1995, the day before his formal declaration of candidacy, Gramm held what was widely described as "the most successful fund-raising event ever held for any federal candidate," a dinner in Dallas that pulled in $4.1 million in contributions.[8] With its own coffers flush, the Gramm campaign then used these funds in an open and deliberate attempt to discourage other potential candidates from entering the race. Any prospective GOP candidate who hoped to be taken seriously, Gramm declared on several occasions, would need to raise "upward of $25 million" before the primaries began. To his Dallas fund-raising dinner he noted, "I have the most reliable friend you can have in American politics, and that is ready money."[9]

The upshot was that the field of Republican candidates turned out to be smaller and thinner than many commentators had anticipated. In the first few months of 1995, a number of major national figures in the Republican Party, including several who had apparently spent the previous year laying the groundwork for a presidential bid, announced that they would *not* be running for president in 1996 (see table 1.2). In almost every instance, news reports indicated that one of the principal factors leading to the declaration of noncandidacy was concerns about fund raising.[10]

TABLE I.2

ANNOUNCEMENT AND WITHDRAWAL DATES IN THE 1996
REPUBLICAN NOMINATION RACE

Declarations of noncandidacy	
	Announcement date
William Bennett	24 August 1994
Dick Cheney	3 January 1995
Jack Kemp	30 January 1995
Dan Quayle	9 February 1995
William Weld	27 February 1995
Lynn Martin	24 March 1995
James Baker	10 May 1995
Tommy Thompson	10 June 1995
Colin Powell	8 November 1995
Newt Gingrich	27 November 1995

Declared candidates		
	Announcement date	*Withdrawal date*
Phil Gramm	24 February 1995	14 February 1996
Lamar Alexander	28 February 1995	6 March 1996
Pat Buchanan	20 March 1995	none
Alan Keyes	26 March 1995	none
Arlen Specter	30 March 1995	22 November 1995
Bob Dole	10 April 1995	—
Robert Dornan	13 April 1995	none
Richard Lugar	19 April 1995	6 March 1996
Pete Wilson	15 June 1995	29 September 1995
Steve Forbes	22 September 1995	14 March 1996

SOURCE: Compiled by the author from contemporary news accounts.

EXIT GINGRICH AND POWELL

Two other noncandidates made longer and noisier exits from the 1996 race. Throughout 1995 the most visible and controversial figure in the Republican Party—and the one who had the most impact on its future prospects—was unquestionably Newt Gingrich, the newly enthroned Speaker of the U.S. House of Representatives. Gingrich had originally seemed to take himself out of the presidential sweepstakes on 13 February 1995, telling reporters, "I think I should stay [in Congress] and focus on what I am doing and get things done." But by late spring, the Speaker began to offer indications that he was reconsidering his decision, that he was dissatisfied with the quality of the announced candidates and might get in the race "if a vacuum developed." There followed a remarkable half-year-long minuet in which Gingrich declined to announce his entry into the race but also refused to rule it out, in which statements that seemed to shut the door were closely followed by suggestions that it was still an active possibility. Perhaps the high point of the "Gingrich for President" craze came in mid-June, when the Speaker spent four days barnstorming around New Hampshire—the trip had originally been billed as a "vacation"—with 130 different news organizations following his every move.[11]

How seriously Gingrich ever entertained the idea of running for president is unclear. Nor is it obvious, if Gingrich had joined the race, how well he would have fared. Almost certainly he would have been a very good fund raiser; unquestionably he would attracted a great deal of press attention. But as the figures in table 1.3 indicate, the Speaker was never especially popular with ordinary Republican voters. In a Gallup survey conducted just before Gingrich's much-ballyhooed trip to New Hampshire, only 9 percent of Republican identifiers listed Gingrich as their first choice for the 1996 nomination, as compared to 45 percent who chose Robert Dole. Even Phil Gramm ran slightly ahead of Gingrich.

The survey evidence also indicates that as the fall budget battle wore on, and the Republicans were accused first of attempting to gut Medicare and then of forcing a government shutdown, the Speaker's popularity fell even further. Any remaining ambiguity about Gingrich's intentions was finally resolved on 27 November, when the Speaker announced that he was "explicitly, definitely clos[ing] the door so there's no more speculation."[12] By that point, however, the bloom was off the rose. Of the major news outlets I have examined, none treated Gingrich's final announcement as an especially significant story.[13]

The exit of Colin Powell, by contrast, *was* a major story—probably one of the most significant events in the 1996 campaign. Powell's situation was, in a sense, the reverse of Gingrich's. No one questioned the former general's popularity with the mass public: surveys routinely showed him as probably the most admired figure in American public life. The uncertainty, in Powell's case, concerned whether that general popularity could be transferred into an effective campaign for the presidency. Would Powell be willing to spend large amounts of time meeting small groups of voters in Iowa and New Hampshire? How much money could he raise? What kind of organizational apparatus would he put together? In sum, could someone who had never campaigned for elective office before really hope to thrive in the almost surreal environment of a contemporary presidential campaign?

If Powell decided to enter the race for the *Republican* nomination,[14] another important question would need to be faced: would Powell's popularity with the electorate at large hold up among the considerably more conservative voters who usually participate in Republican caucuses and primaries? Through the first six months of 1995, Colin Powell's policy views were, outside a narrow range of defense and foreign policy issues, almost completely unknown. As the year progressed, and the general gave more speeches and interviews, he gradually began to fill in the blank spaces. The portrait that emerged was scarcely that of a flaming radical, but neither did it reveal a tried-and-true conservative. Powell was pro-choice on abortion, he supported affirmative action, and he favored some forms of gun control. While Republican officials such as Gingrich, Dole, and national party chairman Haley Barbour were respectful and encouraging, a number of conservative activists made it clear that they were definitely *not* part of the Powell bandwagon and that they would do everything they could to oppose his nomination.[15]

Given his favorable public image, Powell assumed that he could afford to delay his entry into the race far longer than the Doles, Gramms, and Alexanders of the world. Having resigned from his position as chairman of the Joint Chiefs of Staff in late 1993, Powell spent the early months of 1995 finishing his autobiography; in mid-September, he embarked on a richly publicized, nationwide book tour. It was not until late October, then, that Powell seriously began to face up to the hard question whether or not to run for the presidency. For the next several weeks, with the press following his every public move and reporting every obscure hint of his emerging intentions, Powell and a small number of friends carefully weighed the pluses and minuses.

In the end, he decided not to run. On 8 November, Powell told a packed press conference that he would "not be a candidate for president or for any other elected office in 1996." Over the next few days, a number of major news organizations claimed to provide day-by-day, "behind the scenes" accounts of how Powell came to his decision.[16] But the best description of his reasons seems to have been the one he himself offered on 8 November:

> To offer myself as a candidate for president requires a commitment and a passion to run the race and to succeed in the quest; the kind of passion and kind of commitment that I felt every day of my 35 years as a soldier. A passion and commitment that, despite my every effort, I do not yet have for political life, because such a life requires a calling that I do not yet hear.[17]

TABLE 1.3

PRESIDENTIAL NOMINATION PREFERENCES OF NATIONAL REPUBLICAN IDENTIFIERS

DURING THE 1996 "INVISIBLE PRIMARY"

	5–6 Apr. 1995	11–14 May 1995	7–9 July 1995	28–30 Aug. 1995	17–18 Nov. 1995	15–18 Dec. 1995	5–7 Jan. 1996	12–15 Jan. 1996	26–29 Jan. 1996
				Announced candidates only					
Dole	46%	51%	49%	45%	45%	49%	47%	55%	47%
Gramm	13	12	7	11	10	13	10	6	8
Buchanan	8	5	6	7	6	9	7	5	7
Wilson	6	7	8	10	—	—	—	—	—
Alexander	3	3	4	4	4	1	2	3	3
Forbes	—	—	—	—	5	8	11	12	16
Lugar	5	3	3	3	2	3	5	2	3
Specter	2	3	3	2	2	—	—	—	—
Dornan	2	2	1	1	2	1	1	*	1
Keyes	1	1	2	2	1	2	2	3	1
No opinion	14	13	17	15	23	13	15	14	14
(N)	(373)	(459)	(389)		(246)			(485)	

Continued....

TABLE 1.3 — *Continued*

With Gingrich included

	5–6 June 1995
Dole	45%
Gramm	13
Gingrich	9
Buchanan	6
Wilson	5
Specter	4
Lugar	2
Alexander	2
Dornan	2
Keyes	1
No opinion	11
(N)	(438)

	With Powell included	
	22–24 Sept. 1995	*6–8 Nov.* 1995
Dole	31%	34%
Powell	31	33
Gramm	8	5
Buchanan	7	4
Wilson	3	—
Alexander	2	2
Forbes	3	5
Lugar	1	1
Specter	1	3
Keyes	*	1
Dornan	1	1
No opinion	12	11
(N)	(477)	(400)

SOURCE: All results taken from *Gallup Poll Monthly.*

NOTE: Figures through 5–7 January 1996 are based on all Republican identifiers. Results for 12–15 January 1996 and 26–29 January 1996 are based on respondents who were Republican identifiers and registered voters.

* indicates that a candidate was supported by less than 1 percent of the survey respondents.

— indicates that a candidate's name was not on the list read to respondents in that particular survey.

How Colin Powell would have fared in the 1996 presidential campaign must remain a tantalizing speculation. As the data in table 1.3 indicate, before taking himself out of the race, Powell was running about even with Dole in polls of national Republican identifiers. However, surveys of likely caucus attenders in Iowa, which probably provide a better indication of Powell's standing among Republican *activists,* show strikingly little support for the former general (see table 1.4 on page 39). Conceivably, Powell would have outshone Dole on the stump, attracted a huge number of independents and Democrats into the Republican nomination process, and gone on to victory, just as Dwight Eisenhower had in 1952. Alternatively, Powell's candidacy might have gone the way of Edward Kennedy's in 1980: peaking on the day he announced and declining steadily thereafter.

THE FINAL FIELD

Colin Powell excepted, the basic dimensions of the 1996 Republican nomination race had started to emerge by the early summer of 1995. With Jack Kemp and Dan Quayle out of the race, the clear front-runner was Senate Majority Leader Robert Dole, now making his third run at the White House. Polls of the national Republican electorate taken at this time routinely showed Dole with a 30 to 40 percent lead over all his competitors (see table 1.3). The second tier, according to most handicappers, included four candidates: Senator Phil Gramm of Texas; former Tennessee governor and Secretary of Education Lamar Alexander; California Governor Pete Wilson; and former presidential speechwriter and syndicated columnist Pat Buchanan, who had also been a candidate in 1992. One notch below them were two U.S. senators of considerable substance who were, nevertheless, generally regarded as nearly hopeless long shots: Richard Lugar of Indiana and Arlen Specter of Pennsylvania. (Three other candidates—California congressman Robert Dornan, radio host and former State Department official Alan Keyes, and businessman Maurice Taylor—were occasionally invited to debates and candidate forums, but they played no significant role in the 1996 race.)

Fall 1995 brought a few final alterations to the Republican field. Far and away the most significant of these occurred on 22 September, when Malcolm "Steve" Forbes Jr., a multimillionaire publishing magnate with little previous experience in government, announced that he was running for president. As the GOP picked up one new entrant, however, it was losing two old ones. On 29 September, Pete Wilson announced that he was withdrawing from the race. On 22 November, Arlen Specter followed suit.

Specter, as I have indicated, had always been considered a distinct long shot for the Republican nomination, and his departure did not raise many eyebrows.[18] But just six months earlier, Wilson had been regarded as a major player in the 1996 drama; some observers, indeed, thought him to be the single strongest candidate the Republican Party had to offer against Bill Clinton. As R.W. Apple Jr. had declared in a February 1995 article on the front page of the *New York Times,* "It is hard to imagine anyone in a better position to run for the Republican Presidential nomination next year than Pete Wilson."[19]

Wilson's major claim to attention, of course, was the simple fact that he was governor of the largest state in America, a state that could provide one-fifth of the votes needed for victory in the electoral college and that had long been seen as crucial to Bill Clinton's reelection prospects.[20] Being from California also gave Wilson privileged access to an impressive roster of big contributors and fund raisers. In his 1994 reelection race, Wilson had raised almost $30 million. (It is worth pointing out, however, that this feat was accomplished under state campaign finance laws that are significantly less restrictive than those that apply to federal offices.) Finally, although Wilson was pro-choice on abortion and supported gay rights, he had managed to position himself at the forefront of a number of issues that might appeal to social and cultural conservatives and that promised to play a major role in the 1996 elections, including crime, immigration, and affirmative action.

Such apparent advantages notwithstanding, the Wilson campaign had stumbled and staggered from the beginning. Its first major problem was actually medical. On 14 April, shortly after Wilson began to explore his presidential prospects, the California governor had undergone throat surgery to remove a small, benign growth from his right vocal cord. Though the operation was successful, Wilson's recovery was considerably slower than expected: for the next two months, he was almost entirely unable to speak, a condition that obviously retarded his efforts to mobilize party activists and contributors. In early May, the campaign had to contend with revelations that Wilson and his first wife had hired an illegal alien to do housework in the late 1970s and then failed to pay her Social Security taxes. To make matters worse, the Wilson campaign was reportedly plagued by constant dissension and in-fighting, particularly between the governor's long-time California advisers and the more nationally experienced professionals he had brought in to help navigate the unfamiliar waters of a presidential contest.[21]

Even the vaunted California connection ultimately proved troublesome. When running for reelection as governor in 1994, Wilson had promised the state's voters that he would serve out his full four-year term. Bill

Clinton had made the same promise to Arkansas voters in 1990, but apparently had devised a more artful way of going back on his word. Wilson, by contrast, seemed to shift gears almost immediately after his inauguration. Moreover, Wilson's lieutenant governor, and thus his successor as governor if Wilson moved up to the presidency, was a liberal Democrat, a fact that made many California Republicans less enthusiastic about pushing one of their own for national office. Partly for these reasons, and partly perhaps because of California's continuing economic woes, a steady stream of polls raised serious questions about Wilson's popularity within his home state and thus about whether his presence on the national ticket would actually help the Republicans carry the state against Clinton.[22] Lagging in the polls and a million dollars in debt, Wilson first shut down his Iowa campaign and then threw in the towel altogether.

These early withdrawals are worth noting for another reason: Wilson and Specter were the only two candidates in the 1996 Republican field who were clearly and unambiguously pro-choice on the abortion issue.[23] Indeed, both candidates had premised their campaigns partly on the belief that with so many other candidates vying for the support of cultural and religious conservatives, an opening existed for a candidate who united fiscal conservatism with a more liberal stance on social issues, particularly abortion.

Unfortunately for both political strategists and social scientists, reality rarely provides an unambiguous test of a political hypothesis. If both the Wilson and Specter campaigns fizzled quickly, it is unclear how much, if anything, the abortion issue had to do with their fate. Specter probably never had much chance to begin with; and his appeal to socially liberal women, it might be further argued, was substantially undercut by the fact that he had been one of Anita Hill's toughest cross-examiners during the Clarence Thomas confirmation hearings. The Wilson effort collapsed for a variety of reasons. All of which holds out just enough hope for pro-choice Republicans to suggest that someone else will probably try the same strategy next go-around.

FORBES BREAKS OUT OF THE PACK

In its general outlines, then, the 1996 Republican nomination race settled into a familiar pattern: a clear front-runner trailed by a large pack of second- and third-tier challengers. The Republican nomination battles of 1980 and 1988 and the Democratic contest in 1984 were all carved out of essentially the same mold. For the non-front-runners, such a situation carries with it two clear strategic imperatives. First, attack the front-runner—or hope that he self-destructs. Second, try to position yourself as the "principal alternative" to the front-runner: the person who is seen as the most viable option for those who become dissatisfied with the lead candidate. And though Phil Gramm and Lamar Alexander had been trying to accomplish these same goals since the early months of 1995, the first candidate to show any signs of notable success was Steve Forbes.

Forbes got into the 1996 race as the defender of supply-side economics. The principal item in his platform was a proposal to replace the current, graduated income tax system with a "flat tax" of 17 percent applied to all salaried income. (The tax would not have applied, however, to income derived from savings and investments.) A flat tax, according to Forbes, would yield a rich array of benefits: stimulating economic growth, greatly reducing the burdens of taxpayer compliance, strengthening families, and changing the very culture of Washington by eliminating the "principal source of political power, pollution, and . . . corruption."[24]

But with all due respect to the flat tax, Forbes's early success had much less to do with his policy ideas than with the amount of money he was able to spend. As the result of a 1976 Supreme Court decision,[25] federal campaign finance laws have severely limited the amount of money that a person can contribute to someone else's campaign while at the same time allowing candidates to spend unlimited amounts of their own money on their own campaigns. Over the years, a sizable number of wealthy individuals have taken advantage of this situation to finance campaigns for the U.S. Senate and House of Representatives. In 1992 Ross Perot applied the same principle to a presidential campaign, and though $63 million did not buy him victory, it did produce the best showing for a third-party candidate in eighty years.

On joining the Republican race in September, Forbes said he was willing to spend $25 million of his own money on the enterprise. True to his word, the Forbes campaign quickly began to pour enormous amounts of money into states that were holding early caucuses and primaries, especially Iowa, New Hampshire, Delaware, and Arizona. Tradition has it that Iowa and New Hampshire are states where grassroots organization still matters, where any campaign that hopes to succeed must have an extensive, carefully nurtured field organization. But the Forbes campaign challenged the conventional wisdom head on. Almost all of its money went directly into television ads.

Lots of ads. In New Hampshire, Forbes bought enough time on Boston television to ensure that the typical voter saw his ads thirty-four times a week. In the fourth quarter of 1995, according to FEC reports, the Forbes campaign spent $14 million. It then spent another $7.2 million between 1

January and 20 February 1996. In Iowa alone, Forbes spent $4 million —about $400 for every vote he ultimately received.[26]

Inexorably, the ads began to have an effect. By late November, the *New York Times* was reporting that Forbes "has pulled even with or ahead of every candidate except the front-runner, Senator Bob Dole, in New Hampshire or Iowa." A mid-December article in the *Washington Post* quoted a top adviser to a rival candidate as saying, "There is no dispute that [Forbes] is in second place in Iowa and New Hampshire."[27]

By mid-January, Forbes had arrived: he was unquestionably *the* hot candidate in the 1996 Republican field. When all the Republican aspirants gathered in Iowa for a nationally televised debate on 13 January, the candidate who attracted most of the criticism from his rivals was not Bob Dole but Steve Forbes.[28] In the week of 29 January, Forbes was featured on the covers of both *Time* and *Newsweek*. Most important, polls in the early primary and caucus states showed that he was beginning to close in on Dole. In Iowa, where the Kansas senator had once appeared to be a prohibitive favorite, a PSI poll conducted on 22 January found just 26 percent of likely caucus attenders planning to support Dole, while 18 percent favored Forbes (see table 1.4). In New Hampshire, a number of late January polls showed Forbes clearly in the lead. In a *Boston Globe* survey conducted on 29 and 30 January, for example, the results were Forbes 31 percent, Dole 22 percent (see table 1.5). Surveys in Arizona showed Dole and Forbes running even.[29]

Besides pumping up Forbes himself, the millionaire's media blitz had at least three other effects on the tenor of the Republican race. First, it administered a severe pounding to the other candidates, especially Bob Dole. Though Forbes's performance on the stump was sunny, optimistic, and appealingly unpolished, his ads were being crafted by two long-time politicos who had honed their skills working in the bare-knuckle Senate races of Jesse Helms (R-N.C.). While some of their ads trumpeted the virtues of Forbes and the flat tax, many were clearly designed to dirty-up the front-runner, portraying him as a Washington insider who repeatedly voted for tax increases and gaudy congressional perquisites.

At the same time, Forbes made it vastly more difficult for any of the other second-tier candidates to get their messages out and begin to distinguish their campaigns from the rest of the pack. With Forbes dominating the paid media and soaking up an increasing share of the news coverage, Alexander, Gramm, and Buchanan all found themselves temporarily immobilized, stuck at single digits in the Iowa and New Hampshire polls.

Finally, Forbes provoked a counterattack from the other campaigns, es-

TABLE 1.4

PRESIDENTIAL NOMINATION PREFERENCES OF LIKELY
ATTENDERS OF THE IOWA REPUBLICAN CAUCUSES

	PSI						
	16–23 Jan. 1995	*29–30 March 1995*	*31 May– 1 June 1995*	*21–22 Aug. 1995*	*8 Nov. 1995*	*22 Jan. 1996*	*Actual results*
Dole	36%	51%	52%	36%	36%	26%	26.3%
Buchanan	1	5	5	8	9	7	23.3
Alexander	*	1	1	6	6	7	17.6
Forbes	—	—	—	—	8	18	10.2
Gramm	5	10	12	14	8	7	9.3
Lugar	—	*	2	1	2	3	3.7
Powell	7	2	5	4	—	—	
Quayle	9	—	—	—	—	—	
Kemp	6	—	—	—	—	—	
Gingrich	2	—	—	1	3	—	
Wilson	*	3	1	2	—	—	
Specter	*	2	*	2	3	—	
Other	6	2	3	3	8	9	9.6
Undecided	28	23	19	22	18	23	
(N)	(300)	(300)	(300)	(300)	(300)	(300)	

	Iowa Poll			
	6–10 May 1995	*9–13 Sept. 1995*	*26–30 Nov. 1995*	*3–8 Feb. 1996*
Dole	57%	40%	41%	28%
Buchanan	6	7	7	11
Alexander	2	7	6	10
Forbes	—	—	12	16
Gramm	11	18	9	8
Lugar	1	2	3	2
Wilson	2	4	—	—
Specter	1	1	—	—
Other	4	6	6	6
Undecided	16	15	16	19
(N)	(405)	(400)	(407)	(628)

SOURCE: PSI results provided courtesy of Craig Tufty. Iowa Poll results provided courtesy of the *Des Moines Register.*

    * indicates that a candidate was supported by less than 1 percent of the survey respondents.

    —indicates that a candidate's name was not on the list read to respondents in that particular survey.

TABLE 1.5

PRESIDENTIAL NOMINATION PREFERENCES OF LIKELY VOTERS IN THE NEW HAMPSHIRE REPUBLICAN PRIMARY

KRC Communications Research, for *Boston Globe*/WBZ-TV

| | 13–15 Feb. 1995 | | 7–10 Jan. 1996 | 29–30 Jan. 1996 | 9–10 Feb. 1996 | 10–11 Feb. 1996 | 11–12 Feb. 1996 |
	With Powell	Without Powell					
Buchanan	7%	9%	11%	11%	15%	16%	17%
Dole	35	42	33	22	25	24	26
Alexander	2	3	5	9	9	5	5
Forbes	—	—	17	31	26	20	16
Lugar	—	—	2	3	3	4	6
Gramm	6	7	5	7	4	7	5
Powell	20	—	—	—	—	—	—
Weld	8	12	—	—	—	—	—
Specter	2	3	—	—	—	—	—
Wilson	1	2	—	—	—	—	—
Other	2	2	4	4	8	n.a.	n.a.
No opinion	15	20	24	12	11	n.a.	n.a.
(N)	(400)	(400)	(400)	(400)	(400)	(400)	(400)

	12–13 Feb. 1996	13–14 Feb. 1996	14–15 Feb. 1996	16 Feb. 1996	16–17 Feb. 1996	17–18 Feb. 1996	19 Feb. 1996	Actual results
Buchanan	16%	17%	22%	22%	21%	20%	24%	27.2%
Dole	26	27	25	25	24	23	23	26.2
Alexander	8	12	14	18	18	18	21	22.6
Forbes	17	16	14	13	14	13	13	12.2
Lugar	6	3	3	5	6	7	5	5.2
Gramm	5	4	—a	—	—	—	—	.4
Other	n.a.	4	5	5	7	6	9	6.2
No opinion	n.a.	17	17	11	10	12	5	
(N)	(400)	(400)	(400)	(400)	(800)	(800)	(691)	

Gallup Poll

	9–11 Feb. 1996	10–12 Feb. 1996	11–13 Feb. 1996	12–14 Feb. 1996	13–15 Feb. 1996	14–16 Feb. 1996	16–17 Feb. 1996	17–18 Feb. 1996	18–19 Feb. 1996
Buchanan	19%	20%	21%	25%	25%	25%	25%	25%	26%
Dole	25	28	31	32	28	27	26	24	23
Alexander	11	10	11	14	20	23	20	20	20
Forbes	25	21	17	14	13	12	12	14	13
Lugar	4	5	5	5	5	4	5	5	6
Gramm	4	4	5	—a	—	—	—	—	—
Other	4	4	3	4	3	3	5	5	5
No opinion	8	8	7	6	6	6	7	7	7
(N)	(537)	(492)	(496)	(486)	(490)	(600)	(665)	(828)	(841)

Continued...

WMUR–Dartmouth College Poll

	1–4 Oct. 1995	22–25 Oct. 1995	7–10 Jan. 1996	29 Jan.–2 Feb. 1996	13–15 Feb. 1996
Buchanan	9%	9%	10%	12%	22%
Dole	35	37	37	25	22
Alexander	7	6	7	10	16
Forbes	7	10	18	29	14
Gramm	6	6	5	6	—a
Lugar	1	1	2	3	4
Specter	2	2	—	—	—
Other	13	10	12	5	9
Undecided	21	18	12	12	13
(N)	(483)	(530)	(512)	(421)	(343)

SOURCE: KRC results taken from the *Boston Globe.* Gallup results taken from *Gallup Poll Monthly,* February 1996, 18 and 21. WMUR results provided courtesy of the Rockefeller Center at Dartmouth College.

NOTE: Results for 13–15 February 1995 based on all registered voters eligible to participate in the Republican primary. All other results based on likely voters in the Republican primary.

a. Gramm withdrew from the race on 14 February.

— indicates that a candidate's name was not on the list read to respondents in that particular survey.

pecially Dole's, that led them to commit a lot more money to television advertising in Iowa and New Hampshire than they had originally anticipated. Iowa and New Hampshire voters were accustomed to and even expected frequent visits by the candidates and their trailing mobs of reporters. But they were not prepared for the war of dueling television spots that erupted in late January and early February. As the tone of these ads became increasingly negative, the character of the campaign became a major issue in itself. Newspaper and television stories increasingly portrayed a race in which "issues took a back seat to bickering" and "talk [about issues] was drowned out by [the candidates'] complaints about the way their opponents were playing the game." Other reports claimed that the electorates in Iowa and New Hampshire were growing more and more disgusted by the whole spectacle, disenchanted with *all* the candidates. As one Republican precinct official in Iowa told a reporter several days before the caucuses, "From start to finish, this campaign has made it harder for me to decide. It's the ugliest thing I've ever seen."[30]

Into this breach leaped Lamar Alexander. Though Alexander had run what is generally said to be the first negative ad of the 1996 Republican race, in the final days before the Iowa caucuses he began to proclaim as one of the principal virtues of his campaign that he alone among the major contenders was refusing to engage in negative campaigning. When this theme seemed to draw a positive response in Iowa, it became even more prominent in Alexander's final burst of campaigning in New Hampshire. For the last several days before that state's voting, Alexander's favorite prop at rallies and photo opportunities was a pair of L.L. Bean hip boots, designed, he said, to protect him from all the mud being slung by the other candidates.[31]

THE PRIMARIES AND CAUCUSES

It was against this background that the delegate selection season finally began. And just as advertised, it turned out to be a short and wild ride.

The 1996 Republican race began in an unexpected location. Over the last several election cycles, a number of states have attempted to challenge the privileged positions of Iowa and New Hampshire as the first presidential caucus and primary. But both states fought hard to defend their turf and, with assistance from the national parties and many of the presidential candidates, had always managed to fend off their rivals. In 1996, however, the Louisiana Republican Party proved to be just as stubborn: it scheduled its caucuses for 6 February, six days before Iowa, and then refused to move them. A full-blooded showdown with Iowa was averted only because most of the Republican candidates promised that they would not campaign in

Louisiana. But two candidates were willing to defy the ban: Phil Gramm and Pat Buchanan. Louisiana accordingly came to be seen as the first real test of strength between two men who sought to appeal to the same core constituency: what Gramm himself described as "a sort of semifinal to decide who is the real conservative candidate."[32]

Louisiana had originally looked to be fertile terrain for Gramm. He came from a neighboring state; he was endorsed by most of the state's Republican congressmen; he had reportedly built a very strong statewide organization. In January 1995 he had won an overwhelming victory in a straw poll held at the state Republican convention.[33] But Buchanan campaigned extensively in Louisiana in the weeks immediately preceding the caucuses, and proved particularly successful at mobilizing religious conservatives. There is also evidence that the Buchanan effort in Louisiana received some important assistance from the Dole campaign, which at that time saw Gramm as its most formidable long-term rival.[34] Aided by a low turnout, Buchanan won thirteen of the twenty-one delegates at stake that day, to just eight for Gramm.

The Louisiana caucuses had not received much press attention and attracted only 23,000 participants, yet just hours after they were over, the Gramm campaign found itself in serious trouble. A front-page story in the next day's *New York Times* called the result a "stunning upset" that was "shaking the Senator's campaign and devastating his strategy to emerge ... as the leading conservative in the race." Gramm himself told reporters, "If I can run in the top three [in Iowa], we're very much in this race. If I don't run in the top three, we're out of this race. So it's clear cut."[35]

The scene now shifted to Iowa, where the full Republican field was competing. Just as Gramm had been the presumptive favorite in Louisiana, Iowa was long viewed as favorable turf for Robert Dole. Not only was Dole from a neighboring state with a very similar economic base, but Iowa was also the scene of the greatest triumph in his 1988 presidential campaign: a resounding win over George Bush and Pat Robertson that had almost brought Dole victory in New Hampshire. In 1996 Dole won again, but just barely. He received 26 percent of the votes cast by the Republican caucusers, down from 37 percent eight years earlier.

More surprising to the pundits was what happened to the rest of the field. Pat Buchanan, riding the momentum from his victory in Louisiana, came in second with 23 percent. Lamar Alexander, who had been even farther back in the polls several weeks earlier, finished third, with 18 percent. After driving the race through most of December and January, Steve Forbes slumped to fourth place, with just 10 percent of the caucus vote.

Two days later, the forces of winnowing claimed their first victim. As Louisiana had buoyed Buchanan, so it doomed Phil Gramm. The Texas senator finished fifth in Iowa, a percentage point behind Forbes and just two points ahead of Alan Keyes. For all his success at fund raising, Gramm was never able to establish a rapport with the typical Republican voter. Like John Connally in 1980, Gramm found that the tough, abrasive image that worked so well in Texas politics played poorly in the rest of the country. On 14 February, he suspended his campaign.

As Louisiana had helped set the stage for Iowa, so the Iowa results helped define the race in New Hampshire. As the Granite State campaign headed into its final week, it was widely projected as a three-man race. Gramm was finished, and Forbes appeared to be heading in the same direction. The millionaire's standing in the New Hampshire tracking polls fell dramatically in the days immediately after Iowa, and never recovered (see table 1.5). Dole and Buchanan, by contrast, each enjoyed a small surge in support. But the candidate who got the greatest "bump" out of Iowa was clearly Lamar Alexander. Though the former Tennessee governor had been campaigning heavily in New Hampshire for more than a year, it was not until his "better than expected" showing in Iowa that his New Hampshire survey numbers began to take off. In just four days, according to the *Boston Globe*'s surveys, Alexander went from 5 percent to 18 percent.

In the final weekend before the primary, the Dole campaign unleashed one last barrage of negative ads, this time aimed at Lamar Alexander. Alexander's momentum stalled, but Dole's numbers also declined slightly, while Buchanan's support held firm. Thus the former commentator eked out a narrow win: 27 percent for Buchanan to 26 percent for Dole, with Alexander once again in third place, at 23 percent (see table 1.6).

The New Hampshire result was widely interpreted as a significant setback for the Dole campaign. The most immediate casualty of the Granite State primary, however, seemed to be Steve Forbes. Having spent millions of dollars in a state that should have been fertile ground for his antitax, antigovernment message, Forbes finished a distant fourth, receiving just 12 percent of the vote. Yet, over the next week, Forbes was apparently able to deal himself back into the contest.

Forbes's road back to respectability began in Delaware on 24 February. Much like the Louisiana caucuses, the 1996 Delaware primary was a sort of rogue event. It was scheduled to take place four days after New Hampshire, but New Hampshire state law required its primary to be held at least *seven* days before any other. New Hampshire officials accordingly threatened to move up their own primary date and thus throw off the entire early dele-

TABLE 1.6

REPUBLICAN PRIMARY RESULTS

Date	State	Dole	Buchanan	Alex-ander	Forbes	Total vote
20 Feb.	New Hampshire	26.2%	27.2%	22.6%	12.2%	208,993
24 Feb.	Delaware	27.2	18.7	13.3	32.7	32,773
27 Feb.	Arizona	29.6	27.6	7.1	33.4	347,482
27 Feb.	North Dakota	42.1	18.3	6.3	19.5	63,734
27 Feb.	South Dakota	44.7	28.6	8.7	12.8	69,170
2 March	South Carolina	45.1	29.2	10.4	12.7	276,741
5 March	Colorado	43.6	21.5	9.8	20.8	247,752
5 March	Connecticut	54.4	15.1	5.4	20.1	130,418
5 March	Georgia	40.6	29.1	13.6	12.7	559,067
5 March	Maine	46.3	24.5	6.6	14.8	67,280
5 March	Maryland	53.3	21.1	5.5	12.7	254,246
5 March	Massachusetts	47.7	25.2	7.5	13.9	284,833
5 March	Rhode Island	64.4	2.6 [a]	19.0	.9 [a]	15,009
5 March	Vermont	40.3	16.7	10.6	15.6	58,113
12 March	Florida	56.9	18.1	1.6	20.2	898,070
12 March	Louisiana	47.8	33.1	2.1	13.2	77,789
12 March	Mississippi	60.3	25.9	1.8	8.0	151,925
12 March	Oklahoma	59.3	21.5	1.3	14.1	264,542
12 March	Oregon	50.8	21.3	7.0	13.3	407,514
12 March	Tennessee	51.2	25.2	11.3	7.7	289,043
12 March	Texas	55.6	21.4	1.8	12.8	1,019,803

Continued . . .

gate selection calendar, relenting only because most of the candidates promised not to campaign in Delaware. But Forbes refused to march in step, targeting the state with a heavy barrage of television commercials and direct-mail solicitations that were, this time, unanswered by his opponents. Though Dole was supported by most of the state's Republican leadership and seemed to have a comfortable lead in the polls, Forbes edged past him in the final voting, 33 percent to 27 percent.[36]

If Forbes's win in Delaware was heavily discounted by most commentators, his victory in Arizona on 27 February was harder to ignore. Buchanan, Dole, and Forbes all campaigned actively in Arizona in the final week. But the Dole campaign nullified much of its effort by committing one more in a long string of tactical errors, refusing to participate in a televised debate held in Tempe just five days before the voting.[37] Thus Forbes beat Dole, 33 percent to 30 percent, with 28 percent for Buchanan. The Dole

TABLE 1.6 — *Continued*

Date	State	Dole	Buchanan	Alexander	Forbes	Total vote
19 March	Illinois	65.1%	22.7%	1.5%	4.9%	818,364
19 March	Michigan	50.6	33.9	1.5	5.1	524,161
19 March	Ohio	66.4	21.5	2.0	6.0	955,017
19 March	Wisconsin	52.3	33.8	1.9	5.6	576,575
26 March	California	66.1	18.4	1.8	7.5	2,452,312
26 March	Nevada	51.9	15.2	2.3	19.2	140,637
26 March	Washington	63.1	20.9	1.3	8.6	120,684
23 April	Pennsylvania	63.6	18.0	—	8.0	684,204
7 May	District of Columbia	75.5	9.5	—	—	2,941
7 May	Indiana	70.6	19.4	—	9.9	498,444
7 May	North Carolina	71.5	13.0	2.7	4.1	283,213
14 May	Nebraska	75.7	10.4	2.6	6.2	170,591
14 May	West Virginia	68.8	16.3	2.9	4.9	125,413
21 May	Arkansas	76.5	23.5	—	—	42,648
28 May	Idaho	62.3	22.3	—	—	118,715
28 May	Kentucky	73.8	8.1	3.2	3.3	103,206
4 June	Alabama	74.9	15.7	—	—	143,295
4 June	Montana	61.3	24.4	—	7.2	114,463
4 June	New Jersey	82.3	11.0	—	—	209,998
4 June	New Mexico	75.4	8.2	3.9	5.7	67,122
	Totals	58.4	21.6	3.6	10.3	13,876,300

SOURCE: *Congressional Quarterly Weekly Report*, 3 August 1996, 63.

a. Buchanan and Forbes were not listed on the Rhode Island ballot. Votes shown are write-ins.

campaign received modest consolation by posting easy victories in two other primaries held that day, in North Dakota and South Dakota.

The next major event on the tour was the South Carolina primary. Beginning in 1980, South Carolina Republicans had managed to carve out an important niche in their party's nomination calendar. By holding their primary on a Saturday, they established themselves as the first southern primary and thus the first test of strength in a region that now played a central role in Republican presidential planning. Once again, Dole had planned not to participate in a televised debate held just before the primary, but having learned his lesson in Arizona, he changed his mind at the last moment. With strong support from state party leaders, Dole scored his first impressive win of the 1996 season, receiving 45 percent of the vote to 29 percent for Buchanan and just 13 and 10 percent for Forbes and Alexander.

And then, quite suddenly, it was over. With Bob Dole's victory in the South Carolina primary, the competitive phase of the 1996 Republican race effectively came to an end. Never again would Dole's quest for the nomination be seriously challenged. Three days after South Carolina came a mixed assortment of eight primaries, mostly in the Northeast, that the press had dubbed "Junior Tuesday." Dole coasted to comfortable wins in all eight states; his *narrowest* triumph that day came in Georgia, where he still managed to beat his nearest opponent by 11 percentage points. During the next three weeks, Dole then won the New York primary on 9 March, all seven primaries held on "Super Tuesday," all four midwestern primaries held on "Big Ten Tuesday," and the three western primaries, including California, that voted on 26 March. Dole's average margin of victory during this string was 33 percentage points. Most of his opponents quickly got the message and withdrew: Alexander and Lugar on 6 March, Forbes on 14 March. As in 1992, Pat Buchanan never did officially withdraw from the race, but he did make a number of statements conceding the inevitability of Dole's nomination. Most media delegate tallies showed Dole clinching a first-ballot victory as of 26 March (see table 1.7).

WHY DOLE WON

Such are the bare facts; the more daunting task is to explain them. How did Bob Dole win the 1996 Republican nomination? Why did he stumble early in Iowa, New Hampshire, and Arizona? More important, how did he manage to turn things around so quickly right after that and win the next thirty-six primaries in a row?

Of all the major factors working in Dole's favor, one that almost certainly does *not* belong on the list is the candidate's own campaigning skills. On this score, the reviews by journalists, political consultants, and fellow candidates are all but unanimous: Bob Dole has never campaigned very effectively for national office. A variety of important shortcomings were regularly attributed to the 1996 Dole campaign. Above all, it is remarkable that, with all Dole's paid advisers and consultants, he was somehow unable to put together a single, good fifteen-minute stump speech that explained what his candidacy was about and why he wanted to be president.[38]

But if it is easy to disparage the Dole campaign, it is also important to add that one does not get to his position in the Republican Party and the U.S. Senate without some very significant strengths, and through the early months of 1996 these were too often ignored. First, the public opinion polls

TABLE 1.7
ACCUMULATING CONVENTION DELEGATE COMMITMENTS: REPUBLICANS

Date	State	New delegates				Cumulative delegates			
		Dole	Buchanan	Forbes	Other or uncommitted	Dole	Buchanan	Forbes	Other or uncommitted
6 Feb.	Louisiana[a]		13		8		13		8
18 Feb.	Guam[a]	4							
20 Feb.	New Hampshire	4	6	2	4	8	21	2	10
24 Feb.	Delaware			12					
27 Feb.	Arizona			39					
27 Feb.	North Dakota	8	3	4	3				
27 Feb.	South Dakota	11	7			27	31	57	13
2 March	South Carolina	37							
2 March	Wyoming[a]	5		1	6	69	31	58	19
3 March	Puerto Rico	14							
5 March	Colorado	14	7	6					
5 March	Connecticut	27							
5 March	Georgia	39	3						
5 March	Maine	8	4	3					
5 March	Maryland	32							

Continued . . .

TABLE 1.7 — Continued

Date	State	New delegates				Cumulative delegates			
		Dole	Buchanan	Forbes	Other or un-committed	Dole	Buchanan	Forbes	Other or un-committed
5 March	Massachusetts	37							
5 March	Rhode Island	16							
5 March	Vermont	12							
7 March	New York	93				361	45	67	19
12 March	Florida	98							
12 March	Louisiana	9							
12 March	Mississippi	33							
12 March	Oklahoma	38							
12 March	Oregon	14	6	3					
12 March	Tennessee	36	2						
12 March	Texas	121	2			710	55	70	19
19 March	Illinois	59							
19 March	Michigan	34	23						
19 March	Ohio	67							
19 March	Wisconsin	36				933	80	—b	64
26 March	California	165							

Date	State						
26 March	Nevada	14					
26 March	Washington	14	4	1,126	84	—	64
23 April	Pennsylvania^c			1,140	95	—	132
7 May	District of Columbia						
7 May	Indiana						
7 May	North Carolina			1,234	103	2	138
14 May	Nebraska						
14 May	West Virginia						
21 May	Arkansas			1,283	109	—	145
28 May	Idaho						
28 May	Kentucky						
4 June	Alabama						
4 June	Montana						
4 June	New Jersey						
4 June	New Mexico			1,477	141	—	138

SOURCE: Compiled by the author from data reported in Congressional Quarterly Weekly Report and New York Times.

NOTE: Delegate totals are based on the ongoing tallies maintained by the Associated Press and include only delegates who had actually been selected in primaries or caucuses or had been allocated on the basis of primary results.

a. Delegates selected by caucus. All other events listed are primaries.

b. Forbes withdrew from the race on 14 March. Delegates he had won up to that point were reassigned to the alternative candidate they supported, if any, or to uncommitted.

c. After Dole clinched the nomination on 26 March, media organizations stopped reporting the delegate results for individual states.

clearly showed that Dole was better known and better liked than any of his declared opponents. Second, as the Senate Majority Leader, he alone among the Republican candidates had some measure of influence over the ongoing business of government. For the same reason, he also received more press coverage than any of his opponents.[39]

Third, he was very well liked and well respected by almost everybody else in the party who had ever worked with him. The closest thing in the current selection process to a system of peer review is the pattern of endorsements made by governors and senators; it is no accident that in 1996 these people came out overwhelmingly for Dole. Particularly helpful to Dole was the support he received from the Republican governors in Iowa, New Hampshire, and South Carolina. Fourth, for all his problems in articulating an ideology, Dole's *voting record* in the Senate clearly put him in the center of his party, acceptable to all the major Republican factions and interests. Fifth, and partly as a consequence of the first four, he was a prodigious fund raiser, who was thus able to amass the kind of war chest that would allow him to withstand an early setback or two.

Even with all this going for him, there were a few Republicans who might have given Dole a serious run for the nomination—Colin Powell and Jack Kemp being probably his strongest potential competitors. But, as we have seen, neither of them chose to get into the race. And when one looked at the men who did emerge as Dole's principal opponents—Buchanan, Forbes, and Alexander—all had a number of major weaknesses and limitations that made their nomination highly unlikely. This is not to suggest that there was *no* conceivable way for Dole to lose the 1996 race or that winning the nomination did not require a good deal of effort on his part. But it is to say that even during the darkest days of the Dole campaign, after his losses in New Hampshire, Delaware, and Arizona, it was always difficult to construct a plausible scenario as to how anybody but Dole would win the nomination.

Consider, first, Pat Buchanan. Perhaps the most impressive characteristic of Buchanan's vote in the 1996 primaries is how stable it was, how little it varied from state to state (see table 1.8). In almost every state, he got a steady 15–20–25 percent of the vote. He never dipped below this figure: his worst showing was in Connecticut, where he still got 15 percent of the vote.[40] And perhaps more important, he never did much better than this. His best showing was in Michigan where, with just about everybody else out of the race, he still got only 34 percent. In only two other states did the Buchanan vote exceed 30 percent. And lest one think this is somehow a coincidence, or a function of the peculiar makeup of the 1996 Republican

TABLE 1.8

DISTRIBUTION OF THE BUCHANAN, FORBES, AND ALEXANDER
VOTE IN THE 1996 REPUBLICAN PRIMARIES

Vote in	Buchanan		Forbes		Alexander	
the primaries	N	%	N	%	N	%
0–4%	0	0	0	0	0	0
5–9%	0	0	2	10	7	50
10–14%	0	0	10	50	5	36
15–19%	7	26	2	10	1	7
20–24%	9	33	4	20	1	7
25–29%	8	30	0	0	0	0
30–34%	3	11	2	10	0	0
35% or more	0	0	0	0	0	0

NOTE: Vote for Forbes and Alexander is for all primaries before they withdrew in which they were listed on the state ballot. Vote for Buchanan is for all primaries through 26 March in which he was listed on the state ballot.

field, almost exactly the same pattern had occurred when Buchanan ran for president in 1992.

Such figures go a long way toward defining the nature of Pat Buchanan's presidential prospects. On the one hand, it is clear that he *does* have a constituency: he *does* speak for many Americans, articulating their concerns about economic and especially cultural issues. But just as clearly, that constituency is very limited: it makes up far less than a majority of the Republican primary electorate, and of course an even smaller share of the general election voters. As the polling data clearly indicate, Buchanan is simply not popular enough within his own party. Too many Republicans dislike his views, or agree with his views but dislike him, or like him and his views but believe that he is simply unelectable. To cite just one example: In a CBS/*New York Times* poll conducted in late February, only 29 percent of Republican voters expressed a favorable opinion of Buchanan, while 35 percent viewed him unfavorably (the rest were undecided). At the same time, nearly half the Republican electorate called him an "extremist," and 48 percent said he could not win the general election.[41] In the end, according to the network exit polls, Buchanan came close to beating Dole only among the 21 percent of Republican primary voters who described themselves as "very conservative." In every other ideological category, Dole defeated Buchanan by better than 2–1 (see table 1.9).

Under these circumstances, the only way Buchanan could win a primary is the way he did it in New Hampshire: to have so many other candi-

TABLE 1.9

FACTORS AFFECTING THE VOTE

IN THE REPUBLICAN PRIMARIES

Percentage of total vote		Voted for			
		Dole	Buchanan	Forbes	Other
	Age				
10	18–29 years old	52%	25%	12%	11%
30	30–44	50	25	12	11
28	45–59	52	24	13	11
32	60 or older	65	18	10	7
	Education				
3	Not a high school graduate	49	24	8	19
20	High school graduate	57	27	9	7
30	Some college	54	24	11	11
27	College graduate	55	20	13	12
19	Postgraduate	39	12	10	39
	Voted in 1992 for				
12	Bill Clinton	40	24	16	20
66	George Bush	63	20	9	6
13	Ross Perot	38	29	20	13
	Party identification				
75	Republican	61	21	10	8
21	Independent	41	28	15	16
4	Democratic	29	29	11	31

Continued . . .

dates in the race, each of whom takes a large enough chunk of the vote, that he could come in first with only 27 percent. But, as noted earlier, one of the central dynamics of the contemporary presidential selection process is the way it forces candidates to drop out quickly and concentrates the race around two or three central players. And once that started to occur, Buchanan's ability to win the 1996 Republican nomination effectively came to an end.

Much the same verdict can be rendered about Steve Forbes. To be sure, there was one candidate Forbes probably could have bested in a one-on-one race for the Republican nomination, namely, Pat Buchanan. But as long as there were a few other candidates in the field, Forbes's vote was, if anything, even more potentially limited than Buchanan's. Of the twenty primaries in which Forbes was an active candidate, in eighteen of them he received less than 21 percent of the vote. The only two states where he

TABLE 1.9 — *Continued*

Percentage of total vote		Voted for			
		Dole	Buchanan	Forbes	Other
	Ideology				
2	Very liberal	45	19	10	26
7	Somewhat liberal	53	19	14	14
33	Moderate	59	16	13	12
37	Somewhat conservative	59	20	11	10
21	Very conservative	44	38	9	9
	Issues				
38	Favor a constitutional ban on abortion in party platform	49	35	7	9
57	Do not favor antiabortion plank	58	18	15	12
43	U.S. trade creates more jobs in own state	61	14	11	14
39	U.S. trade costs more jobs in own state	49	34	8	9
56	Buchanan is too extreme	71	5	13	11
41	Buchanan is not too extreme	35	47	10	8

SOURCE: *New York Times,* 31 March 1996, 24.
NOTE: Based on combined vote totals and results from Voter News Service exit polls conducted in twenty-eight states (all except Nevada) holding primaries between 20 February and 26 March 1996.

exceeded that figure were Delaware and Arizona, both of which he won with about 33 percent.

Put another way, Steve Forbes could win a Republican primary in 1996 only when two things occurred. First, he had to spend *enormous* amounts of money. Dropping a few million bucks here and there over a large state like New York just would not do it. Forbes absolutely needed to blanket the airwaves with his commercials, as he did in Iowa, New Hampshire, Delaware, and Arizona.

Money initially gave Forbes some prospect of winning Iowa and New Hampshire—until his opponents, especially Bob Dole, launched a counterattack that ultimately sent Forbes reeling to a fourth-place finish. This emphasizes a second condition necessary for Forbes to win a primary: not only did he need to spend a lot of money, but he needed to have his major opponents largely ignore the state. Absent those two obviously special circumstances, Forbes's showing in the 1996 Republican primaries was consistently unimpressive.

Why did Forbes do so poorly? His first limitation was the simple fact that he had never held any significant governmental office before. For all the loose talk about how much Americans distrust career politicians, there is also a great deal of evidence to indicate that, especially in presidential elections, the voters value experience; they recognize that the job is a very challenging one and do not want to turn it into an amateur-hour performance. In one *Time*/CNN poll, for example, respondents were asked if they would be more likely to vote for a candidate "who never held public office or one who has served as a public official." Just 24 percent preferred the "outsider," while 56 percent wanted someone with previous governmental experience.[42]

Another major problem with Forbes's candidacy was that the much-publicized centerpiece of his campaign, his call for a flat tax, proved to be far less appealing than he apparently expected. How widely the public supported a flat-tax proposal depended, not surprisingly, on the way the survey question was worded; but most polling organizations found that only about 40–50 percent of Americans endorsed the basic concept. And this was before they learned that the Forbes proposal would have eliminated the highly popular deductions for mortgage interest payments and charitable contributions.

Finally, even if Forbes had managed to surmount these obstacles and become a real threat to win the nomination, he would have been hobbled by some of his positions on social and cultural issues, which were well to the left of the Republican mainstream.[43] So again, unless every other candidate in the race except Buchanan had dropped out, Steve Forbes probably never had a realistic shot at winning the Republican nomination.

That brings us to Lamar Alexander. And unlike Buchanan and Forbes, Alexander could plausibly have won the nomination, but his opportunity to do so was far more limited than was generally recognized. Given Bob Dole's initial advantages in money, organization, and popularity with the voters, Alexander's only real hope of winning was to do essentially what Gary Hart almost did in 1984: to finish "better than expected" in Iowa, parlay that into a victory in New Hampshire, and then ride a huge tidal wave of press attention and momentum that would sweep him to an early victory.

Unfortunately for Alexander, it appeared for quite a while that he would never even make an initial breakthrough. Of all the major Republican candidates, it was probably Lamar Alexander whose campaign plan was most seriously disrupted by the unexpected Republican victory in 1994.

Prior to that time, early reports from the presidential campaign trail suggested that Alexander was doing quite well, wowing the Republican faithful with his attacks on the mess in Washington and his suggestion that the only way to deal with Congress was to "cut their pay and send them home." But this message obviously took on a very different set of overtones once the Republicans assumed control of Congress. Suddenly deprived of his best applause lines, Alexander spent the next year or so looking for a new theme and never did find one that was entirely satisfactory. Through most of 1995, he struggled to portray himself as the "Washington outsider" in the race, an odd way to describe a career that included a stint in the Nixon White House and two years as George Bush's secretary of education. When Steve Forbes's entry into the race further undercut his outsider credentials, Alexander borrowed a theme from the 1984 Gary Hart campaign and tried to bill himself as the candidate of "new ideas."

In the final confusing week before the Iowa caucuses, both Forbes and Gramm fell off the pace and Alexander came in third, or, as the media invariably described it, "a strong and surprising third." That turn of events gave Alexander an eight-day "window of opportunity"—the only eight days when he may have had a plausible shot at winning the nomination. What has to be stressed, though, is that Alexander needed to *win* the New Hampshire primary. Another "strong and surprising" third or even second just would not give him the huge burst of money and publicity he needed as the campaign headed into the next round of primaries.

In the days immediately after Iowa, Alexander did show some signs of real movement in New Hampshire. In the *Boston Globe* tracking polls, as we have already seen, his support jumped from 5 percent to 18 percent in just four days. But the Dole people were reading the same polls, and knew quite well what had happened to Walter Mondale in 1984. So, unlike Mondale, they did not wait until the day after the primary to launch a counteroffensive. If there was one campaign decision in the 1996 race that may have been crucial, it was the decision of the Dole campaign to launch a huge media blitz on the weekend before the New Hampshire primary, aimed not at Pat Buchanan but at Lamar Alexander. That blitz was quite effective in driving up Alexander's negatives, with the result that the former governor wound up in third place.[44]

Many reporters and commentators misread this result, calling it a "strong" (though apparently no longer surprising) third. But in fact, Alexander was never a serious factor in any primary after New Hampshire. His average vote in the thirteen remaining primaries before he dropped out was about 9 percent. His best showing was in Rhode Island, where, even with

Forbes and Buchanan not listed on the ballot, he still received only 19 percent of the vote.

The Democratic Nomination

In its own way, the Democratic presidential nomination race of 1996 was every bit as remarkable as anything that occurred on the Republican side. What was noteworthy about the Democratic nomination, of course, was what did *not* happen: Bill Clinton won the nomination without any significant organized opposition from within his own party. The 1996 Democratic National Convention never did hold a formal roll-call vote: Both Clinton and Gore were nominated by acclamation. Such consensus had not been in evidence at a Democratic convention since the nomination of Lyndon Johnson in 1964. But even Johnson had one major announced opponent in the 1964 Democratic primaries: George Wallace, then governor of Alabama, who ran quite impressively in three northern primaries. So an argument can be made that Clinton is the first person to win the Democratic nomination without opposition since Franklin D. Roosevelt accomplished the same feat in 1936.

If this result seemed at the time to be the "natural" or expected outcome, it was definitely not seen that way as recently as a year and half earlier. Especially after the stunning Democratic losses in the 1994 midterm elections, it was frequently predicted that Bill Clinton would have at least one significant opponent on his route to renomination. To be sure, there was never much likelihood that the president would lose such an encounter. The more realistic worry for the White House was that Clinton would face the kind of challenge that Pat Buchanan had offered to George Bush in 1992: someone who would hound, harass, and criticize the president, stir up resentments within his own party, divert his attention and resources, and delay the point at which he could begin to focus on the general election campaign. Among the major Democratic figures named most often as potential challengers to the president were the Reverend Jesse Jackson, House Minority Leader Richard Gephardt, Senator Bob Kerrey of Nebraska, and Senator Bill Bradley of New Jersey.[45]

But in the end, no such challenge ever materialized. There was one near-miss: On 25 March 1995, former Pennsylvania governor Robert Casey announced that he was setting up an "exploratory committee" to begin raising money and seeking support for a possible presidential campaign. But four weeks later, Casey bowed out of the race. Having had a heart and liver transplant two years earlier, Casey doubted his own capacity to "sustain the extraordinary energy level required by a national campaign."[46] From that point on, Clinton had essentially a free ride to the nomination. With only Lyndon LaRouche and a few other fringe candidates to draw votes away from him, Clinton breezed through the Democratic primaries with 90 percent of the vote (see table 1.10).

Like the "dog that didn't bark" in the famous Sherlock Holmes story, the Democrats' smooth renomination of an incumbent president in 1996 cries out for explanation. In fact, there are four principal reasons for Clinton's success in this regard. In the first place, it reflected Clinton's own substantial political skills, especially his ability to position himself in the center of the Democratic Party while nonetheless offering some measure of sympathy and support to those who were more liberal or more conservative than he was. Back in the days when Richard J. Daley was mayor of Chicago, one group leader said of him, "The mayor doesn't give us everything we want, but he knows what we have to have—and that he gets for us."[47] The same can generally be said of Clinton. For all his ideological drifting, Clinton had a very sure instinct for the political lines that had to be drawn, for the issues on which he could not compromise or surrender. In his 1996 State of the Union speech, for example, Clinton boldly proclaimed that "the era of big government is over." But he also understood that there was at least one major symbol of big government that he had to continue supporting, namely, affirmative action. That decision may have cost him a few votes in the general election, but doing otherwise would have been just the kind of "slap in the face" that would have antagonized several key Democratic constituency groups and possibly served as a rallying point for an anti-Clinton candidate in the Democratic primaries.

Second, the search for Democratic unity was surely aided by the 1994 midterm election results. What the Republican takeover of Congress did, in effect, was to confine political debate to a very narrow part of the ideological spectrum. A substantial segment of the Democratic Party—perhaps as much as 40 percent of its mass base and an even larger share of its elected officials—emphatically does not believe that the era of big government is over. To the contrary, they would like to see the federal government take on a number of important new responsibilities, especially in such areas as health care, education, and environmental protection. But the events of November 1994 made any proposal to expand government politically unthinkable. In practical terms, the debate in Washington over the past two years has been about whether to cut federal spending by a whole lot or by just a little. This way of posing the question temporarily united the liberal and moderate wings of the Democratic Party, making the party appear a good deal less divided than it actually was.[48]

TABLE 1.10

DEMOCRATIC PRIMARY RESULTS

Date	State	Clinton	Total vote
20 Feb.	New Hampshire	83.9%	91,557
24 Feb.	Delaware	90.3	10,740
5 March	Colorado	88.9	54,527
5 March	Georgia	100.0	95,103
5 March	Maine	88.4	27,027
5 March	Maryland	84.2	293,829
5 March	Massachusetts	87.1	155,470
5 March	Rhode Island	89.1	8,780
5 March	Vermont	96.5	30,838
12 March	Louisiana	80.8	154,701
12 March	Mississippi	92.5	93,788
12 March	Oklahoma	76.2	366,604
12 March	Oregon	94.8	369,178
12 March	Tennessee	88.9	137,788
12 March	Texas	86.4	921,256
19 March	Illinois	96.2	800,676
19 March	Ohio	92.6	765,298
19 March	Wisconsin	97.6	356,168
26 March	California	92.8	2,523,062
26 March	Washington	98.5	98,946
23 April	Pennsylvania	92.0	724,069
7 May	District of Columbia	98.2	20,441
7 May	Indiana	100.0	296,896
7 May	North Carolina	80.6	572,160
14 May	Nebraska	86.9	94,176
14 May	West Virginia	86.5	297,121
21 May	Arkansas	75.8	315,503
28 May	Idaho	87.7	40,228
28 May	Kentucky	76.8	272,899
4 June	Alabama	79.9	200,145
4 June	Montana	90.0	91,725
4 June	New Jersey	95.2	266,740
4 June	New Mexico	90.3	121,362
	Totals	89.7	10,668,801

SOURCE: *Congressional Quarterly Weekly Report,* 17 August 1996, 79.

Third, the same front-loaded primary calendar that helped thin out the ranks of Republican presidential contenders also upped the ante for anyone contemplating a challenge to Bill Clinton. As the incumbent president, Clinton was assured of a substantial war chest: By the end of 1995, his campaign had collected $26.8 million, with another $11 million in matching funds.[49] For anyone else, raising money for a Democratic presidential nomination campaign is generally even more difficult than it is for a race in the Republican Party.

Finally, and least auspiciously for the Democrats, Clinton's smooth path to renomination is a backhanded testimony to the fact that the Democratic nomination is not worth what it used to be. In 1968 and 1980, when the last two sitting Democratic presidents were challenged for renomination, most Democrats still believed that they were the clear majority party in the United States, that Democrats tended to win presidential elections at least as often as they lost them, and that anyone who won the Democratic nomination therefore stood a better-than-even chance of triumphing in November. By 1996, all these assumptions looked a good deal more dubious, which in turn meant that any Democrat who might have thought about running against Clinton had to wonder if the prize was worth the effort.

The Spring and Summer Campaign

With both parties' nominations effectively decided by the end of March, the 1996 campaign entered a phase that cannot readily be classified as part of the nomination process or part of the general election. Much of what the parties and candidates did during the months of April through August clearly involved tasks associated with the nominations: writing the party platforms, organizing the conventions, and (for the Republicans) choosing a vice-presidential candidate. Yet, just as plainly, this was the time when both parties began their general election campaigns, testing and refining the issues and tactics they would use more fully in the fall.

For the Dole campaign, the original plan had been to "run from the Senate floor": to showcase Dole in his role as Senate majority leader, to pass a series of bills that would show him as "a doer, not a talker," to make him look almost like a "co-president" holding court at the opposite end of Pennsylvania Avenue. Above all, Dole hoped to put Clinton in a position where he would have to veto several major bills passed by the Republican Congress, thus sharpening the differences between Dole and the president and casting Clinton as the principal source of "gridlock" and obstruction in American national government.[50]

Unfortunately for Dole, the strategy never worked half so well in practice as it looked on paper. The rules of Senate procedure were never designed to foster the values of speed and efficiency; and in the first weeks of April, Dole found that many of the tactics he had used so effectively to thwart the Clinton agenda in 1993 and 1994 were now being used against him by Senate Democrats. Where Dole had hoped to be laying out the broad themes of his fall campaign, he found himself mired in legislative minutiae and arcane procedural matters. The pressing demands of legislative work also made it more difficult for Dole to campaign outside Washington and to distance himself from some of the more unpopular policies championed by House Republicans. During the first three months of 1996, according to numerous national polls, what had once been a close race between Dole and Clinton had turned into a comfortable Clinton lead. The Dole campaign had hoped that this disadvantage was temporary and would be erased once the Republican nomination race was settled. Instead, Clinton's lead actually grew larger: by late April, the polls routinely showed Dole trailing the president by more than 20 percentage points.

Needing a dramatic move that would reenergize his faltering campaign, on 15 May Dole announced that he was resigning from the Senate (effective 11 June), ending his thirty-five-year congressional career in order to campaign full-time for the White House. At the time, Dole's decision was widely depicted as a daring and dramatic gamble "that will either be remembered as a bold masterstroke or a colossal blunder."[51] But in retrospect it is difficult to make much of a case for either prediction: Dole's standing in the polls seems to have been neither helped nor hurt very much by his resignation. Freeing Dole from his Senate duties did solve some immediate strategic problems and open up some new opportunities, but Dole proved almost entirely incapable of taking advantage of them. Instead, his early summer campaign was characterized primarily by a long series of missteps and blunders.

On 13 June, just two days after leaving the Senate, Dole made a speech in which he seemed to challenge the idea that smoking was addictive; the next day, he compared the health harms from tobacco with those from drinking milk. And rather than admit his error, over the next several weeks Dole compounded it by engaging in a contentious debate on the topic on the NBC *Today* show and accusing former Surgeon General C. Everett Koop of having been "brainwashed" by the liberal media. On 9 July, Dole planned to deliver a speech in which he would announce that he no longer wanted to repeal the ban on nineteen assault weapons passed by Congress in 1994. But at the last moment, Newt Gingrich persuaded Dole to drop the crucial sentence, substituting in its place a remarkably nebulous claim that "we've moved beyond the debate over banning assault weapons" that was criticized by both supporters and opponents of gun control. A few days after that, Dole accused Kweisi Mfume, the head of the National Association for the Advancement of Colored People (NAACP), of "trying to set him up" by inviting him to speak at the civil rights group's national convention.[52]

On a tactical level at least, the Clinton campaign seemed to be performing far more effectively. Such, at any rate, was the all-but-unanimous verdict of the reporters covering the presidential contest.[53] Particularly high marks were given to the Clinton "rapid response" team, which demonstrated a remarkable capacity to anticipate and answer each new charge or criticism from the Dole campaign, often within minutes after it was made. The president also proved quite adept at getting political mileage out of fairly small policy ideas. With little prospect of getting most of the legislation he wanted through the Republican Congress, Clinton nevertheless managed to appear very active, announcing a steady stream of new initiatives on such issues as truancy, teenage smoking, and domestic violence—all of which could be implemented with little or no money and without congressional approval.[54]

The more troubling question for the Democrats was whether they were winning the battle and losing the war. So determined was the president to preserve his lead, many within his own party complained, that he too often conceded the substance of public policy to the Republicans. Especially controversial was Clinton's decision, announced on 31 July, to sign a "welfare reform" bill that dismantled many of the most significant federal welfare programs created during the New Deal. On another occasion, Congress passed a law designed to stem the legalization of same-sex marriages, only to have the president announce that he, too, opposed such marriages and would readily sign the bill.

Vice-Presidential Selection and the Party Conventions

Dole also encountered a rocky road when he sought to reunite his own party and heal the wounds left over from the nomination campaign. The most contentious matter facing the Republican Party in the summer of 1996 was the shaping of the national platform, especially its stance on the abortion issue. Since 1984, the Republican platform had included a forthright, unqualified declaration that "the unborn child has a fundamental individual right to life that cannot be infringed" and had endorsed a "human life amendment" to the Constitution. On 6 June, Dole reaffirmed his support for these provisions, but also said that he wanted to add a "declaration of tolerance," recognizing that many Republicans held different views on the issue. This announcement provoked a huge outcry from conservative and pro-life groups; and as the platform began to be drafted and debated, it became increasingly clear that this was one issue where the delegates would *not* march in lockstep behind their nominee-to-be. Though Dole at one point declared that finding an acceptable compromise would be a "piece of cake," the abortion issue dominated news coverage about the Republican campaign through June, July, and early August.[55]

Eventually, Dole was forced into a series of retreats from his original position. First, he agreed to take the tolerance section out of the abortion plank and put it elsewhere in the platform. Next, he consented to change the wording so that the tolerance provisions applied to other issues besides abortion. Finally, the word "abortion" was dropped altogether from the tolerance section. In the end, the platform's sole concession to pro-choice Republicans was to add an appendix to the end of the document that listed all the measures and amendments rejected by the platform committee, about a dozen of which dealt with abortion.[56] To underline the Republicans' discomfiture, the Democrats, who had refused to allow a pro-life Democratic governor to address their 1992 convention, promptly added some tolerance language to their 1996 platform.[57]

Dole fared better in his search for a running mate. As a reflection of Dole's decision-making style and his own experiences as a prospective vice-presidential nominee in 1988, the Republican vice-presidential selection process of 1996 was an unusually secretive one, the precise contours of which are often difficult to reconstruct. A large number of names seem to have been seriously considered at one point or another. The top prospect on most people's lists was Colin Powell, but Powell himself repeatedly said that he did not want the position. If Powell was truly unavailable, the early betting line held that Dole would turn to one of four popular midwestern governors: John Engler of Michigan, Tommy Thompson of Wisconsin, George Voinovich of Ohio, or Jim Edgar of Illinois. When the open competition among these four reportedly annoyed Dole, a succession of other possibilities got a brief moment in the spotlight: Senators John McCain of Arizona and Connie Mack of Florida, Governor Tom Ridge of Pennsylvania, former Governor Carroll Campbell of South Carolina, even Dan Lungren, the attorney general of California.[58]

One name rarely mentioned during June and July was the man Dole ultimately selected: Jack F. Kemp, former congressman and secretary of housing and urban development. Kemp had unusually broad support within the Republican Party. He was pro-life on abortion, he was a leading proponent of supply-side economics, and he had developed a special reputation as one of the few major figures in the GOP with an active concern for the problems of poor and minority voters. Equally important, Kemp was a known quantity. As someone who had run for president himself in 1988, putting Kemp on the ticket would avoid the sort of "feeding frenzy" visited on Geraldine Ferraro in 1984 and Dan Quayle in 1988, in which coverage of the candidates' personal foibles overshadowed every other aspect of their potential appeal.

Given all this, and the fact that many of Dole's top campaign advisers had previously worked for Kemp, it is likely that Kemp would have been an instant front-runner for the vice-presidential slot had it not been for the tangled, often prickly personal relationship between the two men. Dole and Kemp had frequently clashed on economic issues, especially over the relative priority of balancing the budget versus cutting taxes. Any lingering warmth between them had apparently been destroyed when Kemp endorsed Steve Forbes for the Republican nomination just days before Forbes withdrew. But Dole had significantly narrowed the ideological distance between them by embracing a supply-side-driven proposal for a 15 percent cut in income taxes, and was apparently willing to overlook the personal differences if it enhanced his prospects of winning the election. In the short term at least, Dole's choice was a huge success. Though Kemp's performance in the general election would receive mixed reviews, most Republicans greeted the announcement with unfeigned enthusiasm, providing the Dole campaign with one of its few good moments during the summer of 1996.[59]

Over the past half century, the national party conventions have played a progressively less important role in the presidential nomination process. In 1996 they were, if anything, even further diminished. With both party tickets clearly set before the conventions were gaveled to order, with all major platform issues carefully resolved, the three major television networks all made a decision to reduce the amount of live coverage they provided to an hour per night.

In 1992 many Republicans blamed their party's showing in November on the image presented at the Republican convention, especially a controversial speech by Pat Buchanan in which he had spoken of a "religious war going on in this country for the soul of America." As a result, the 1996 Republican conclave, which was held in San Diego from 12–15 August, barred Buchanan from the speaker's rostrum and almost entirely banished any dis-

TABLE I.II

1996 CONVENTION APPORTIONMENTS AND ROLL-CALL VOTES

	Democratic delegate apportion- ment	Republican delegate apportion- ment	Dole	Buchanan	Other	Not voting
Alabama	66	40	40			
Alaska	19	19	16			3
Arizona	52	39	37			2
Arkansas	47	20	16			4
California	424	165	165			
Colorado	58	27	27			
Connecticut	67	27	27			
Delaware	21	12	12			
District of Columbia	33	14	14			
Florida	178	98	98			
Georgia	91	42	42			
Hawaii	30	14	14			
Idaho	23	23	19			4
Illinois	193	69	69			
Indiana	88	52	52			
Iowa	56	25	25			
Kansas	42	31	31			
Kentucky	61	26	26			
Louisiana	71	30	17	10	3	
Maine	32	15	15			
Maryland	88	32	32			
Massachusetts	114	37	37			
Michigan	156	57	52	5		
Minnesota	92	33	33			
Mississippi	47	33	33			
Missouri	93	36	24	11	1	
Montana	24	14	14			
Nebraska	34	24	24			

Continued ...

cussion of social and cultural issues. The major speakers—General Colin Powell, Elizabeth Dole, and keynoter Susan Molinari—attempted to show a party of broad and diverse views, but may have missed a chance to press some of their most potent electoral appeals and galvanize an important part of their base.

TABLE I.II — *Continued*

	Democratic delegate apportionment	Republican delegate apportionment	Dole	Buchanan	Other	Not voting
Nevada	26	14	14			
New Hampshire	26	16	16			
New Jersey	122	48	48			
New Mexico	34	18	18			
New York	289	102	102			
North Carolina	99	58	58			
North Dakota	22	18	17			1
Ohio	172	67	67			
Oklahoma	52	38	38			
Oregon	57	23	18	5		
Pennsylvania	195	73	73			
Rhode Island	32	16	16			
South Carolina	51	37	37			
South Dakota	22	18	18			
Tennessee	83	38	37			1
Texas	229	123	121	2		
Utah	31	28	27	1		
Vermont	22	12	12			
Virginia	97	53	53			
Washington	90	36	27	9		
West Virginia	43	18	18			
Wisconsin	93	36	36			
Wyoming	19	20	20			
American Samoa	6	4	4			
Guam	6	4	4			
Puerto Rico	58	14	14			
Virgin Islands	4	4	4			
Democrats abroad	9					
Totals	4,289	1,990	1,928	43	4	15

SOURCE: Compiled by the author from information provided by the Democratic and Republican National Committees.

NOTE: No roll-call vote was held at the 1996 Democratic National Convention. Both Clinton and Gore were nominated by acclamation.

The Democratic National Convention took place in Chicago from 26–29 August; like the Republican gathering two weeks earlier, it was designed principally to entertain what little remained of the television audience. Its major speakers hammered at several themes that were to serve as the basis of Clinton's fall campaign: the extreme and irresponsible character of the Republican Congress, the achievements of the president. The Democrats also sought to inoculate themselves against what they presumed would be a major Republican tactic in the fall, by arguing that campaigns should be about issues, not personalities. The only unexpected event at either convention came on the final day of the Democratic gathering, when Dick Morris, a political consultant often credited with helping revive Clinton's reelection prospects, resigned from the campaign after a tabloid revealed that he had repeatedly engaged the services of a Washington-area prostitute.

Third-Party and Independent Candidates

In most years, this would be the end of our story. But since 1992 was the year when Ross Perot had run the strongest third-party presidential bid in eighty years, the 1996 campaign was inescapably filled with speculations about the possibilities and prospects of another major third-party or independent run at the White House. The list of people who were allegedly exploring the possibility of a third-party presidential candidacy is an impressive one. It included, at one time or another, General Colin Powell, Pat Buchanan, the Reverend Jesse Jackson, retiring New Jersey Senator Bill Bradley, former Connecticut Governor Lowell Weicker, former Massachusetts Senator Paul Tsongas, and, of course, Perot.

But there were also a number of significant obstacles facing a third-party presidential bid. Of these, perhaps the most significant was one too often glossed over in the press coverage: fund raising. Under current campaign finance laws, the two major-party candidates have their fall campaigns financed entirely by the federal government. Minor-party and independent candidates, by contrast, generally do not receive such funds, unless they received at least 5 percent of the vote in the last presidential election.[60] Yet, even though most independent challengers never see a dime in federal money, they are still required to abide by the federal contribution limits, under which no individual may contribute more than $1,000 to a presidential candidate. Without the possibility of large contributions, third-party and independent candidates are usually caught in a vicious cycle in which they cannot raise money because they do not have enough supporters, and they cannot get more supporters because they do not have the money to run an effective campaign.[61]

The only sure way around this dilemma is the one Perot had used in

1992: financing the campaign almost entirely out of his own pocket. But this option is available only to the superrich. Powell, Weicker, Bradley et al. are not poor men—most of them, in fact, are millionaires—but none of them had the capacity to pour $63 million of his own money into a long-shot run at the White House. In the end, then, none of the "merely wealthy" third-party hopefuls ever pursued a presidential campaign beyond the exploratory stage. As for Perot, his path to the 1996 general election did nothing to dispel his image as one of the most erratic and self-willed individuals in all of American politics.

In October 1994 Ross Perot had urged his followers to vote Republican in the upcoming congressional elections, on the grounds that the Democrats had been in power for too long and the Republicans now deserved "a turn at bat." Apparently that turn was a very brief one; by mid-August 1995 Perot was already complaining about the performance of the 104th Congress. On 25 September, in one of his now-regular appearances on the *Larry King Live* television program, Perot announced that he was forming a new political party—the Independence or Reform Party—that would field its own candidate for the presidency and try to be the "swing vote" in congressional races.[62]

If the Perot vehicle for 1996 was formally called a "party," it was, in most respects, just as much a one-man show as the Perot campaign of 1992. For all the populist strains in Perot's own rhetoric, the major decisions that shaped the new Reform Party were announced from the central headquarters in Dallas, with only the thinnest pretense of consulting the wider membership.[63]

And who would serve as the party's first presidential candidate? Again, Perot's conduct almost begs for a cynical interpretation. For almost a year after his September 1995 announcement, Perot refused to make his intentions clear, repeatedly insisting that he didn't want the job but also declining to rule it out. "I can think of six or seven people who would just be incredible candidates," he said on several occasions. But he refused to name any of them or to set up a process for recruiting them. In the end, Perot maintained his reticence just long enough to attract one other candidate into the race. On 9 July 1996, Richard Lamm, a maverick Democrat who had served three terms as governor of Colorado, announced that he would be a candidate for the Reform Party's nomination. Just two days later, Perot declared that he was in the race as well.[64]

To decide upon a national standard-bearer, Reform Party officials in Dallas set up a complicated process that culminated in a nationwide vote by party members, conducted by mail, telephone, and the Internet. To no one's great surprise, Perot won that election. Well before the vote was announced, a torrent of complaints emerged about the efficiency and impartiality of the process. Many party supporters complained that they never received a ballot; and of the 68,000 people who attempted to vote by telephone, more than 94 percent had their ballots declared invalid. And though Perot would later display great indignation about being excluded from the fall debates between Dole and Clinton, he himself declined to debate Richard Lamm. Of the 1.13 million ballots sent out to Reform Party supporters, less than 50,000 were returned. The final tally showed Perot 65 percent, Lamm 35 percent.[65]

One final step remained: choosing a running mate. Characteristically, the Reform Party membership seems to have played no role in this selection process. On 10 September, Perot announced on television that he had chosen Pat Choate, an economist and author who shared the Texan's skepticism about current American trade policies.

The Process in Retrospect

Ever since 1968, political observers have watched presidential nomination races with two major questions in mind. The first, of course, is who is going to win? But the second and sometimes more significant question is how well is the process working? Is this really the best way to select our presidential candidates, and if not, how can we make the system better?

Curiously enough, one of the central criticisms of the 1996 process that has surfaced in the immediate postelection commentary is almost the exact opposite of one that was frequently made just a few years earlier. Especially after the 1976 election, the view emerged that we had created a presidential nomination system that was uniquely favorable to candidates like Jimmy Carter: unknown "fresh faces," without any significant governing responsibilities, who could parlay a vague image and a lot of personal campaigning in Iowa and New Hampshire into a few early victories that generated unstoppable momentum. Once he got to the White House, however, Carter's lack of experience was vastly more of a liability than an asset, and many political scientists worried that the future held a lot more of the same.

In fact, Carter's 1976 nomination campaign has proven to be probably the most copied political strategy in modern times, providing the clear model for such well-known White House seekers as George Bush in 1980, Gary Hart in 1984, and Lamar Alexander in 1996. As that list suggests, however, nothing quite like the Carter phenomenon has occurred in any election since then. Indeed, the record since 1976 suggests that the contemporary nomination process is one that is actually quite favorable to front-runners and party leaders.[66]

Perhaps *too* favorable. After Bob Dole's uninspiring fall campaign, many Republicans and conservatives complained that the system gave too much of an advantage to candidates who were already nationally known and well financed and thus prevented the emergence of fresh new talent within the party. As conservative writer David Frum argued two days after the election:

> The Republicans lost in 1992 and 1996 because the party leadership has built a nominating process that favors bland candidates who care much more about building a political machine than they do about ideas and principles....Party leaders—governors, senators, state committee chairmen, big donors—matter much more in the GOP than in the Democratic Party. These leaders are not altogether comfortable in the party Reagan built.... And so, sometimes without fully understanding what they were doing, they have constructed a nominating process that shuts the rank and file out.[67]

In one of the best books on the theory and practice of presidential selection, James Ceaser argued that one important objective of a well-designed selection process is that it "provide for the proper amount of choice and change."[68] And perhaps the new criticism only proves that it is difficult to find the proper balance between continuity and change and that, regardless of where you draw the line, some people will never be satisfied. But it might also be argued that *both* criticisms stem, at least in part, from a common source: the heavily front-loaded delegate selection calendar. The great worry about front-loading is that it takes a system that is already quite frenetic and chaotic and makes it even less careful and deliberative. With the delegate selection season so radically compressed, voters and party activists are given little or no opportunity to change their minds or reconsider their first impressions as new information becomes available and new circumstances develop.

Depending on the other rules and the particular field of candidates, front-loading can lead to two quite different kinds of undesirable outcomes. One is a situation in which early front-runners become prohibitive favorites because other challengers are scared out of the race or lack the resources to mount a credible campaign after Iowa and New Hampshire. But front-loading may also make it possible for a relatively unknown candidate, who may have significant flaws, to win a few early primaries and caucuses and then ride a huge burst of momentum that permits him to clinch the nomination before most voters have any real opportunity to learn very much about him. To judge from 1996, the first outcome seems more likely than the second, but neither is an advertisement for the glories of American democracy.

The other aspect of the 1996 process that has a lot of people worrying is the Steve Forbes candidacy, and what it says about the role of money in presidential politics. Forbes, as we have seen, took advantage of the strange mismatch in the current campaign finance laws that places very tight restrictions on the money a candidate can raise from other people but allows the candidate to spend unlimited amounts of his own money. The experience of Ross Perot in 1992 and now Steve Forbes makes one wonder whether we have created a system where at least one candidate in every presidential campaign will come from what David Letterman has called "the Wacky Billionaires' Party."

For all the reasons suggested earlier, Forbes fell short in 1996, but that does not mean that some other megamillionaire might not prove more successful in some future nomination race. Moreover, Forbes did succeed to this extent: he made himself a national figure, and if Ross Perot is any indication, it seems most unlikely that he will now quietly retire to a life of golf and shuffleboard. Forbes also succeeded in gaining a great deal of attention and publicity for his favorite policy issue, the flat tax. And some might say that this is a *good* thing: the American political system should be open to new ideas; an individual with strong convictions ought to be able to take his case directly to the American people. The problem, of course, is that there are hundreds, even thousands, of people with similarly strong beliefs who would love the chance to proselytize for *their* favorite policy proposal, but who lack the $25 million or $63 million in spare cash.

If we are soon to embark on another major round of "reforms" in the presidential selection process, one hopes that this time around the reformers will have a better sense of history than those who shook up the system in the early 1970s. Parties ought to be open to new talent and new ideas; but as the Democrats learned in the 1970s, there is also much to be said for a process that values experience and proven capacity. For all of Dole's weaknesses as a candidate, it is far from obvious that any of his principal rivals would have done much better.

Acknowledgments

The author would like to thank Tami Buhr, Clark Hubbard, Sharon Pilmer, Craig Tufty, Jonathan Moore, David Shribman, Gerald Pomper, and Amy Logan for their assistance with this chapter.

Notes

1. For a more detailed discussion of this Commission and its work, see especially Byron Shafer, *Quiet Revolution: The Struggle for the Democratic Party and the Shaping of Post-Reform Politics* (New York: Russell Sage, 1983); and Nelson W. Polsby, *Consequences of Party Reform* (New York: Oxford University Press, 1983).

2. This point has been copiously documented. See especially Michael J. Robinson and Margaret A. Sheehan, *Over the Wire and On TV: CBS and UPI in Campaign '80* (New York: Sage, 1983), 174–80; and William C. Adams, "As New Hampshire Goes . . . ," in *Media and Momentum: The New Hampshire Primary and Nomination Politics,* ed. Gary R. Orren and Nelson W. Polsby (Chatham, N.J.: Chatham House, 1987), 42–59.

3. For a more extended discussion of these points, including a complete list of candidate withdrawal dates from 1952–1992, see William G. Mayer, *The Divided Democrats: Ideological Unity, Party Reform, and Presidential Elections* (Boulder, Colo.: Westview Press, 1996), 35–41.

4. See *New York Times,* 23 September 1993, A16.

5. For good accounts of this early maneuvering, see Emmett H. Buell Jr., "The Invisible Primary," in *In Pursuit of the White House: How We Choose Our Presidential Nominees,* ed. William G. Mayer (Chatham, N.J.: Chatham House, 1996), 1–43; Arthur T. Hadley, *The Invisible Primary* (Englewood Cliffs, N.J.: Prentice Hall, 1973); and Jules Witcover, *Marathon: The Pursuit of the Presidency, 1972–1976* (New York: Viking, 1977), chaps. 3–13.

6. On this point, see *New York Times,* 14 November 1994, A1; and *Time,* 21 November 1994, 76–77.

7. For early news commentary on this point, see *New York Times,* 2 February 1995, A1; 5 February 1995, sec. 4, 1; and 5 March 1995, sec. 4, 14; *Time,* 13 February 1995, 26; and 13 March 1995, 93–94; and *Congressional Quarterly Weekly Report,* 29 April 1995, 1195–97; and 19 August 1995, 2483–88.

8. *Time,* 13 March 1995, 80.

9. The two quotations from Gramm are taken from *Congressional Quarterly Weekly Report,* 25 February 1995, 630; and 22 April 1995, 1124.

10. See, for example, *New York Times,* 31 January 1995, A12; and 10 February 1995, A14.

11. *New York Times,* 14 February 1995, A13; 22 May 1995, A13; 31 May 1995, B6; 3 June 1995, A8; 11 June 1995, A1; and 13 June 1995, A20.

12. *New York Times,* 28 November 1995, A21.

13. Gingrich's final withdrawal from the race appeared on page 6 of the *Washington Post* and page 21 of the *New York Times. Time* magazine allotted the matter exactly one sentence, buried in the middle of an article about Gingrich's ethical problems. *Newsweek* appears not to have mentioned it at all.

14. Like Dwight Eisenhower in 1952, Colin Powell began the 1996 election cycle without ever having formally declared himself to be either a Democrat or a Republican. As indicated later in the text, this prompted some speculation that he

would enter the race as an independent or third-party candidate, though this option was apparently ruled out at a relatively early stage in his deliberations. Not until his 8 November 1995 press conference did Powell commit to speaking out on the issues "as a member of the Republican Party and try[ing] to assist the party in broadening its support."

15. On the varying reactions to speculation about a Powell candidacy, see *New York Times*, 3 October 1995, A1; 27 October 1995, A22; 30 October 1995, A12; 2 November 1995, B11; and 3 November 1995, A26; and *Time*, 20 November 1995, 48 and 54–55.

16. See, in particular, "Variation on a War Game: How Powell Arrived at No," *New York Times*, 12 November 1995, 1; Evan Thomas, "Why He Got Out," *Newsweek*, 20 November 1995, 43–45; and Nancy Gibbs, "General Letdown," *Time*, 20 November 1995, 48–57.

17. For the full text of Powell's statement, see *New York Times*, 9 November 1995, B13.

18. For some early assessments of Specter's chances, see *New York Times*, 30 March 1995, A1; and *Congressional Quarterly Weekly Report*, 3 June 1995, 1588–93.

19. R.W. Apple Jr., "Pete Wilson and '96 Race: A (Coy) Natural," *New York Times*, 9 February 1995, A1.

20. For a demonstration of the latter point, see William G. Mayer, "The New American Electoral Map," *Public Perspective* 5 (November/December 1994): 24–27.

21. See *New York Times*, 15 April 1995, 9; 4 May 1995, A16; 6 May 1995, 6; 21 May 1995, 30; and 15 June 1995, A18; and *Time*, 15 May 1995, 40; 5 June 1995, 29; 25 September 1995, 31–32; and 9 October 1995, 54.

22. See, for example, *New York Times*, 14 March 1995, A20; and *Washington Post*, 16 June 1995, A2.

23. Two others, Lamar Alexander and Steve Forbes, were also generally pro-choice, but rarely talked about it. Alexander, in particular, had a remarkably convoluted position that he sometimes described as "pro-life" even though he opposed federal action to ban abortions.

24. As quoted in *Washington Post*, 20 December 1995, A14.

25. *Buckley et al.* v. *Valeo*, 424 U.S. 1 (1976).

26. See *Time*, 12 February 1996, 31; and *New York Times*, 13 February 1996, A19.

27. See *New York Times*, 25 November 1995, 1; and *Washington Post*, 20 December 1995, A14.

28. *New York Times*, 14 January 1996, 1.

29. For the Arizona results, see *Congressional Quarterly Weekly Report*, 27 January 1996, 228.

30. The three quotations are taken from *New York Times*, 18 February 1996, 18; and 17 February 1996, 8; and *Boston Globe*, 9 February 1996, 1.

31. *New York Times*, 12 February 1996, A1; 16 February 1996, A1, A27;

and 19 February 1996, A1.

32. As quoted in *New York Times,* 6 February 1996, A18.

33. For assessments of Gramm's prospects in Louisiana, see *New York Times,* 6 February 1996, A18; and *Congressional Quarterly Weekly Report,* 3 February 1996, 313–14.

34. See *Time,* 18 March 1996, 40.

35. *New York Times,* 7 February 1996, A1; and 8 February 1996, B12.

36. *New York Times,* 23 February 1996, A22; 25 February 1996, 1; and 26 February 1996, B7.

37. On the influence of this event, see *New York Times,* 23 February 1996, A22; 25 February 1996, 18; and 28 February 1996, A1.

38. This is a regular theme in the coverage Dole received throughout 1995 and 1996. It is also my personal observation, based on having watched Dole campaign in New Hampshire.

39. For a vivid demonstration of this, see Buell, "Invisible Primary," 24–32.

40. As noted, the summary statistics on the Buchanan vote in table 1.8 exclude the Rhode Island primary, since Buchanan's name was not on the ballot there.

41. See *New York Times,* 27 February 1996, A19.

42. *Time,* 20 January 1996, 27.

43. For some early indications of Forbes's troubles with cultural conservatives in the Republican Party, see *Boston Globe,* 10 February 1996, 1.

44. For an excellent account of this decision and its consequences, see Michael Kranish, " 'Deliberate Feint': The Dole Turnaround," *Boston Globe,* 26 March 1996, 1.

45. On the possible opposition to Clinton for the 1996 Democratic nomination, see *New York Times,* 21 November 1994, A1; 26 December 1994, 15; and 31 January 1995, A12; and *Time,* 21 November 1994, 77; 23 January 1995, 37; 13 February 1995, 27; and 13 March 1995, 74–75.

46. See *New York Times,* 25 March 1995, 8; and 19 April 1995, B12.

47. As quoted in Andrew M. Greeley, "A Scrapyard for the Daley Organization?" *Bulletin of the Atomic Scientists* 29 (February 1973): 11.

48. On the continuing divisions within the Democratic Party, see Mayer, *Divided Democrats,* chaps. 4 and 5.

49. See *Time,* 5 February 1996, 29.

50. On Dole's attempt to campaign from the Senate floor, see *New York Times,* 18 April 1996, A1; and 29 April 1996, A1; and *Time,* 6 May 1996, 30–33.

51. The quotation is from *Congressional Quarterly Weekly Report,* 18 May 1996, 1400. For a similar sentiment, see *New York Times,* 16 May 1996, A1.

52. For more details on these incidents, see *New York Times,* 3 July 1996, B6; 10 July 1996, B8; 11 July 1996, B11; 12 July 1996, A1; 13 July 1996, 19; and 14 July 1996, 18; and *Time,* 15 July 1996, 20–23; and 22 July 1996, 31.

53. See, for example, *New York Times,* 1 May 1996, A1; 28 May 1996, A1; and 3 July 1996, B6; and *Time,* 6 May 1996, 30–33; and 19 August 1996, 31–39.

54. *New York Times,* 24 July 1996, A1; and *Time,* 22 April 1996, 54–57; and 13 May 1996, 40–43.

55. *Congressional Quarterly Weekly Report,* 4 May 1996, 1237–40; and *New York Times,* 7 June 1996, A1; 8 June 1996, 1; 11 June 1996, A1; 12 June 1996, A1; 14 June 1996, A20; 20 June 1996, A1; 22 June 1996, 7; 23 June 1996, 1; 24 June 1996, B6; and 2 July 1996, A1. As one indication of the prominence of the abortion issue for the Republicans, notice that it appeared on the front page of the *New York Times* on seven days between 7 June and 2 July.

56. See *New York Times,* 13 July 1996, 1; 6 August 1996, A12; and 8 August 1996, A1; and *Congressional Quarterly Weekly Report,* 10 August 1996, 2267–68.

57. *New York Times,* 11 July 1996, B11; and 6 August 1996, A11; and *Congressional Quarterly Weekly Report,* 13 July 1996, 1989; and 10 August 1996, 2269.

58. For accounts of the Dole vice-presidential selection process, see *Time,* 20 May 1996, 26–29; *Congressional Quarterly Weekly Report,* 3 August 1996, 18–20; and *New York Times,* 18 March 1996, A1; 30 March 1996, 9; 15 May 1996, A18; 27 June 1996, A20; 6 July 1996, 8; 23 July 1996, A12; 26 July 1996, A20; 2 August 1996, A20; 8 August 1996, B9; and 9 August 1996, A1.

59. *Congressional Quarterly Weekly Report,* 10 August 1996, 2260–61; and 17 August 1996, 2296–97; *Time,* 19 August 1996, 21–25; and *New York Times,* 10 August 1996, 1; and 11 August 1996, 1.

60. Candidates who receive 5 percent of the vote in the current election may become eligible for a retroactive subsidy. The problem, of course, is that they do not receive any of this money until after the election.

61. This discussion draws on Emmet T. Flood and William G. Mayer, "Third-Party and Independent Candidates: How They Get on the Ballot, How They Get Nominated," in Mayer, *In Pursuit of the White House,* 318–20.

62. *New York Times,* 6 October 1994, D22; 10 October 1994, A15; 9 April 1995, 1; 14 August 1995, A8; 26 September 1995, A1.

63. Micah L. Sifry, "Perot's Sham Party," *New York Times,* 17 October 1995, A25; and *New York Times,* 11 November 1995, 12.

64. *New York Times,* 26 September 1995, A1; 20 November 1995, B9; 19 March 1996, A15; 10 July 1996, A1; and 12 July 1996, A1.

65. *New York Times,* 18 August 1996, 1.

66. For an elaboration on this point, see William G. Mayer, "Forecasting Presidential Nominations," in Mayer, *In Pursuit of the White House,* 44–71.

67. David Frum, "GOP, We Could Have Won," *USA Today,* 7 November 1996, 19A.

68. James W. Ceaser, *Presidential Selection: Theory and Development* (Princeton: Princeton University Press, 1979), 10.

2

Candidate Strategies and the Media Campaign

MARION R. JUST

Your large speeches may your deeds approve,
That good effects may spring from words of love.
— *King Lear* (I, i)

The politics of 1996 posed problems and opportunities for candidates and the mass media. In the glow of their midterm sweep of Congress, Republicans expected 1996 to be a banner year. Eyeing the tepid approval ratings of the incumbent president and gloomy public assessments of the economy, Republican challengers crowded into the ring in early 1995. But one year later, in media "trial heats," incumbent president Bill Clinton handily defeated the most likely Republican nominee, Bob Dole.[1]

This sharp reversal of political fortune overshadowed the start of the 1996 campaign. The most immediate problem faced Bob Dole. He had to prove to his own party that he deserved the nomination in spite of ominous portents in the polls. Then, in the face of a healthy economy and public complacency, Dole had to get voters to reject the incumbent and choose him instead. The strategic environment facing Bill Clinton was less daunting. With no challengers in his own party, he could focus his energies on the general election campaign. The president's task was to make sure that the public gave him credit for the economic expansion, acknowledged that he deserved reelection, and ignored any reservations it might have about his personal integrity.

As in the past, the vehicle for these candidate appeals was the media. The candidates considered what was reported about them in the press crucial to their success. Their campaigns would pay special attention to key media events: the party nominating conventions and the candidate debates. Although the candidates would have an opportunity for direct communication with the public through television advertising, they knew that even there the judgments of journalists could be important.

Newspeople faced the 1996 campaign with a different kind of trepidation. If the economy stayed healthy, perhaps nothing could dislodge the president. And if the increasingly popular Clinton held on to his double-digit lead over Dole—a far from magnetic challenger—would there be any news?

How the candidates and the media coped with the political context of the 1996 campaign and how they coped with each other are the subjects of this chapter. How well did the candidates craft their messages, and how did those messages play in the press? How well did the media cover the campaign? If the horserace proved unexciting, did that leave room for more substantive and innovative coverage?

The Candidates and the Media

It is typical in political campaigns around the world that incumbents defend their records and challengers call for change. The 1996 American presidential campaign was no exception. But in the light of a strong economy, the incumbent's message was more persuasive than the appeals of any of the challengers.

BOB DOLE

Even before challenger Bob Dole could try to make a case for change he had to win his party's nomination.

The Primaries: Dole's First Hurdle. —Since 1976, reporters have looked to the early nominating contests in Iowa and New Hampshire to identify the most "viable" candidates. Handicapping the candidates is a staple of election news, but it also serves a practical purpose. When there is a large field of candidates, it is difficult for news organizations to cover all of them, even superficially. The sooner reporters can target the most likely candidates, the more in-depth coverage they can provide. In winnowing the field of challengers, the media had their work cut out for them. In September

1995 there were nine candidates active in New Hampshire: Dole, Forbes, Buchanan, Alexander, Gramm, Keyes, Lugar, Dornan, and Taylor.

In the eyes of the press, the man to beat was Bob Dole: "By almost any measure, Mr. Dole is far and away the leading Republican," wrote one reporter. "In the year since the campaign began to take shape behind the scenes, none of his multiple challengers has shown any serious traction against him. [He has] more than $24 million in the till, 20 of the nation's 31 Republican governors working their states for him and a deeper organization than he fielded in his two prior and failed efforts for the presidential nomination."[2] The press saw the early nominating contests as a test of Dole's ability to translate his money, experience, and name recognition into votes.

The first serious challenge to Dole came from a candidate with both money and message: Steve Forbes. Although a late entry in the Republican field, Forbes banked on television advertising in New Hampshire to establish himself as a viable candidate. Forbes's ads emphasized a single issue position: replacing the graduated income tax with a 15 percent flat tax. With that issue he seized control of the discourse. Several other Republican candidates, including Phil Gramm and Pat Buchanan, embraced their own versions of the flat tax.[3] In January, two weeks before the Iowa caucuses, Forbes's picture appeared on the covers of *Time* and *Newsweek* featuring stories on the flat tax, and a January *New York Times*/CBS poll found that 58 percent of voters had heard or read about the flat tax, up from 34 percent the previous year.

Forbes was unsuccessful in transferring his advertising strategy to the Iowa caucuses. He spent more than $4 million on ads,[4] many of them attacking Dole as a Washington insider. The media labeled Forbes "the most negative" candidate in the presidential race, and he finished a poor fourth behind Dole in the Iowa caucuses. National media criticism of Forbes's negative strategy in Iowa caused his "not favorable" ratings to rise sharply in the New Hampshire race, which followed two weeks later.[5] Forbes came in third in New Hampshire, trailing Buchanan and Dole.

Dole's second-place finish in New Hampshire diminished his stock of a precious media resource: momentum. His lead began to be called "fragile" and "vulnerable." Dole probably suffered longer from this kind of coverage than his performance merited because of a media survey glitch. In 1992 and again in 1996, the major networks got together to pay for exit polling by the Voter News Service (VNS), rather than going to the expense of conducting their own surveys. As a result, when one news outlet made an incorrect call, it was backed up by several others. For reasons that no doubt will be argued by survey professionals for years to come, VNS incorrectly predicted the outcome in two early primaries. In Louisiana and Arizona, news stories based on exit polls featured election outcomes that were contradicted by the actual returns.

In Louisiana, exit polls overestimated the strength of Dole's most right-wing challenger, Pat Buchanan, and underestimated the appeal of Phil Gramm, but the relative order of finish was correct. In the Arizona case, exit polls presented Dole as a weak third-place finisher, behind both Forbes and Buchanan. ABC's *Nightline* that evening focused on Dole's faltering appeal to the electorate. The next morning, election results indicated that Buchanan had finished third and Dole was actually in second place.

In spite of upsets in New Hampshire and Arizona, Dole faced down his challengers. In March all the primaries went to Dole. The flurry of media attention to his challengers ended abruptly. The second- and third-place challengers left the field or were buried by the successful arithmetic of the Dole campaign.

Crafting the Dole Campaign Message ("... or whatever").—During the primaries Dole helped his candidacy most when he stayed above the fray and looked "presidential."[6] Although he was respected for his integrity, his campaign appeal was limited by a lackluster speaking style. Even supportive press noted: "there's still no way to make Bob Dole exciting."[7] Oddly enough, Dole was well known for a quick, dry wit that had gotten him into trouble in the past. Possibly the dullness of his delivery may have resulted from a conscious effort to rein in his sharp-edged humor. Although sorely tempted to give as well as he got in the primaries, Dole put off attacking his primary opponents. His previous candidacies had earned him the sobriquet "hatchet man,"[8] and in this election he wanted to present a cooler head and a warmer personality. He softened his image with smiles, self-deprecating remarks, and appearances with his devoted wife, Elizabeth.

In presenting him to the 1996 electorate, the Dole campaign needed to keep questions of his age and health out of the picture. Age was probably the most difficult quality to camouflage, even though the candidate had a youthful appearance. His three decades in public life, much of it reported in the national press, made his age only too apparent to the electorate. Open-ended poll questions about the candidate as early as October 1995 found that the most frequent description of Bob Dole was "old."[9] But health was another matter, and here the press cooperated. Dole's bout with prostate cancer was almost never mentioned, even in articles about candidate health. Dole goaded the president into releasing his medical report, and when both men's medical records were made public, the press drew flattering comparisons between Dole's health and that of the much younger but somewhat overweight president.

Within his own party, Dole had to make special efforts to reassure conservatives that he merited their support in spite of his reputation as a pragmatist. He made a number of moves to protect his right flank, such as attacking Clinton's surgeon general, opposing late-term abortions, supporting repeal of the assault weapons ban, and standing by the view that tobacco was not addictive. This strategy appeared to work for Dole in the primary campaign. In an ideological coup that particularly weakened his most conservative opponent, Pat Buchanan, Dole received the endorsement of the Christian Coalition.

After Dole sealed the Republican nomination in March, he took a month off from the presidential campaign. He did not begin to focus on his message until late spring. Crafting the Dole appeal was not going to be easy. The economic evidence that shored up the Clinton campaign was a millstone for the Republican challenger. Dole could not talk about what was wrong with the economy when the public thought it was going well, and it was risky to remind people about the Republican Congress.

As majority leader, Dole was, in fact, a symbol of that Congress. Furthermore, he was forced to take public positions on every item on the legislative agenda. News stories about his leadership in the Senate made at least a passing reference to the impact of Dole's positions on his electoral chances: Was his stance sufficiently popular with conservatives in his party? Was this the same position he would have taken if he weren't running for president? Was this the same position he took last year?

With Dole lagging in the polls, prominent Republicans began to talk about ways to reduce his exposure as Senate majority leader. In a surprise move Dole stepped down from the Senate altogether on 15 May. His resignation from the Senate was a media coup. By making a dramatic gesture, he received a good deal of positive news coverage. But his resignation from the Senate also resulted in diminished and less flattering attention to his candidacy in the succeeding months. Without the legislative news to report, journalists began to pay more attention to Dole's campaign. News stories began to surface that Dole did not have a message.

In response, Dole made another heroic gesture just prior to the convention, announcing that he—an advocate of fiscal responsibility—would support a 15 percent across-the-board tax cut and an end to the Internal Revenue Service "as we know it." In embracing the tax-cut strategy Dole was playing to the public's view of Republicans as most likely to keep taxes low. The tax-cut maneuver looked like just the kind of issue that could turn the election around. As Ronald Reagan demonstrated in 1980, cutting taxes appeals to Americans in every class and region. Surprisingly, however, Dole ran into heavy weather with his tax plan. Whatever the public might forgive and forget, reporters recalled Dole's previous positions.

Announcement of the Dole plan was accompanied by suspicion in the press. One lead story began: "A longtime skeptic of the supply-side economics championed by President Reagan, Mr. Dole today adopted the Reagan formula as he tried to appeal to what he described as the besieged middle class."[10] News stories quoted experts, voters, and even pollsters to cast doubt on the tax cut. Media polls were produced to show that most Americans did not believe Dole would actually cut taxes if elected.[11] Democratic pollster Peter Hart explained that the problem with the Dole tax plan was that "you have an economy that's working and you have a candidate who is trying to sell a new economic fix."[12]

Dole had several months to see if the tax-cut proposal would catch on; if it did not, his strategic options appeared limited.

BILL CLINTON

Bill Clinton had the luxury of crafting his campaign message from a position of economic strength. The appeal was a one-two punch: "I've done a good job" followed by "the alternative is risky." Circumstances conspired to make both messages believable to a majority of the electorate.

Crafting a Credible Appeal.—Peace and prosperity were the basis for Clinton's positive appeal. By the second quarter of 1996, the economic news was almost too good: the GDP grew, the stock market soared, disposable income for middle-class earners finally rose, inflation stayed low, and the deficit was down. By the spring of 1996, economic growth clearly inoculated the president against calls for political change. During the campaign, the economy never garnered more than 15 percent in any list of "most important problems facing the country," yet Clinton's campaign slogan might have been "it's the economy—again."[13]

Clinton reinforced his credit-taking for the nation's economic performance with a list of accomplishments and proposals aimed at showing what government could do for the American family: expanded family leave; school uniforms; the anti-TV-violence "V-chip"; connecting every classroom and library to the Internet by the year 2000; tax breaks for college tuition; portable health care. The president launched these ideas in his State of the Union message and over the course of several months highlighted each proposal with a media event. The aim was to portray himself as a president who knew how to use government to address the needs of families. These appeals were targeted at married women and female heads of house.

The corollary to Clinton's positive message was that change was dangerous. Here the Republican majority in Congress provided Clinton with plenty of ammunition. Led by Speaker Newt Gingrich, Republicans bet on humiliating the president and forcing him to concede direction of the national policy agenda. In news coverage, the congressional Republicans were portrayed as the perpetrators of the budget crisis. Not surprisingly, polls then showed that the public blamed the Republicans in Congress, rather than the president, for the impasse.

Clinton was able to paint the Republicans as dangerous Medicare meddlers and himself as a guardian of the elderly. One voter remarked: "I have an elderly mother lying in the hospital right now and she has Medicare, but it's not enough. . . . If they have to put her in a nursing home, we'll have to pay for it. . . . I give [President Clinton] credit. If he hadn't vetoed, who knows what would have happened with the budget and Medicare and that?"[14] By early October a *Times Mirror* poll[15] showed Clinton's increasing favor among women and older Americans. That support never flagged.

The Clinton strategy of holding himself out as the safer alternative to the Republicans was given a substantial boost after Dole clinched the nomination. As majority leader, Dole could be tied to alleged Republican extremism in Congress. While Dole was in the Senate, the Democratic National Committee (DNC) went on the offensive for Clinton, producing ads spotlighting the Dole-Gingrich congressional axis. One DNC ad aired that spring used a visual in which Dole appeared to slide from left to right behind Gingrich as a kind of *eminence grise,* while the voiceover accused the pair of threatening Medicare.

Inoculating the President against Political Liabilities.—Clinton was lucky in the timing of the economic recovery and miscalculations of the Republican Congress. But the lesson of 1992 was that presidents would be held to their campaign promises.[16] In presenting himself for reelection, Clinton was obliged to address a number of weaknesses in his own record. The centerpiece of his 1992 campaign had been a plan to stimulate the economy and reduce the deficit—and on these he delivered. On two other issues he was less successful. Clinton's health-care initiative was a legislative disaster, and there was no progress on "ending welfare as we know it." With the election looming, both the president and Congress were finally ready for compromise. Clinton happily signed a bipartisan health-care measure and reluctantly acquiesced to a stringent welfare bill.

Clinton earned plenty of negative press for appearing to do the expedi-

ent thing on welfare instead of leading in an unpopular direction. His action on welfare was seen as further evidence that he wavered and waffled in
the winds of public opinion. Clinton paid for that move both in the subsequent news coverage of the Democratic convention, where the welfare bill
was a staple of media commentary, and in media interviews. But signing the
welfare bill meant that Clinton could campaign on having made good on
his campaign promises and essentially took the welfare issue out of play in
campaign discourse.

The "Hillary factor" was another potential problem that the Clinton
campaign managed to overcome. The president's wife was a controversial
figure in the 1992 campaign, and during Clinton's administration she became a liability on two fronts. She absorbed much of the blame for Clinton's health-care initiative, which she led, and she became a major target of
ethics investigations concerning the Rose law firm where she worked before
Clinton's election. It seemed that the safest role for the first lady was to disappear as a political figure, which she did for several months before the
campaign. She reemerged as a spokesperson for women, families, and children. Press reports of a round-the-world trip with daughter Chelsea, during
which she focused on health issues, were positive. She strengthened her position as a nonpolitical defender of women and children with the publica-
tion of her book, *It Takes a Village*. Mrs. Clinton appeared on several popular talk shows, touting her book and refashioning her image.

The Achilles heel of the Clinton candidacy was ethics. His first bid for
the presidency had been dogged by scandal, and the tempo of ethics charges
against the Clinton administration increased after the Republican congressional victory in 1994. For the first part of the campaign, however, Clinton
was relatively fortunate on this front. In spite of regular news stories about
the Whitewater investigations and resulting trials, the public seemed unin-
terested, and Clinton's approval ratings did not falter. The Whitewater special prosecutor, Kenneth Starr, announced that he would not make a report
until after the election, eliminating the possibility of an "October surprise."
After several extensions, the Senate Whitewater Investigation Committee
led by Al D'Amato wrapped up its activities in the spring without substanti-
ating any wrongdoing by the president. Also in the spring Clinton gave
video testimony in two trials of his associates. The first trial ended ominously in May with convictions of two of his business associates, but the
second verdict, in early August, was "not guilty." The acquittal seemed to
help the White House face down the press on Whitewater in the weeks before the party conventions.

During this time, network coverage of the campaign fell substantially below that of the two previous presidential elections (see figure 2.1). Clinton was able to dominate the reduced coverage by using the office of the presidency (see figure 2.2, p. 89). In the slack period between the end of the Republican primaries and the party conventions in August, the president led the anniversary mourning for victims of the Oklahoma City bombing, comforted relatives of the victims of the TWA Flight 800 air disaster, and opened the International Olympic Games in Atlanta. The Dole campaign, its federal matching funds depleted by expenditures on the primaries, had to sit tight while waiting for an infusion of cash after the Republican nomination.

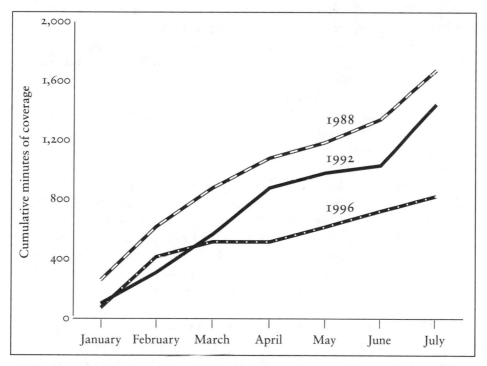

FIGURE 2.1

PRESIDENTIAL CAMPAIGN COVERAGE IN NETWORK NEWS:
THE FIRST SIX MONTHS OF 1996, 1992, AND 1988

SOURCE: Media Studies Center/ADT Research.
NOTE: Includes CBS, NBC, and ABC weekday nightly newscasts.

Media Events

The conventions and debates gave the major party candidates opportunities to expound their own messages and challenge their opponents. The anemic coverage of the Reform Party and the exclusion of Ross Perot from the debates forced the third-party candidate to rely almost exclusively on advertising in order to reach the public. Clinton and Dole also spent great sums on advertising, but the president's strategy proved more effective.

THE PARTY CONVENTIONS

The Dole campaign pursued a strategy of building excitement for the convention by releasing information in the days preceding the opening ceremonies. The big question in the news was who would be Dole's vice-presidential nominee. From October 1995, polls showed that a Bob Dole/Colin Powell ticket could beat Clinton and Gore, but Powell reiterated his refusal to run. The press wondered whether Dole might be able to find another running mate with that kind of electoral appeal.[17] Given the gender gap in Dole's support, the press speculated that perhaps a woman might help the Dole ticket. New Jersey's governor, Christine Todd Whitman, was mentioned so often that she made a public announcement declining the vice-presidential spot. In what turned out to be a diversion, the Dole campaign focused attention on several Republican governors. In the week before the convention, the *New York Times* ran biographical stories on each of them. The announcement of the vice-presidential nominee was scheduled for Dole's hometown: Russell, Kansas.

The name was successfully kept out of the press until the day before the announcement. Jack Kemp, a former congressman and President Reagan's secretary for housing and urban development, would be Dole's vice-presidential running mate. The press judged Kemp a good choice. He was seen as more politically moderate than Dole, with good ties to minority communities. Kemp was also known to the press as a lively campaigner, making up, it was suggested, for Dole's rather wooden delivery on the stump.

The Republican Platform Committee denied the media an expected conflict over abortion and opened the convention with a show of unity by Dole's potential challenger, Colin Powell. The African American former chair of the Joint Chiefs of Staff drew a large television audience and gave the party a much-sought-after image of diversity. Following a traditional approach to visuals, network cutaway shots during the Powell speech featured some of the few African Americans who were in attendance. Although the convention delegates were overwhelmingly white, middle-aged, and male, subsequent speeches were also accompanied by "appropriate visuals" of minorities, young people, and women. Some journalists, however, were uncertain about how to report a convention scripted to the minute. Was it news or was it, as some said, a partisan "infomercial"? Ted Koppel took most of the *Nightline* crew home after two nights of set-piece speeches; but the rest of the press and the public generally disapproved of such a radical move, arguing that the very successful scripting of a unified convention was itself news.[18] Elizabeth Dole's speech, using a folksy delivery from the floor of the convention rather than from the podium, made a big hit with the public and the press. Numerous speeches (by Elizabeth Dole, Colin Powell, and Senator John McCain of Arizona, a decorated veteran of the Vietnam war) emphasized Dole's status as a war hero. In his acceptance speech, Dole promised to reduce taxes 15 percent without increasing the deficit and to strengthen traditional values, building a bridge to the virtues of the past. It appeared that the Republican challenger had found the elements of his message.

Dole and the Republicans scored a major success at their August convention. The event was a media triumph—"a meticulously choreographed pageant of unity."[19] Although very few people watched the actual conventions (viewership was down 20 percent from 1992), press reports and news clips were strongly positive. The networks gave the Republican candidates a great deal of coverage. The number of network news stories about Dole was equal to Clinton's at the Democratic convention (see figure 2.2), and network news stories about Kemp in the first half of August were two or three times the peak coverage for Clinton's vice-president, Al Gore.[20]

The Democrats opened their convention only ten days after the close of the Republican convention. There was positive press for most of the speeches, including Hillary Clinton's address and the president's acceptance speech. Clinton's speech scored a minor press coup, by turning around one of Dole's convention metaphors. Dole had asked: "Let me be the bridge to a time of tranquility, faith, and confidence in action. To those who say it was never so, that America has not been better, I say, you're wrong: And I know, because I was there. I have seen it. I remember." In contrast, Clinton emphasized that he would not be building a bridge to the past but "a bridge to the twenty-first century." That theme became the mantra of the Clinton/Gore general election campaign, highlighting the team's relative youth and vision. Although the Republican convention got a good ride in the press, the parties entered the general election with Clinton still in the lead.

An Alternative Message:
Perot and the Reform Party

In his second bid for the presidency Ross Perot added something to the campaign with lots of press appeal—the element of uncertainty. If Perot could catch on in 1996 as he had in 1992, he could conceivably cut into the president's lead enough to put the election in doubt.

Once Perot announced his willingness to run for the nomination (via his favorite communications channel, *Larry King Live),* he managed to eliminate most of the excitement about his candidacy. Perot took his movement, United We Stand America, down the road of a traditional political party, rather than maintain the grassroots organization that had attracted so much positive press in 1992. The media response to the new reality of Perot's campaign was mixed. One reporter rhetorically asked: "Perot's back. But did voters ask for an encore?"[21]

In order to get his party listed on state ballots, Perot had to move up his party's convention prior to Labor Day (his original choice). But there was precious little room for the Reform Party in the August calendar, already crowded with both the Republican and Democratic conventions. In the end, the Reform convention was split into two unfavorable time slots. Nominating ballots were mailed out two weeks in advance and candidates receiving 10 percent of the ballots in ten states (Perot and former Governor Richard Lamm) addressed the first Reform conclave only hours before the opening of the Republican convention. Party voters were given a variety of ways to signal their support for the nominees, including electronic balloting. Then the acceptance speeches were scheduled for the week between the two major party conventions. Neither Reform Party affair achieved much media coverage. Perot's misadventures and heavy hand in the nominating process resulted in a number of critical stories, but more significant was his disappearance from the news altogether, as seen in figure 2.2.

Perot's candidacy received two major blows in September. He found that it was difficult to buy all the television time he thought he would need to take his candidacy to the American public. Networks were reluctant to sell him the half-hour time slots he sought for his infomercials. At the end of September he took his case to the Federal Communications Commission, but the FCC found that Perot had been given adequate access to the airwaves.[22] He expected to popularize his candidacy by participating in the scheduled presidential debates. Here he was disappointed by the decision of the Presidential Debate Commission (a group of private citizens often referred to as the Bi-Partisan Commission). Although Perot's support stood at the same level as it had four years before—5 percent—the technical rule un-

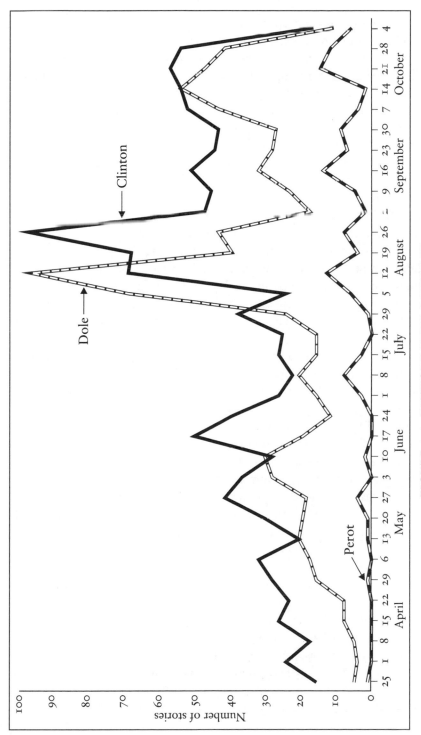

FIGURE 2.2. NETWORK NEWS COVERAGE

der which the commission operated in both years required 10 percent in the polls. The commission bent the rule in 1992 but refused to do so again in 1996. With little time to spare, Perot took the commission to court. Here, too, he lost his bid. His supporters and most Americans thought he had been unfairly excluded from the debates, but that judgment did not appear to add to the newsworthiness or the appeal of his candidacy.

THE CANDIDATE DEBATES: ONE ON ONE

The 1992 presidential debates surprised everyone by attracting a large audience that grew with each succeeding debate. The 1996 debates did not meet that standard. Only one-third of American households tuned in to the first debate, the lowest level in more than thirty years. By agreement, Bob Dole and Bill Clinton faced off, with only Jim Lehrer, the chief interviewer for the Public Broadcasting System's *Newshour*, asking the questions. The two candidates appeared equally well prepared with facts and themes.

In a "gift" question early in the debate, Lehrer asked Dole to comment on Clinton's ethics. Surprisingly, Dole declined to do so. The challenger, however, did not eschew all attacks. He remarked that in the debate he would refer to his opponent as Mr. President, even though in the 1992 debates Clinton had not used the title in addressing President George Bush. A large NBC focus group tracking the debate illustrated just how much the public disapproved of even that mild attack. Dole's remark about Clinton's title was greeted with a steep downturn on the "people meter."

The postdebate analysis in the press reached a consensus: the debate was civil and Dole did well, but not well enough to make a difference in the outcome of the campaign.[23] In making this judgment, the press seemed inescapably tied to the horserace metaphor. The focus of reporters' postdebate banter was, as usual, who "won" and who "lost." The routine postdebate judgment was also made: "the candidates said nothing new." Clearly, if the public had not heard what the candidates had to say in the months leading up the debates, the reporters certainly had.

The vice-presidential debate a few days later showed two candidates evenly matched—one with more passion and the other with more facts. Kemp had been nominated, in part, to express the more compassionate side of the Republican ideology. He was a good, if verbose, speaker and could hold his own in debate. But his ideological differences with his running mate were a chink in his armor, easily targeted by his Democratic opponent. Gore was known as a rather wooden speaker, and his recitation of campaign themes did little to disprove that assumption. But the vice-president was easily the better prepared, and his points went virtually unanswered.

Kemp manfully defended his running mate, and in a move he must have immediately regretted, Kemp reassured the audience that Bob Dole would not stoop to attack the president.

But after the first debate, fellow partisans begged Dole to go on the offensive. Dole was faced with a strategic dilemma. If he attacked Clinton, he would reinforce his image as "Nixon's hatchet-man," "the mean Bob Dole, the old Bob Dole." A *Time*/CNN poll released after the debate showed that twice as many people thought Dole had already been too negative as thought he had not.[24] But if Dole held back, Clinton might win in a walk. Throughout the campaign Dole had behaved in a gentlemanly way to the president. He insisted on calling the Democrats his "opponents" rather than his "enemies." He met with the president early in the campaign and reassured him he would not discuss his problems with Whitewater.[25] Between the first and second debates, however, Dole changed tactics. He consulted crowds of supporters, asking whether they thought he should attack the president. The answer was resoundingly yes. The day before the second debate, Dole launched his first salvo on the "integrity gap."

The second presidential round was billed as a "citizens' debate," but it did not come off as the citizen triumph that it had been in 1992. Jim Lehrer, while a good interviewer, was less experienced in the role of talk-show host. He gave the citizens little help in framing their questions. During the debate, Dole continued to carry out an assault on the president's ethics, but his public agonizing over whether to attack dulled some of the effect. Also, the evidence from the first debate was that the public disliked personal confrontation. Apparently Dole's aggressive posture in the debate reinforced the view that he was running a negative campaign, for afterwards his "not favorable" ratings rose, while the public credited Clinton with an even bigger "win" than in the first round.

Following the debates, and with little more to lose, Dole's rhetoric on the stump stayed in attack mode. Seizing on Clinton's brewing foreign campaign contribution scandal, he accused the president's campaign of laundering money. He shouted to a crowd in his home state of Kansas, "Come on, Mr. President.... Come clean, Mr. President!"[26] This last turn in campaign strategy seemed to relieve the self-conscious Dole from having to talk about himself and allowed him to enjoy the final weeks of campaigning.[27]

ADVERTISING STRATEGIES

The presidential ad campaign generated less press attention than in previous elections, in part because both candidates pursued a targeted state strategy, rather than making national ad buys. The strategy—selecting media markets in key electoral college states—was the same approach Clinton had used in his 1992 campaign. Dole's team adopted a similar plan in 1996, but had to switch gears when the candidate fell behind in a large number of states. Targeting is an effective way to use scarce funds only if a relatively small number of markets are involved. Once the candidate is losing broadly, efficiencies of scale make national media buys expedient. Even where the Dole campaign targeted its buys, however, the strategy did not always pay off. A great deal of Republican money was spent in California, for example, before the campaign decided to pull its ads.

In the spring and early fall the Dole campaign aired a number of positive ads about the candidate and his proposals. In September the campaign released a five-minute biographical spot about the candidate (ignoring what must have been seen as a liability—his thirty-year career in the U.S. Senate).[28] The Dole camp did not sponsor an attack ad until the last week in September.[29] In contrast, most of the Clinton ads were a mix of praise for the president (in full color) and attacks on the Dole record (in believable black and white). The blend of positive and negative appeals echoed the overall Clinton strategy.[30] Although in debates and speeches Clinton made a point of praising Dole's public service, his ads hit hard on Dole's political record, especially Medicare, which Dole had originally opposed. Clinton ads even accused Dole of voting for millions of dollars in tax increases, and one presented a chronology of the Dole record in which the candidate visibly aged before the camera.

Clinton's advertising strategy was in contrast to Reagan's in 1984. The circumstances were similar: good economic times, a president with good approval ratings, and a not very popular opponent. Reagan's managers stayed on the high road throughout the campaign, never airing the negative ads they had prepared because they felt their substantial lead meant they "didn't have to."

In the language of most ad critics, Clinton's ads were "comparative" because they attacked Dole's record and not his personal qualities. Still it was hard to find a strictly positive Clinton ad that merely extolled the candidate's own record and virtues. The two-pronged approach suggests that the Clinton campaign was not sufficiently confident that the president's record could stand on its own, without a comparison to the "risky" opposition.

Even though Dole used more positive spots than Clinton, the public judged Dole to be the more negative campaigner. One explanation is that Clinton's ad campaign, which was more attack oriented than Dole's, was far less visible to the public than Dole's campaign speeches. Dole's assaults on

Clinton were carried in the evening news, while Clinton's ads were aired only in selected media markets. As a whole, the 1996 campaign will go down as less negative than previous campaigns because both sides tended to focus on the records.[31] The public appeared to recognize this: a much larger percentage than in previous years rated the 1996 campaign more positive than previous elections.[32]

Perot's ads attracted much less attention in 1996 than they had in 1992. Part of the reason was that the novelty had worn off. Perot also delayed his advertising assault until the very last weeks of the campaign. Then he let loose with a vituperative attack on Clinton, focusing on ethics and on foreign donors in particular. Perot contributed mightily to focusing public attention on the growing scandal over the Indonesian connection and the questionable practices of Democratic fund raiser John Huang. If anything slowed Clinton's campaign momentum, it was the combined attack of Dole's speeches, Perot's ads, and investigative news reports on the ethics of his campaign contributions; but in terms of the election outcome, it was too little, too late.

The Media and the Candidates

The campaign was affected not only by the candidates' use of the media but also by the media's treatment of the candidates. As in all recent presidential elections, candidates and their supporters scrutinized the media coverage for evidence of bias. While Clinton had more good press than Dole, the bottom line for the 1996 campaign was less press. The lack of suspense regarding the outcome of the election decreased coverage of the horserace and the campaign overall.

GOOD PRESS AND BAD PRESS

Throughout the long campaign year, the news did not neglect stories about the Clintons' "ethics problems": Travelgate (the peremptory firing of the White House travel staff, which resulted in the alienation of much of the White House press corps); Filegate (the discovery that a White House security officer had requested FBI files on numerous people, including a large number of prominent Republicans); the mysterious disappearance and reappearance of documents associated with rumors and conspiracy theories about the death of White House adviser Vincent Foster and the possible financial wrongdoing of Hillary Clinton when she was a partner in the Rose law firm. In spite of extensive news coverage of each of these problems, the press seemed compelled to report that the president's popularity did not decline in the face of these allegations of wrongdoing. In June, for example, a story based on a *New York Times*/CBS poll announced: "Clinton Lead Is Unaffected by Troubles," and an interior box concluded that the public saw Whitewater "as a matter of politics, not ethics."[33] Both Clinton's opponents and the press seemed dismayed by the public's lack of interest in these ethical issues. By the end of the campaign, the media's frustration with Clinton's unassailable popularity in the face of well-covered scandals led to a new story: why didn't the public care about presidential character?

With Dole, a candidate who was on the losing end for most of the campaign, the press harped, not on ethics, but on tactics. News reports repeatedly discussed the candidate's inability to generate enthusiasm, his lack of a clear "message," and disorder in his campaign organization. These factors were often seen as causally related. Dole appeared to heed the warnings not only of the press but also of his own party, and he fired and rearranged his campaign staff several times throughout the campaign. While the public seemed deaf to the Clinton scandal stories during the campaign, they accepted the press's view of the Dole campaign. In a Pew Research Center poll, the public graded the Dole campaign a *C* compared to a *B*+ for Clinton.

Although some celebrities claim that bad publicity is better than none at all, political partisans are highly sensitive to the way they are covered in the media. Losing candidates often blame the press for favoring their opponents. Republicans, in particular, have long held that liberal journalists are biased against them. Given the outcome of the election, it is reasonable to ask whether Dole suffered from an excess of negative press.

Figure 2.3 charts the "tone" of coverage for Clinton and Dole from the end of the primaries to election day. Every evaluation of a candidate in a network news story was rated either positive or negative. Simple inspection shows that the neither candidate was especially favored in the tone of coverage. In fact, the dominant pattern until Labor Day was alternating ups and downs for Clinton and Dole. Dole's convention peak is higher than Clinton's, and two of the general election campaign weeks had especially positive coverage for the Republican. In the network news coverage overall, 48 percent of the evaluations of Dole on network news were positive, compared to only 41 percent for Clinton.

These findings appear to go against the common view that Clinton got better coverage than Dole. The explanation lies in the candidates' strategies. Typically, challengers attack incumbents, and Dole was no exception. There were, in fact, twice as many Dole attacks in the news as Clinton attacks.[34] Clinton pursued the standard front-runner strategy of talking mostly about himself and not even mentioning his opponent's name.[35] Since Clinton

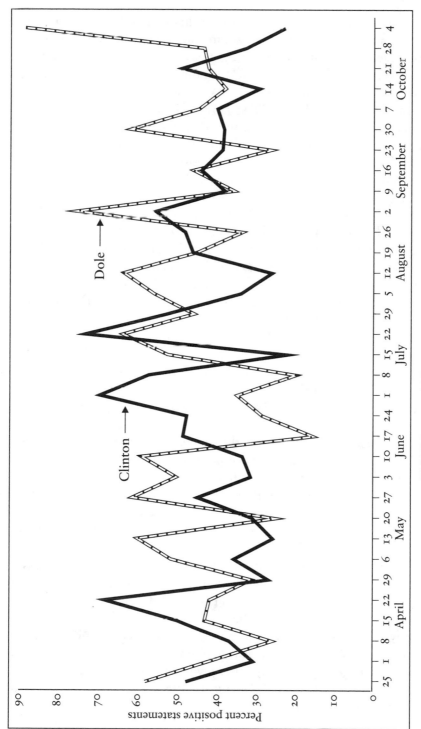

FIGURE 2.3. NETWORK NEWS TONE

would not respond to Dole, journalists evaluated Dole's attacks. Clinton's self-praise attracted far less journalist attention. Figure 2.3 shows that journalists achieved a rough balance in the tone of news about the candidates —but at some cost. The public concluded that Dole was the more negative candidate, and that if the press was biased, it was against Dole.[36] What's more, with *both* candidates talking mostly about Clinton, the public felt more informed about what the president stood for than about his challenger's positions. Twice as many Clinton as Dole supporters claimed they voted for their candidate rather than against the opponent, and twice as many Clinton supporters said their choice was based on their candidate's stand on the issues.[37]

WHAT IF THERE WERE AN ELECTION AND NOBODY CAME?

To the dismay of the press, the general election campaign stagnated despite the unfolding of many events that could have made for an exciting story: a successful Republican convention; the choice of Jack Kemp, a lively campaigner, as Dole's running mate; the entrance of Ross Perot and his Reform Party into the race; and the resignation of Clinton's campaign manager, Dick Morris, in a sex scandal. The immutability of the race was demonstrated the day after Morris was forced out, when a widely cited ABC poll showed Bill Clinton leading Bob Dole by 20 points, one point more than the week before. Even the presidential debates made only a ripple in the surface of the campaign. By the time the debates took place in October, most votes were set in stone.[38]

Were the media to blame for the voters' lack of interest in the campaign? For years, media critics have harped on the press's preoccupation with the horserace, arguing that it drives out the substantive coverage voters need to make informed decisions. Early reports of the 1996 campaign echoed the same theme. One analyst found the news seriously deficient in providing "extensive, detailed, and contextually meaningful issue discussions."[39]

Even more disturbing to some analysts,[40] when the news did discuss issues, the candidates' positions were framed in terms of the horserace. For example, in a CNN report on "stagnant wages and standards of living," the real focus of the piece was "Who [i.e., which candidate] is helped and who is hurt by the economy?"[41] Even a routine campaign news story was introduced this way on NBC: "President Clinton called on Congress to allow new mothers longer hospital stays after giving birth—*a big issue for women voters*. In Omaha, Senator Bob Dole *went after conservative voters* by attacking the president on crime."[42]

Notably, press coverage of Clinton's performance at the key campaign events—the conventions and debates—focused on his position in the horserace. Pre-event coverage emphasized that he was expected to do well, and postevent coverage found that he had, in fact, done well. Given their expectations, the press view was that a really poor showing might hurt Clinton, but that Dole had to perform spectacularly well to move the numbers. Even after the successful Republican convention, poll stories emphasized that Clinton still led Dole by 11 percent and that Dole had not yet succeeded in generating a favorable public image, had not convinced voters that he would lower their taxes, and had not told them enough about his economic plan.[43] After a debate in which each candidate laid out his positions on a wide range of issues and outlined his plans for the nation's future, Tom Brokaw's emphasis was typical: "[The debate] did not cause any seismic shifts in voter support."

Dole was, not surprisingly, resentful of this kind of coverage and in the last week of the campaign vented his spleen on the "liberal media." He called the *New York Times* (which endorsed his opponent) "the apologist for President Clinton for the last four years and an arm of the Democratic National Committee."[44] When the inevitable occurred, and Dole lost the election, press reports focused not on the difficulty of defeating an incumbent presiding over a healthy economy but on all of the "mistakes" Dole had made along the way. One front-page headline the day after the election read: "Missteps Doomed Dole from the Start."[45] Clinton, the winner, was credited with having run a flawless campaign.

Though often framed in terms of a horserace, the election lacked drama and was therefore short on news value. The campaign got less coverage than previous campaigns, even those with big candidate leads.[46] Scant attention was paid to the campaign on local television, even on stations that carried two or three hours of news. In the words of Larry Perret, news director of KCBS-TV in Los Angeles, "The polls are the polls. If it were a real close race, ... then I think that might be a different situation."[47] By the end of the campaign one estimate was that, compared to 1992, network coverage had declined 55 percent and newspaper coverage had dropped 40 to 45 percent.[48] When confronted with the decrease, the press was philosophical. Bill Wheatley of NBC thought the amount of coverage was "about right," explaining "every campaign has its own reality."[49]

Interestingly, the public did not appear to be unhappy with the cutbacks. Polls generally showed that a majority of Americans thought well of the coverage and gave the media higher marks at the end of the campaign than in the beginning.[50]

And Now for the Good News

If the campaign was a yawn, the coverage did not lack achievement or innovation. While a number of disappointing trends persisted—short sound bites (candidate quotes on the evening news averaged 8.2 seconds),[51] decreasing viewership for television news and newsmagazines, declining attention to news among young people,[52] predominance of horserace news, cynical reporting, negative campaigning, and deceptive advertising—there were some positive signs as well. A report by the Annenberg Center found that strategy stories made up a smaller proportion of newspaper and network coverage than in the recent past and poll stories declined even more precipitously. As a result, the proportion of policy coverage increased.[53]

The figures suggest that although the horserace drives the amount of coverage, the lack of excitement in the 1996 campaign created opportunities for serious reporting.

Campaign Innovation

In the face of (and perhaps because of) the decline in overall news coverage, 1996 was marked by a number of innovations in campaign communications, including civic journalism, free media, and the use of computers and the World Wide Web.

Civic Journalism

The "civic journalism" movement was based on the premise that the candidates and the media ought to be covering issues that the people, rather than journalists, are concerned about. In media outlets that embraced civic journalism, the public's issue priorities were made to lead the news agenda. The movement continued to make headway in 1996 but had little impact at the presidential level, where it was vigorously opposed by national journalists. The approach came in for particular criticism during the North Carolina Senate rematch between Jesse Helms and Harvey Gantt. Political and journalism critics[54] accused the coordinated civic journalism coverage by the state's major media outlets of ignoring the blatant racism of the Helms campaign because the issue was not identified as important by voters before the campaign began.

Those news outlets that did not practice civic journalism, however, made a point of including interviews with the public in their coverage of the campaign. Both print and television reporters accosted people in malls, diners, and on Main Street so that they could include their views along with those of pundits and pollsters. CBS News aired a segment in the fall entitled "In Touch with America—Issues That Matter to You." NBC sent one reporter on the road to record reaction to the campaign in towns around the country, while another reporter, Lisa Meyers, conducted roundtables soliciting voters' opinions. During the first presidential debate, a large focus group on NBC provided a second-by-second reaction to the candidates' remarks. Even local stations followed the trend of increased citizen participation in the coverage.[55]

FREE MEDIA

While journalists were willing to broaden the voices in their coverage to include the public, they were less willing to cede time to the candidates. Beginning in 1988, news analysts with stopwatches have eyed the shrinking candidate "sound bite" with alarm.[56] They argue that candidates have too much trouble getting out their messages in the interstices of journalist commentary.

In 1996 there was considerable pressure to develop a format of candidate communication closer to the European model of free air time, which would compete with political advertising and perhaps make it unnecessary. Paul Taylor, with the help of news dean Walter Cronkite and Senator John McCain of Arizona, organized the Free Media for Straight Talk Coalition in the spring of 1996, when it was clear that Clinton and Dole would be the major party nominees. The group included a number of former newspeople and pressured the networks to yield some time to candidates to speak without journalist commentary or interpretation. In spite of the initial opposition, each of the major broadcast networks made some concession to the concept of unfiltered time. CNN offered five minutes of air time to major candidates on its evening news program *Inside Politics* each week for the last four weeks of the campaign; ABC offered to provide a one-hour live special during the final week of the campaign; NBC offered candidates time on *Dateline* as well as opportunities to appear on its evening news specials "In Their Own Words"; and Fox, which had been the first to endorse the idea, guaranteed each candidate ten one-minute segments to talk about the issues in the last two months of the campaign. The concept also found its way into print. The *New York Times* used a box, "In Their Own Words," next to regular news stories about the campaign. The *Jim Lehrer Newshour* on PBS and the *Nightly News* on NBC used the same title for video clips of the candidate speeches, and the CBS *Evening News* aired excerpts from stump speeches. Although numerous surveys showed that the public overwhelmingly favored greater access to what the candidates had to say unimpeded by journalists,[57] only 20 percent claimed to have seen "free" media—a figure no doubt inflated by overreporting.[58]

COMPUTERS AND THE WORLD WIDE WEB

Only a small percentage of the electorate is at present connected by computer to the Internet or World Wide Web—about 11 percent of households subscribe to an online service.[59] Most people who contact political sites on the World Wide Web are regular users of other campaign media; most are white, male, and highly educated.[60] Because of its limited user base, the World Wide Web exhibited more potential than impact during the 1996 campaign.

In 1996 the Web made a big hit with candidates and their consultants. As an inexpensive means of communication, the World Wide Web has the potential for leveling the playing field for less-well-funded candidates and small parties. With only limited resources, a candidate can provide the audience with up-to-date information, find out about potential supporters, and even solicit donations. In 1996 most primary candidates set up sites on the World Wide Web and were pleased with the results. For example, Phil Gramm's Web site was accessed 197,425 times for a set-up cost of only $8,000. The candidate calculated that he made eight times as many contacts with the public by way of the World Wide Web as he could have made with first-class mail.[61]

In the 1996 campaign the Web also demonstrated its capacity for interactive political communication. Users expressed their views to candidates, journalists, and each other. In one stunning display of interactivity, a six-week online poll of *AllPolitics* users—the VPick Game—resulted in naming Jack Kemp the best choice for Dole's running mate three days before the official announcement and two days before it was leaked to the press. The Web also had an indirect impact on the campaign. News stories about "hot" Web sites found their way into regular election coverage.[62] And political junkies had a new outlet for checking up on election results. Traffic on political Web sites increased manyfold on election night, although the increase mostly represented a shift by regular users from entertainment or business sites to politics.[63] Postelection polls found that somewhere between 6 and 10 percent of the public visited a political Web site or claimed to have gotten information about the election from the World Wide Web.[64] The small number of actual users suggests that the time for the Internet as a tool of mass communication has not yet come and may have to wait until public access is relatively cheap and widespread.

Judging the Candidates and the Media

When political campaigns are over, the candidates are often judged by how well their messages were received by the media and the public. The media are also judged: were they equitable to the candidates and did they help the public make informed decisions? In rendering a verdict on the candidates and the media in 1996, it is important to take into account the circumstances in which they found themselves.

When Bill Clinton campaigned for president in 1996 and 1992, he asked people the same question: Are you better off today than you were four years ago? In 1996, most Americans thought the answer was yes! Four years earlier, when Clinton challenged incumbent president George Bush, most people thought the answer was no. Clinton's success suggests that it is easier to design a campaign around yes when you are the incumbent and no when you are the challenger.

Bob Dole did not have Clinton's advantage. He was a challenger in good times. Furthermore, in the first few months of the 1996 campaign, he was preoccupied with contesting his party's nomination; but once he had it in his grasp he was admittedly slow to design a strategy for the election campaign. The message he finally hit on—a 15 percent tax cut—had two defects. First, it was unlikely to resonate with an economically complacent public, and second, it was not congruent with his personal history as a fiscal conservative. News coverage amplified both message problems.

Dole's difficulties were compounded by Clinton's lead in the polls. Expectations for Dole's performance were set higher and higher the closer the campaign got to election day. In these circumstances almost nothing that Dole did could be framed as a success in the media. Journalists, however, helped Dole in one significant respect. They originated the story about Clinton's foreign campaign contributions, which engaged the public in the last few weeks of the campaign. Both Dole and Perot were able to focus their attacks on Clinton around the unfolding scandal.

The public seemed quite perceptive about the way the candidates were covered in the media. A poll by the *Washington Post*/Kaiser Family Foundation found that most of the public, regardless of which medium they depended on for news, thought that the candidates were treated equally by the press. But those who thought the media were too negative to Dole believed the press paid too much attention to his standing in the polls and to his campaign problems, while those who thought the media were too negative to Clinton overwhelmingly cited too much media attention to his personal character.

In evaluating the media's performance, it is important to recognize that the public and the journalists thought that the 1996 campaign was singularly lacking in suspense. The media responded to an unexciting horserace with a predictable decline in overall campaign coverage. But they also made substantive innovations in news coverage: more citizen involvement, deeper investigation of issues the public cared about, more attention to campaign financing, and more time for candidates to speak unfiltered to the audience. The public had no complaints about the amount of campaign coverage and gave the media adequate marks.[65]

Whether it was the revamped mix of campaign stories, innovations in coverage, new media, or the sheer familiarity of the candidates, the great majority of the voters in 1996 thought they had enough information to cast their ballots.[66] Survey evidence showed that the voters were not bluffing. On key points of campaign discourse the voters knew where the candidates stood (see chapter 3). The losing candidates were much less generous to the media than was the public. Dole and Perot blamed journalists for not covering them enough or for covering them unfairly.

Whether there was enough coverage of the campaign is debatable. Like the candidates, the media had to play the hand they were dealt. There was less news than in previous elections, but apparently enough to cover the subject. Even if the amount is judged disappointing, the media can take credit for increasing the proportion of substantive and creative coverage. The campaign of 1996 also saw media innovations that may flower in future, more competitive elections.

It is probably easier to say that the coverage was enough than to say it was fair. The public judged the coverage equitable, and analysis shows that it was balanced, but in a troubling way. When Clinton did not answer Dole's attacks, the press did—underscoring impressions of press bias and negativity toward Dole. In this sense the effect of the reporting was not neutral. The campaign of 1996 shows that fairness, balance, and neutrality are not the same things and demonstrates why achieving those goals remains a compelling challenge for the candidates and the media.

Notes

1. *New York Times*/CBS News poll release, "State of the Union Poll, January 18–20, 1996," with trends.

2. See, for example, Katharine Q. Seelye, "Issue for Dole Isn't Courage, but Convictions," *New York Times*, 26 December 1996, A1.

3. *New York Times*, 18 January 1996.

4. *New York Times,* 14 February 1996.

5. The *New York Times*/CBS News poll, February National Poll, 22–24 February 1996, showed an increase in Forbes's not favorable ratings from 14 to 37 percent.

6. As described by focus groups in *New York Times,* 10 October 1996.

7. *Boston Globe,* 6 February 1996.

8. See, for example, the description in the *New York Times* candidate biographical series in December 1995: "... skeptics say voters formed their impressions of Mr. Dole long ago—first as President Richard M. Nixon's 'hatchet man,' then as a split-the-difference compromiser in Congress" (26 December 1996).

9. WMUR-Dartmouth poll, 1–4 October 1995, director Linda Fowler, data analyst Tami Buhr.

10. Katharine Q. Seelye, "Dole Offers Economic Plan Calling for Broad Tax Cut Aimed at Spurring Growth," *New York Times,* 6 August 1996.

11. Fifty-one percent of respondents in the *New York Times*/CBS News poll.

12. *New York Times,* 6 August 1996, A13.

13. David Rosenbaum with Steven Lohr, "With Stable Economy Clinton Hopes for Credit," *New York Times,* 3 August 1996.

14. Quoted by Michael Winerip, "Backers of Bush in '92 Are Turning to Clinton," *New York Times,* 27 May 1996, 10.

15. Reported in *New York Times,* 9 October 1995.

16. See Marion Just, Ann Crigler, Dean Alger, Timothy Cook, Montague Kern, and Darrell West, *Crosstalk: Citizens, Candidates, and the Media in a Presidential Campaign* (Chicago: University of Chicago Press, 1996).

17. *New York Times,* 11 July 1996.

18. Media Studies Center, *The Media & Campaign 96 Briefing,* no. 4, October 1996, 9.

19. *New York Times,* 13 August 1996, A1.

20. Data collected by the Center for Media and Public Affairs and analyzed by the Consortium for Campaign Media Analysis, Wellesley College, supported by a grant from the Pew Charitable Trusts.

21. Richard Berke, "Week in Review," *New York Times,* 14 July 1996, sec. 4, p. 7.

22. *New York Times,* 24 September 1996.

23. Howard Kurtz, "No Debate about It: TV Analysts Say Clinton's a Winner," *Washington Post,* 18 October 1996.

24. *Boston Sunday Globe,* 13 October 1996, 36.

25. Somewhat disingenuously in the first debate, Dole described his undertaking not to mention Whitewater (thereby, of course, mentioning Whitewater).

26. *New York Times,* 19 October 1996.

27. Adam Nagourney, "Dole Warms to Task of Attacking Clinton," *New York Times,* 19 October 1996, 8.

28. *New York Times,* 5 September 1996.

29. Eleanor Randolph, "Two Campaigns Escalate the Rhetoric in Ad War,"

Los Angeles Times, 28 September 1996.

30. "Accentuating the Negative—Quietly," *U.S. News & World Report,* 30 September 1996, 43–44.

31. "Clinton, Dole Unveil Attack Ads," *Boston Globe,* 18 September 1996.

32. In the *New York Times*/CBS poll (16 October 1996), 29 percent of respondents thought the campaign was more positive, compared to 11 percent in 1992. The Pew Research Center for the People & the Press News Release, 15 November 1996, reported that 36 percent thought the campaign was less negative than previous campaigns, compared to only 16 percent in 1992.

33. *New York Times,* 26 June 1996.

34. Dole evaluated Clinton in 727 messages on the network news compared to less than half that number for Clinton. Both candidates had mostly negative things to say about the other (92 percent for Dole and 88 percent for Clinton). Research shows that media coverage of candidate attacks is the most important factor in the total amount of negative coverage a candidate receives. Attacks are newsworthy activities by acknowledged newsmakers, making them irresistible subjects of campaign coverage. See Marion Just, Ann Crigler, and Tami Buhr, "Discordant Discourse: Communication in the 1992 Presidential Election Campaign" (paper presented at the annual meeting of the American Political Science Association, Chicago, 1995).

35. There are more positive statements by Clinton on Clinton than by Dole on Dole (583 compared to 520) in network news, in spite of the Republican's penchant for referring to himself in the third person.

36. A Pew Research Center poll found that one-third of respondents labeled the press "unfair" to Bob Dole's campaign, compared to only a quarter for Clinton's. The Pew Research Center News Release, 15 November 1996. The Kaiser Family Foundation postelection poll found that 36 percent thought the press was too negative to Dole, compared to only 12 percent for Clinton. "Campaign '96: Knowing the Candidates and the Issues," *Washington Post*/Kaiser Family Foundation/Harvard University Survey Project, prepared for the Shorenstein Center and the Kaiser Family Foundation Meeting of News Executives, 4 December 1996.

37. Pew Research Center for the People & the Press News Release, 14 November 1996.

38. According to a Pew Research Center postelection poll, 72 percent of the voters had made up their minds how to vote prior to the debates. The Pew Research Center News Release, 15 November 1996.

39. S. Robert Lichter and Richard Noyes, "Campaign '96: The Media and the Candidates, First Report to the Markle Foundation: The Road to New Hampshire," Center for Media and Public Affairs, Washington, D.C., June 1996.

40. See Thomas Patterson, *Out of Order* (New York: Knopf, 1993).

41. Bruce Morton, CNN News, 10 April 1996.

42. Brian Williams, NBC *Nightly News,* 11 May 1996.

43. *New York Times*/CBS News poll, reported in *New York Times,* 20 August 1996, A1.

44. *New York Times,* 28 October 1996, A15.

45. *New York Times,* 8 November 1996.

46. According to the Center for Media and Public Affairs, the amount of coverage on network news averaged 12 minutes per day in 1996, 25 in 1992, and 17 in 1988. See *Media Monitor* 10, no. 5 (November/December 1996).

47. *New York Times,* 19 October 1996.

48. Figures by the Annenberg Public Policy Center, reported in the *Virginian-Pilot* (Norfolk), 17 November 1996, J1.

49. Kaiser Family Foundation/Shorenstein Center Meeting of News Executives, 4 December 1996.

50. Media Studies Center, *The Media & Campaign 96 Briefing,* no. 4, October 1996; Pew Research Center poll, the Pew Research Center for the People & the Press News Release, 15 November 1996; Campaign Discourse and Civic Engagement 1996 poll, directed by Marion Just and Ann Crigler, Wellesley College, conducted by the Institute for Social Research, University of Michigan; *Washington Post*/Kaiser Family Foundation/Harvard University Survey Project, "Campaign '96: Knowing the Candidates and the Issues."

51. Figure from the Center for Media and Public Affairs, director Robert Lichter.

52. Media Studies Center, *The Media & Campaign 96 Briefing,* no. 4, October 1996, 4.

53. Reported by Tony Wharton in the *Virginian-Pilot* (Norfolk), 17 November 1996, J1. The Center for Media and Public Affairs also reported a decline in "horse race" coverage, from 58 percent in 1992 and 1988 to 48 percent in 1996 (*Media Monitor* 10, no. 6, November/December 1996).

54. For example, Michael Kelly, "Media Culpa," *New Yorker,* 4 November 1996, 45–49.

55. Natalie Jacobson of WCVB in Boston explained, for example, that "we went out and solicited the voters' opinion right from the start in the New Hampshire primary." Kaiser Family Foundation/Shorenstein Center Meeting of News Executives, 4 December 1996.

56. See Kiku Adatto, "Sound Bite Democracy," Kennedy School Press/Politics Center Research Paper (June 1990); Daniel C. Hallin, "Sound Bite News: Television Coverage of Elections, 1968–1988 (Symposium: Television News and Its Dis-Contents)," *Journal of Communication* 42, no. 2 (1992): 5–25; Patterson, *Out of Order;* S. Robert Lichter, Daniel Amundson, and Richard Noyes, *The Video Campaign: Network Coverage of the 1988 Primaries* (Washington, D.C.: American Enterprise Institute for Public Policy Research, 1988).

57. Media Studies Center, *The Media & Campaign 96 Briefing,* no. 4, October 1996.

58. *Washington Post*/Kaiser Family Foundation/Harvard University Survey Project poll, "Campaign '96: Knowing the Candidates and the Issues."

59. *New York Times,* 21 April 1996, sec. 4, pp. 1, 6.

60. Times Mirror Center for the People & the Press, News Release "Tech-

nology in the American Household: Americans Going Online ... Explosive Growth, Uncertain Destinations," 16 October 1995.

61. Media Studies Center, *The Media & Campaign 96 Briefing,* no. 1, April 1996, 9.

62. This was a regular feature in the *Wall Street Journal.*

63. The overall traffic on the Web barely increased. See *New York Times,* 7 November 1996.

64. The Media Studies Center/Roper Survey reported 6 percent (*The Media & Campaign 96 Briefing,* no. 4, October 1996); the Pew Research Center found 7 percent (Pew Research Center for People & the Press News Release, 15 November 1996); and Wirthlin Worldwide reported 14 percent (David Winston, "The Internet and Campaign '96," *Politics Now, Poll Track,* 16 December 1996).

65. *Washington Post*/Kaiser Family Foundation/Harvard University Survey Project poll, "Campaign '96: Knowing the Candidates and the Issues."

66. About two-thirds of the respondents in the *Washington Post*/Kaiser Family Foundation poll and three-quarters in the Pew Research Center postelection survey, the Pew Research Center for the People & the Press News Release, 15 November 1996.

3

Public Opinion and the Election

SCOTT KEETER

> Thus play I in one person many people . . .
> — *Richard II* (V, 5)

> He was saying yes and saying no at the same time.
> He was stealing the center, creating the center.
> — George Stephanopoulos

Bill Clinton played many parts in the political drama of his first four years, including occasional stints on stage in multiple roles simultaneously. He proved to have the versatility to do this well, and in doing so, excelled in one important role demanded of elected officials: he reflected public opinion in all its ambivalence and changeability. Ultimately, though, he was defined by who he was not, and the public was provided with a relatively clear choice about the direction of the country and what role the government should play.

As in most modern American elections, the election of 1996 was shaped by three important aspects of public opinion, which will be the main focus of this chapter. The first was the underlying division in opinion about the appropriate scope and role of government, and the extent to which voters of differing viewpoints could be mobilized to vote. Although the election did not provide a clear referendum on the conservative revolution of House Speaker Newt Gingrich and his colleagues, opinion about what the government should be doing was the most important criterion used by voters. The public was deeply divided over the role of government; paradoxically, both the president and the Republicans running for Congress were able to position themselves in ways to take advantage of the shifting center of gravity in American politics. Although it was not a conscious wish of most voters, the result—divided government—reflects the near-equal balance of the parties and their underlying ideologies in the public today.

The second key aspect of public opinion was the relatively high level of voter satisfaction with the direction of the country in general and approval of the condition of the economy more specifically. For the nonideological voter, generalized approval or disapproval of the incumbent party's management of the economy is often the most important criterion in the vote. Voter dissatisfaction with the economy is usually hazardous to the health of incumbents, as George Bush discovered in 1992. Conversely, good economic conditions, or at least the perception of them, can make voters overlook other flaws an incumbent president might have. Good economic conditions can and did help congressional incumbents as well.

The candidates' personal qualities constitute the third key element of voter choice and are especially important in presidential elections where voters come to know—or at least believe they know—both of the major party candidates very well. Despite Republican hopes that Bill Clinton's widely perceived character problems would become a key criterion for voters, the president turned out to have a much more complex public persona, manifesting a very human mixture of strengths and weaknesses. Ultimately, the favorable aspects of Clinton's personal qualities reinforced his strengths on the issues—his arguments on behalf of preserving the safety net, improving education, and protecting the environment seemed consistent with the public's image of him as a warm and empathetic human being—while his personal flaws, especially in view of the public's low expectations for the ethics of public officials, seemed irrelevant to his conduct of the presidency.

Take a Left, Then a Hard Right, Then Veer Slightly Left Again

The essence of democracy is that the government should reflect the views of the people. If the public changes its mind about what the government should be doing, then we expect this change to have an impact on what the government actually does. To what extent can we find congruence between public opinion and the outcome of the election and, more generally, the direction taken by government over the past several years?

This question is especially relevant in view of the dramatic outcome of the 1994 congressional elections, in which the Republicans emerged with control of both the House and Senate for the first time in forty years. No

Republican incumbent at either the national or state level was defeated, while many liberal Democratic icons (such as New York Governor Mario Cuomo and Texas Governor Ann Richards) lost. Among the many explanations for the Republicans' triumph was the view that the public had become markedly more conservative, in reaction to perceived excesses of the first two years of the Clinton administration. This belief provided much of the energy and justification for the efforts made by the GOP Congress in 1995 and early 1996 to reduce the size and scope of the federal government.

Polls in 1992, 1994, and 1996 suggest that voters were divided over what the federal government should be doing and that sentiment about the proper scope of government did indeed shift over the period, moving right ward from 1992 to 1994, and then slightly leftward from 1994 to 1996 (see table 3.1). Among voters interviewed on election day in 1992, a majority (54 percent) said the government should be doing more to solve problems; 46 percent disagreed, saying that the government does too many things better left to businesses and individuals. The electorate of 1994 was much more conservative, with 59 percent of voters saying that the government does too much. By 1996, voter sentiment was slightly less conservative, but a majority (55 percent) still felt that the government was doing too much.[1] Among voters who felt this way, only 30 percent voted for Bill Clinton. Among those who felt the government should be doing more, Clinton won 72 percent of the vote.

TABLE 3.1

VOTER OPINION ABOUT THE SCOPE OF GOVERNMENT,
1992, 1994, 1996

	1992	1994	1996
Government should do more to solve problems	54%	42%	45%
Government is doing too many things better left to businesses and individuals	46	59	55

SOURCE: Election day voter surveys conducted by Voter News Service (1994 and 1996) and Voter Research and Surveys (1992).

A more nuanced analysis of polls conducted over the past several years yields two key conclusions about the elections of 1994 and 1996. First, there was a clear, if relatively small, shift to the right in public opinion up through 1994 on several important issues, with the largest conservative shift occurring on issues of welfare and assistance to the poor. Following 1994, conservative sentiment abated slightly on some of the issues. Second, *voter*

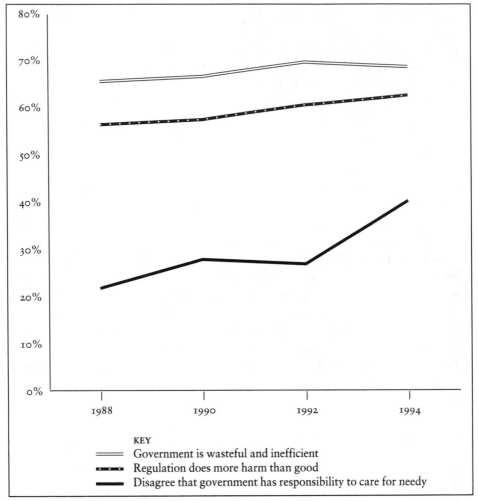

FIGURE 3.1

ANTIGOVERNMENT SENTIMENT, 1988–94

SOURCE: Surveys conducted by the Times Mirror Center for the People and the Press.

opinion is not the same as *public* opinion: voter turnout was critical in the outcomes of the 1994 and 1996 elections. The voters of 1994 and 1996 were considerably more conservative than those who stayed home.

Figure 3.1 shows results from three items asked by the Times Mirror Center for the People and the Press from 1988 to 1994. The percentage of the public agreeing that government regulation does more harm than good rose from 57 percent in 1988 to 63 percent by 1994. A more dramatic increase (18 points) is seen in the percentage of respondents disagreeing that "it is the responsibility of the government to take care of people who cannot take care of themselves." And while the segment of the public agreeing that "government is almost always wasteful and inefficient" rose only 3 percentage points over the period, the percentage who agreed "completely" was up 9 points.

The sharp rise in opposition to the government's social welfare function can also be seen in the General Social Survey's long-running series of questions about government spending. As recently as 1991, only a minority of the U.S. public (40 percent) felt that too much was being spent on welfare (figure 3.2). By 1993, this sentiment had spiked sharply upward, and it peaked in 1994 when 62 percent of respondents felt this way.

But two other important points can be gleaned from figure 3.2. The first is that the antiwelfare sentiment of the mid-1990s is not unprecedented. Comparable levels of opposition to welfare spending were seen in the late 1970s, presaging the election of Ronald Reagan as president and a Republican majority in the U.S. Senate. During the 1980s, as a conservative administration attempted to roll back benefits for the poor, public opinion shifted back in a more liberal direction.

The second point is that although it is too early to tell if a trend is developing, the data suggest that a similar moderation in public opinion may be occurring, with antiwelfare sentiment in 1996 showing a 6 percentage point decline from the 1994 reading. Evidence from other surveys also shows a slight decline in antigovernment opinion. The percentage of respondents believing that government is always wasteful and inefficient dropped by 8 points from 1994 to 1996, and the percentage who believe that government regulation does more harm than good declined by 9 points. The percentage saying that poor people have it easy because they can get government benefits without doing anything for them increased by 6 points from 1994 to 1995, but then fell by 8 points in 1996.[2]

The upshot of these changes in public opinion is that the pool of potential voters in 1996 was somewhat more conservative than it was in 1992, but also somewhat *less* conservative than in 1994. This pattern alone is consistent with the broad outcome of the elections of 1994 and 1996: a stunning, deep, conservative Republican victory in 1994, and a mixed but still generally successful result for congressional Republicans in 1996.

But one other element of opinion needs to be examined: voter turnout. A prominent journalistic theme of the 1996 election was the relatively low

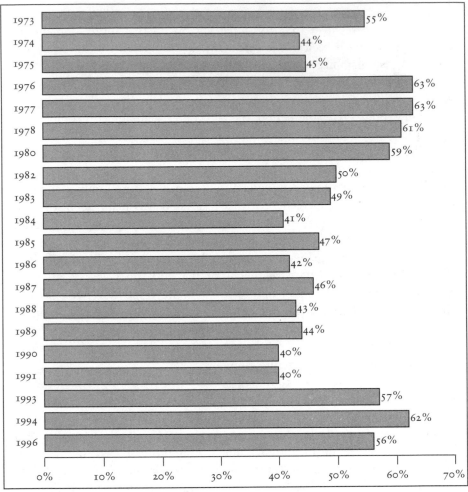

FIGURE 3.2

PERCENTAGE OF THE PUBLIC SAYING THAT THE U.S.
SPENDS "TOO MUCH" ON WELFARE

SOURCE: General Social Surveys conducted by the National Opinion Research Center,
1973–96.

level of public attention to the campaign, culminating in the lowest rate of
voter turnout since 1924, when women were newly enfranchised. Both to
understand the dynamics of the election and to assess the extent to which
the results reflected the will of the people, we need to compare the opinions
of voters and nonvoters.

As with all off-year elections, the level of voter turnout in 1994 was considerably lower than in presidential years.[3] But the election of 1994 featured a high degree of mobilization by conservatives, with the effect that voters were considerably more likely to favor Republican House candidates than were nonvoters. Voter turnout in 1996 was higher than in 1994, but a similar ideological and partisan skew in the electorate was evident, with voters more conservative and Republican than nonvoters. Clinton's lead among likely voters in the Pew Research Center's mid-October survey was 9 percentage points, but he led Dole among the poll's registered but likely nonvoters by a whopping 63 percent to 26 percent. Similarly, likely voters divided about evenly between Democratic and Republican candidates for the House, but among registered but nonvoting citizens, the Democrats led by a margin of 59 percent to 41 percent.[4]

An instructive way to look at the effect of the "hyperactive conservative" is through the prism of the Pew Research Center's voter typology, which sorts citizens into ten groups based upon responses to questions about core political values and partisanship.[5] The most conservative and Republican of the groups is the "Enterprisers," who hold conservative views on issues across nearly all domains of politics: they are probusiness, promilitary, antiregulation, antitax, antiwelfare, antiabortion, and antihomosexual. As figure 3.3 shows, the turnout of Enterprisers in 1996 was estimated at 72 percent, a figure over 10 points higher than the next most active group. (In 1994, the Enterprisers were estimated to have turned out at a rate of 70 percent, which was nearly 20 twenty points higher than any other group). Virtually all Enterprisers voted Republican in the House elections. Enterprisers constituted one-eighth of the general public, but were a disproportionate one-fifth of citizens who actually voted.

Indeed, two of the top three groups in terms of turnout were highly Republican. The group called the "Moralists," which includes most evangelical and fundamentalist Protestants, cast nearly 90 percent of its votes for GOP House candidates and was estimated to have turned out at a 59 percent rate, nearly 10 percentage points higher than the next most active groups (the "New Dealers," the "Partisan Poor," and the "New Democrats"). Of the liberal and Democratic groups in the typology, the most active was the "Seculars," a well-educated group that tends to be supportive of regulation and social welfare programs and also socially tolerant. Sixty-one percent of Seculars were estimated to have voted, and 92 percent of them voted Democratic in House races.

Three other Democratic groups turned out at about 50 percent, the average rate for the entire electorate. The New Dealers, an older, socially

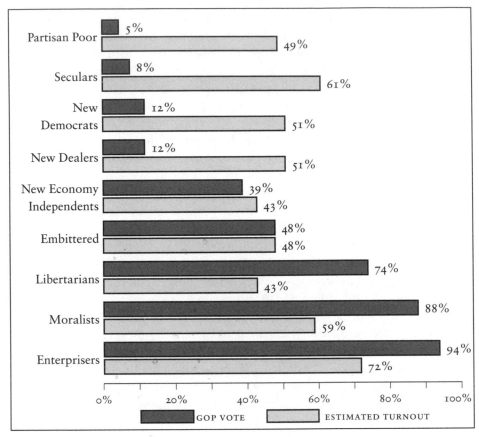

FIGURE 3.3

PARTY PREFERENCE AND TURNOUT IN THE ELECTIONS
FOR U.S. HOUSE IN 1996, BY VOTER GROUP

SOURCE: October 1996 survey conducted by the Pew Research Center for the People and the
Press.

conservative group that provided many votes to Ronald Reagan in the
1980s, cast nearly 90 percent of its votes for Democratic House candidates,
and gave Clinton nearly three-fourths of its votes. The Partisan Poor, a disadvantaged, pro–social welfare group, was as strongly supportive of Clinton and House Democrats as the Enterprisers were of Dole and Republican
House candidates. And the New Democrats, a moderate, female-dominated
group targeted by Bill Clinton, gave Clinton and Democratic House candidates about nine out of ten of their votes.

Collectively, these three groups, plus the strongly Democratic Seculars, constituted about 36 percent of the public and were about 40 percent of the actual electorate. By contrast, the two most active Republican groups—the Moralists and the Enterprisers—were about 27 percent of the public but on election day made up over 37 percent of the voters who turned out.

Reversal of Fortunes: Public Perceptions of the President and Congress

Bill Clinton dubbed himself the "Comeback Kid" during the 1992 campaign, but even he could hardly have imagined how well the moniker would fit by election day in 1996. Socks the cat was a perfect pet for a man who seemed to have multiple political lives. But Clinton was not the only politician with the ability to resurrect himself. The Republicans in Congress staged an impressive comeback, too.

CLINTON'S JOB RATINGS
As figure 3.4 shows, President Clinton's approval ratings shifted substantially throughout his first term in office. His first weeks in office were exceptionally troubled, characterized by self-inflicted wounds over cabinet appointments and rancorous political battles over divisive issues such as changes in the policy regarding homosexuals in the military. In April, his package of economic stimulus measures was defeated in Congress, and the siege of the Branch Davidian compound in Waco, Texas, ended in tragedy. Although a majority (55 percent) still approved of his performance, it was the lowest rating for a president after the first 100 days in office since Gallup began collecting this datum in 1953.

May and June were even worse, and Clinton's approval rating fell to 41 percent following the controversy over the firing of seven members of the White House travel office staff and widely reported stories about his expensive and airport-closing haircut aboard *Air Force One* in Los Angeles. The fall of 1993 was better for the president, with significant accomplishments including hosting the signing of the Israeli-Palestinian peace accord and the passage of the North American Free Trade Agreement. By January his ratings were back up to 55 percent.

But 1994 brought new troubles. Stories about the Whitewater affair became a regular feature of the evening news, the president was slapped with a sexual harassment lawsuit, and the White House's health-care reform proposal was under fierce attack. The reform effort ended in failure in September, when Democrats pulled the legislation. By election day, the president's approval rating was down to 42 percent. Following the election,

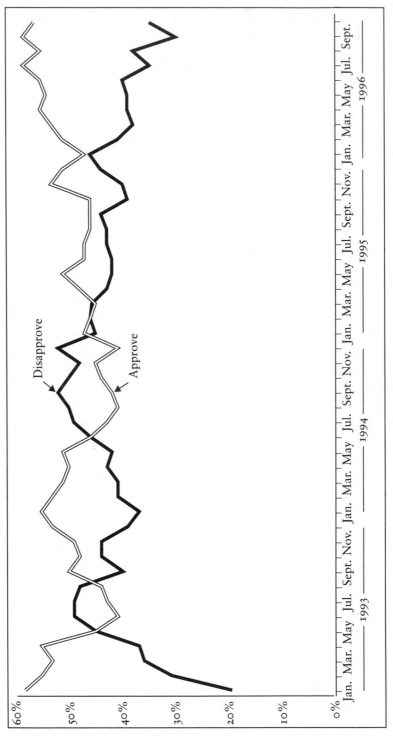

FIGURE 3.4. PRESIDENTIAL APPROVAL AND DISAPPROVAL, 1993–96

SOURCE: Gallup data, monthly averages.

Clinton was reported to be depressed and frustrated. "I want my presidency back," he was quoted as saying to an aide.[6]

Clinton's next comeback began in April, when he was called upon to reassure the nation and console victims and families of the bombing of the federal building in Oklahoma City. As discussed below, Clinton's impressive performance in the days and weeks after the bombing improved his standing with the public and positioned him for further gains later in the year when he went into battle against the Republican Congress.

CLINTON VERSUS CONGRESS

Upon assuming the majority in Congress, the Republican leaders—followed eagerly and sometimes led by the conservative group of House freshmen—moved quickly to act on a wide range of initiatives that included a mix of popular reforms and highly controversial rollbacks of government functions and services. The aggressive manner in which the GOP agenda was pursued was off-putting to many citizens, and disapproval of Congress's performance rose steadily through the spring of 1995 (see figure 3.5).

Meanwhile, President Clinton was confronted with critical decisions about how much to cooperate and how much to oppose, in short how to become politically relevant again. Relying upon his instincts, along with a great deal of polling information and advisers across a wide spectrum of opinion, he charted a very careful path that led him—against the wishes of many Democrats in Congress and the more liberal of his advisers—to accept the necessity of a plan for a balanced federal budget, and, in 1996, to sign a very conservative welfare reform bill. But he also defended affirmative action programs, environmental regulation, and the current contours of the Medicare system. During the summer and fall of 1995, he spent millions of dollars in targeted advertising attacking the Republican agenda and vowing to fight to preserve popular government programs. Most important, he chose not to strike a budget deal with the Republican leadership. This impasse led to two partial shutdowns of the federal government, for which Congress and not the president received most of the blame. In November 1995 during the first of the shutdowns, disapproval of Congress reached 68 percent (figure 3.5). By contrast, disapproval of President Clinton was only 40 percent (figure 3.4).

THE STRATEGY OF "TRIANGULATION":
TWO CAN PLAY THIS GAME

Republican leaders observed, contemptuously but with obvious frustration, that Clinton had appropriated numerous Republican ideas as his own, even

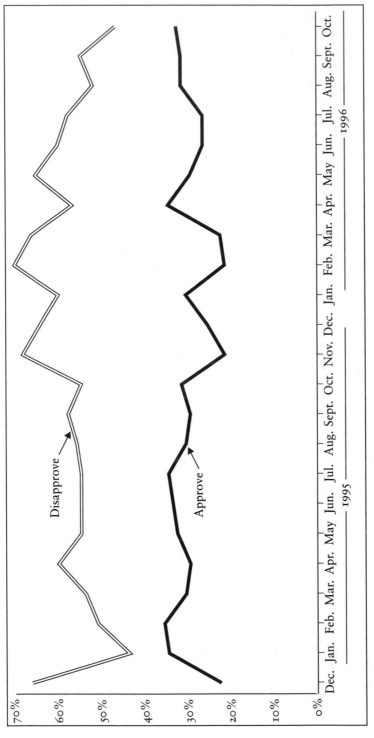

FIGURE 3.5. CONGRESSIONAL APPROVAL AND DISAPPROVAL,
DECEMBER 1994–OCTOBER 1996

SOURCE: Polls by CBS News, the *New York Times*, and the Gallup Organization.

taking credit for several GOP congressional initiatives in his acceptance speech at the Democratic National Convention. Having successfully co-opted the Republicans on key issues where they had traditionally enjoyed an advantage over the Democrats in public opinion, he was free to move the campaign debate to issues on which he and the Democrats were pre-ferred by voters—"M2E2," as E.J. Dionne Jr. called it: Medicare, Medicaid, education, the environment.[7]

But the Republicans in 1996 moved at least as consciously and strategi-cally in the direction of Democratic positions as Clinton had moved toward Republican positions. In the face of polls showing overwhelming public support for the proposals, the Republican Congress acquiesced in the pas-sage of an increase in the minimum wage and of the Kassebaum-Kennedy bill mandating the portability of health insurance. Gone, too, was the stri-dent rhetoric of revolution. No serious effort was made to repeal the ban on assault weapons or to push environmental and regulatory reforms after the defeats of early 1996. The Republican National Convention featured a prime-time lineup of women and moderates and many reassuring words about the concern of the party for the disadvantaged and the helpless. The phrase "wolves in sheeps' clothing" was invoked by Democrats, and occa-sional glimpses of Republican strategy memos seemed to reveal the stitching here and there (e.g., Republican lawmakers were counseled to soften the party's environmental image by holding tree-planting ceremonies back home in their districts). But, in fact, the public's view of the Republicans softened considerably in the summer and fall, and overall disapproval of Congress declined from 70 percent in June to 52 percent in August, ending up at 47 percent in October, just before the election (see figure 3.5). While a majority of the public (52 percent) felt that the Republicans in Congress had tried to change too many things too fast, a plurality of 42 percent nev-ertheless felt that Congress had accomplished more than it usually does in a typical term. On election day, a majority of voters (55 percent) said they were not concerned that a reelected Republican Congress would be too conservative. Instead, a plurality of 49 percent said they feared a Demo-cratic Congress would be too liberal (see chapter 6).

The Mood of the Electorate

Even as most voters chose a candidate based on issues and values, the rela-tively equal division of the public on questions of the appropriate scope of government, combined with the energetic efforts of both Democrats and Republicans to move to the safety of the center, necessarily rendered the outcome of the election ambiguous. As Gerald Pomper writes in chapter 5, "the election conveyed a mood more than a message."

The success of President Clinton in particular, and congressional incumbents of both parties in general, can be attributed in part to the mood of the public, which, in the fall of 1996, was more sanguine about the condition of the country than it had been in several years. An October Gallup/CNN/*USA Today* poll found 39 percent of respondents satisfied with the way things were going in the country. By comparison, only 20 percent were satisfied in 1992. Over the past 16 years, vote for the incumbent president's party has been strongly correlated with this general measure of voter mood.

Another measure of voter mood told a similar story. An NBC News/*Wall Street Journal* survey item asked citizens if they believed the country was going in the right direction or off on the wrong track. Through June 1996, about half or more of the public said the country was off on the wrong track, with less than a third saying the direction was right (figure 3.6). In August and September, positive and negative views were nearly balanced, and in October, those who thought the country was moving in the right direction finally outnumbered those who thought it was on the wrong track. On election day, 55 percent of exit-poll respondents said the country was moving in the right direction, and 70 percent of these voters chose Clinton. (By contrast, only 40 percent of voters in 1994 thought the country was going in the right direction.)

Why did so many voters feel that the country was on the right track? The answer may be found in the notorious slogan posted in Clinton's 1992 campaign "War Room": "It's the Economy, Stupid!" Figure 3.6 also shows the percentage of respondents in Gallup/CNN/*USA Today* polls who felt that the condition of the economy was either excellent or good. This measure of citizen opinion tracks almost perfectly with the sentiment that the country was moving in the right direction. Further evidence for the economic basis of the public mood can be seen in a September 1996 NBC News/*Wall Street Journal* poll, which found the public nearly evenly divided about the direction of the country. When asked why they felt the way they did, over half of those who said the country was going in the right direction mentioned some aspect of the economy—unemployment was down, the minimum wage was going up, or the economy in general was good. Only about a fifth mentioned President Clinton explicitly, and hardly anyone mentioned Congress. Among those who thought the country was on the wrong track, reasons divided roughly evenly among concerns about crime, taxes, family and moral values, education, and President Clinton.

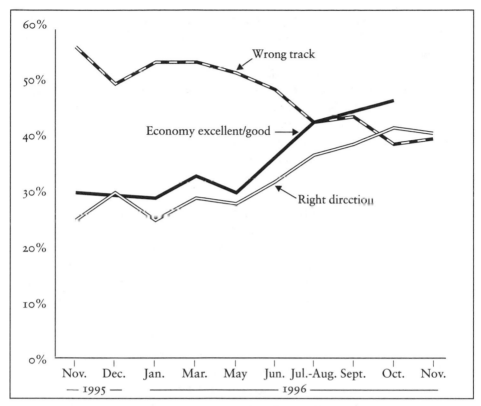

FIGURE 3.6

OPINION ABOUT THE DIRECTION OF THE COUNTRY
AND THE CONDITION OF THE ECONOMY

SOURCE: Questions on direction of country from polls conducted by Hart/Teeter for NBC News and the *Wall Street Journal*. Questions on condition of economy from polls conducted by Gallup for CNN and *USA Today*.

The Candidates as People

Elections select leaders, not just ideas. Despite differences on the issues, the Democratic and Republican presidential candidates of 1996 were similar in many respects. Both Clinton and Dole were life-long politicians. Both were known and respected for their strong grasp of the details of public policy and for their pragmatic approaches to problem solving. But they were very different in temperament and personal style.

BILL CLINTON

The public came to know Clinton's strengths and weaknesses, and ultimately enough voters accepted him, warts and all. On the negative side, Gallup surveys during 1996 found majorities of the public disagreeing that Clinton is an effective manager (54 percent), keeps his promises (59 percent), or is honest and trustworthy (an average of 51 percent during 1996). Voters were relatively divided over a few other personal qualities: "tough enough for the job" (51 percent yes, 46 percent no); "puts the country's interests ahead of his own political interests" (50 percent yes, 45 percent no); "a man of strong convictions" (51 percent yes, 47 percent no).

Although Clinton was viewed as ineffective by many voters, especially following the 1994 election, he entered the fall campaign with a strong majority of the public believing that he was a man who "can get things done" (62 percent in a late August Gallup poll). But his most important personal quality to many voters was his empathy—the sense, as captured in the Gallup poll item, that he "cares about the needs of people like you." Entering the fall campaign, 63 percent of voters said this statement fit the president; only 34 percent disagreed. Even earlier in the year, when the public had many questions about the president's ability to do his job, majorities saw him as genuinely caring about them.

Clinton first developed his public reputation for conspicuous compassion during the 1992 campaign, but it was not until the bombing of the federal building in Oklahoma City that he was called on to put these talents to use in the presidential role of consoler and healer. Clinton received high marks from the public for his handling of the Oklahoma City tragedy. Polls conducted in the weeks following the bombing consistently found over 80 percent saying they approved of how the president responded to the event. Oklahoma City provided a double opportunity for the president. In addition to the enormous human tragedy for which people needed consolation and reassurance, there was a palpable political dimension as well. After the arrest of suspect Timothy McVeigh, speculation about the motive for the bombing moved from international terrorism to domestic antigovernment radicalism. Clinton's speech on 24 April attacking the "loud and angry" voices of talk radio was criticized by some observers as an effort to politicize the tragedy, but a majority of the public agreed that these voices pose a problem for society. It was clear that the more vociferous critics of the federal government in general, and of Clinton in particular, were placed on the defensive, if only temporarily.

BOB DOLE

Bob Dole's image among the public was in many ways a mirror of Clinton's. Clinton's honesty was viewed with skepticism by voters, but two-thirds (66 percent) felt that Dole was honest and trustworthy. Similarly, 67 percent thought that Dole was a man of strong convictions. And majorities felt that he could get things done (67 percent felt this way just after the Republican National Convention). But the public was about evenly divided over the degree to which Dole "cares about the needs of people like you," and by a 55–35 margin disagreed that he had "a clear plan for solving the country's problems." Dole's age troubled a minority of voters. Numerous polls asked about the age issue, with an average of 28–35 percent of respondents saying that Dole was too old to be president. (Typically, fewer than 10 percent of voters said that his age would actually be an asset to him.) When asked by a CBS News/*New York Times* poll why Dole's age was a problem, more respondents (41 percent) said that it was because he was out of touch with the younger generation than said was it because he would not have enough stamina to be president (36 percent). A fifth (22 percent) said both of these were problems.

But, for at least two important reasons, Dole was never able to capitalize on his comparative advantage over Clinton on the "character issue." One problem was that Dole changed his position on two major issues during the campaign, reversing his support for affirmative action programs and his opposition to large tax cuts as a stimulus to economic growth. These changes undercut his ability to criticize Clinton for being irresolute on issues and left him vulnerable to charges of political opportunism. The shift on affirmative action probably did relatively little harm, since he was unlikely to get the votes of very many proponents of affirmative action regardless of his stand. (By the same token, most voters who opposed affirmative action were probably not going to vote for Bill Clinton, regardless of what Dole did.)

Dole's embrace of a 15 percent across-the-board tax cut, however, raised serious questions about the depth of his commitment to deficit reduction, a core belief for which he had fought valiantly in the Senate for over a decade. It also reflected a misreading of public sentiment about government and the economy. Concern about the budget deficit was greater than antitax sentiment among the public. By a 55–39 margin, respondents to a CBS News poll in August 1996 said they would prefer reducing the deficit to cutting taxes. More surprising was the fact that majorities of Democrats, Independents, *and* Republicans felt this way (table 3.2). And Dole's motives were questioned: an August poll for *Newsweek* found that, by a whopping 70–19 margin, respondents thought that Dole had proposed the 15 percent tax cut to win votes rather than to help the economy.

A more general reason for Dole's inability to gain traction with the

TABLE 3.2

PUBLIC PREFERENCES FOR REDUCING THE DEFICIT
VERSUS CUTTING TAXES, AUGUST 1996

	All	Republicans	Democrats	Independents
Reduce the deficit	55%	55%	54%	57%
Cut taxes	39	39	42	35
Don't know	6	6	4	8

SOURCE: CBS News poll conducted 12–13 August 1996. Cited by *Polling Report* 12, no. 16 (19 August 1996).

character issue is that while the public certainly questioned Clinton's ethics, public expectations for ethical conduct among public officials, especially when the officials are perceived as sympathetic to the average American, are simply not very high. And character questions involving sexual morality and family life have never been especially important to most of the voting public. Enough voters have "been there, done that" that there is an appreciation for the frailties of the human condition.

The limitations of the character issue as a club against Clinton were illustrated when Dole casually asked audiences in April 1996 who would make a better guardian for their children if something happened to them —President Clinton or himself. The idea for the statement came from a focus group in which participants were said to have remarked that they would be more likely to trust their children with Dole than with Clinton. But when the *Washington Post* posed the question to a national sample, 52 percent said they would prefer Clinton, and just 27 percent would pick Dole to care for their children.[8] The incident was doubly damaging for Dole. In addition to the embarrassment of having a plausible contention about public opinion contradicted by a reputable poll, and thus making Clinton's character problem seem less serious, it also provided an opportunity for critics and journalists to raise questions about Dole's character by reminding voters of his unsuccessful first marriage. A Pew Research Center poll in July 1996 found 45 percent of voters saying that Clinton better represented their views on family values and sexual issues. Only 40 percent picked Dole.

NEWT GINGRICH

President Clinton found a remarkable, if involuntary, ally in House Speaker Newt Gingrich. Even before the GOP Congress ran afoul of the public, Gingrich did not enjoy high ratings from the public. Through the period from January to October 1995 (when the confrontation with the president over the federal budget developed), approval of Gingrich's performance ranged between 35 and 45 percent, while disapproval fluctuated between about 25 and 45 percent. Through most of this time, the public was fairly evenly divided about him (see figure 6.3, p. 215).

Gingrich was thrust into the public eye over the budget battle and the government shutdown in mid-November, and the public did not like what it saw. His image problem was compounded by his casual remark to reporters that he was being tougher in the budget negotiations because of the way he was treated by the president aboard *Air Force One* during the trip to Israel for Prime Minister Rabin's funeral. His disapproval rating soared to 65 percent in one poll, and it remained near or above 50 percent throughout 1996. His efforts to stay out of the spotlight did little to improve his public image.

Negative opinion about Gingrich went beyond mere disapproval of his performance or disagreement with his positions on issues. A Hart/Teeter poll conducted in July 1996 for MSNBC asked which of five national figures—Bill Clinton, Hillary Rodham Clinton, Bob Dole, Ross Perot, or Newt Gingrich—was the most annoying. Gingrich won in a landslide, beating his nearest competitor, Hillary Clinton, by a margin of 45 percent to 22 percent. Ross Perot trailed at 17 percent, and Clinton and Dole barely registered (12 and 10 percent, respectively).

Does the Public Really Want Divided Government?

The election left the country with different parties in control of the presidency and Congress for at least two more years. A number of polls during the campaign suggested that this particular outcome may have been favored by a significant portion of the public, engaging in a conscious effort to promote the natural checks and balances of the system. A more pragmatic version of the argument held that while the public was inclined to reelect Bill Clinton, many voters were concerned about what he might do if left unchecked by a Republican Congress. As election day approached, some Republican congressional candidates even tacitly conceded Dole's defeat by appealing for votes so that they could serve as a restraint on Clinton. An October poll conducted by the Pew Research Center asked voters the following question: "If Bill Clinton is reelected president in November, would it be better for the Republicans to control Congress or the Democrats to control Congress?" Forty-six percent of registered voters chose the Republicans, while 42 percent picked the Democrats.

But responses to this question were largely a reflection of the underlying partisan affiliation of the voters, and hence their preferences for which party should control the government, rather than an abstract commitment to Madisonian checks and balances.[9] Among likely voters who were Republicans, 84 percent said they preferred that Republicans control Congress. Among Democrats, 74 preferred Democrats (19 percent picked the Republicans). Among the 5 percent of likely voters who were "pure" independents (unwilling to indicate that they leaned toward either the Democrats or the Republicans), 57 percent indicated a preference for a Republican Congress if Clinton won. Altogether, about 16 percent of likely voters in the Pew survey answered the question in a way that represented a split preference that was not simply a reflection of their underlying partisan sentiment.[10] And on election day, the VNS exit poll indicated that only about 14 percent of voters actually split their tickets between parties in the presidential and House races. Thus, for the vast majority of voters, divided government was simply a desirable alternative to unified control by the party they opposed.

Opinions about the Campaign

The public was generally satisfied with the choice of candidates and with the conduct of the campaign in 1996. They just didn't find it very interesting or pay much attention to it.

In an October Pew Research Center survey, 59 percent of voters said they were at least "fairly satisfied" with the choice of candidates for president, somewhat higher than the 51 percent who felt this way in October 1992. And a majority of registered voters (59 percent) said the candidates had indeed been talking about issues of importance to them (only 35 percent disagreed). But the public expressed ambivalence on this point. In a postelection survey by Pew, only 25 percent of voters said the candidates discussed issues more in 1996 than in the past, and 65 percent said issues were discussed less. By contrast, a 1992 poll found that 59 percent thought issues had been discussed more than in the past, and only 34 percent thought they had been discussed less.

The public in 1996 was more sanguine than the public of 1992 about the tone of the campaign. In 1996, about half (49 percent) said there had been more mudslinging and negative campaigning than in the past, but this was nearly twenty points lower than in 1992, when 68 percent said there was more negative campaigning than in the past. In 1996, the percentage saying that there was less mudslinging (36 percent) was twenty points higher than in 1992.

The candidate debates were much less of a factor in 1996 than they were in 1992. This was, in part, a consequence of the low level of public interest in the campaign compared with 1992, and the resulting small audiences for the debates. Public sentiment about the candidates changed very little after the 1996 debates, in contrast with 1992, when both Clinton and Perot used the debates effectively to improve their images. Voters in 1996 judged the debates as much less helpful in their decision making than voters in 1992, or even in 1988. Only 13 percent of 1996 voters said the debates were "very helpful," and another 28 percent said they were "somewhat helpful." By contrast, in 1992, 31 percent found the debates "very helpful" and 39 percent thought they were "somewhat helpful." Even in 1988, an election in which the dynamics of the campaign were reasonably similar to those of 1996, 48 percent found the debates at least "somewhat helpful."[11]

What Did They Know and When Did They Know It?

One important criterion for judging the campaign is what voters learned from it. There was good news and bad news. The good news was that most voters knew where the candidates and the parties stood on major issues in the election. For example, according to surveys conducted by the *Washington Post* in conjunction with Harvard University and the Kaiser Family Foundation, 73 percent could correctly state which candidate proposed to spend the least on Medicare, 70 percent knew which candidate had proposed a 15 percent tax cut, 67 percent knew who proposed a greater increase in defense spending, 75 percent knew who wanted to expand the family leave act, and 81 percent knew which party wanted to make it harder for women to obtain an abortion (see table 3.3).[12]

The bad news was that most of this knowledge was acquired by mid-September, with little gain thereafter. The most intense period of the campaign, which included the candidate debates, appeared to add little to voter knowledge about the basic issue positions of the candidates and their parties. The largest increase in public awareness in the *Washington Post* poll was the ability to name the Republican candidate for vice-president. In September, 68 percent named Kemp. In the postelection survey, 79 percent could do so.

More troubling was the relatively large minority of voters who misperceived the candidates' positions on several key issues. Overall, 50 percent of voters in the postelection survey could correctly identify Bob Dole as the

TABLE 3.3

VOTER KNOWLEDGE

	September (likely voters)	November postelection (reported voters)
Named Jack Kemp as GOP VP candidate	68	79
Named Pat Choate as Reform Party VP candidate	10	13
Aware that GOP had majority in House/aware that GOP won House majority in election	79	80
Which party in the U.S. Congress would favor:		
Making it harder for women to get abortions	83	81
Greater increase in defense spending	68	67
Keeping the ban on assault weapons	69	74
Expanding family leave	72	75
Did either candidate propose 15 percent tax cut?	65	70
Which candidate proposed:		
Spending the least on Medicare	Not asked	73
Constitutional amendment to allow voluntary prayer in schools	52	52
Goverment vouchers for school choice	43	50
Constitutional amendment to balance the budget	52	52
Government maintaining affirmative action efforts in hiring, contracting, and college admissions	72	72
Development of an antimissile defense system	54	49
Do presidential candidates receive campaign funds from U.S. government?	70	70

SOURCE: Surveys conducted 20–26 September and 6–10 November 1996 by the *Washington Post*, the Kaiser Family Foundation, and Harvard University.

candidate who supported government vouchers for school choice, an increase of 7 percentage points from the September survey. But a third of all voters thought that Clinton was the candidate who supported vouchers, and among Clinton's voters, nearly half thought this. Similarly, only about half (52 percent) the voters correctly identified Dole as the candidate who supported a constitutional amendment to require a balanced federal budget. Twenty-three percent said Clinton was the candidate who favored this, and another 15 percent said both did. And Clinton's supporters were even more likely to misperceive his position on this issue.

The Performance of the Preelection Polls

Just as they had done for several months, all the polls conducted during the week before the election indicated that Bill Clinton would beat Bob Dole. Most of the polls, however, overestimated the actual margin of victory. The Clinton lead averaged about 12 percentage points, 4 points higher than the actual margin on election day. In addition, several polls overestimated the level of Democratic support in the "generic House vote." A number of critics, especially among conservatives, were strongly critical of the polls and journalists' use of them. Everett Carll Ladd, director of the Roper Center for Public Opinion Research at the University of Connecticut, described the election polls as "An American Waterloo."[13] What happened?

One problem is that some of the polls probably overestimated the likely turnout of Democratic-leaning voters. Throughout the fall, political observers noted the low level of interest by the public and the press, a result in part of the large and steady Clinton lead. This relative lack of interest led to speculation that turnout would be low, and Republicans in particular were worried that Dole's supporters would be discouraged from voting. But, as the analysis of turnout earlier in this chapter indicates, Democratic supporters appear to have been the ones most likely to fail to show up. Pollsters try a variety of techniques to forecast who will vote: interest in the campaign, past voting history, knowledge of where to vote, self-described likelihood of voting. For nearly all these measures in 1996, the more stringent the test (i.e., the smaller the predicted turnout), the more Republican the likely electorate became.

The other reason for the underprediction of the Republican vote is that public opinion apparently shifted in the direction of the Republicans in the closing days of the campaign. Although few of the preelection polls indicated a significant shift, there was other evidence of change. According to the VNS exit poll, among the 17 percent of voters who said they made their choice in the presidential race in the last week before the election, Dole won about 42 percent to Clinton's 34 percent (Perot also did well in this group, winning about 20 percent). If the exit poll is accurate, then a valid reading of public opinion early in the weekend preceding election day would have shown Clinton with about a 10-point lead.

Even stronger evidence is seen in the pattern of forecast errors by different polls. Polls conducted closer to election day were more accurate. Figure 3.7 shows that (with one exception) the earlier the poll, the larger the overestimate of the margin of Clinton's victory. The relationship between the error and the timing of the poll is almost linear.[14]

Why did public opinion shift? One answer is that the most salient cam-

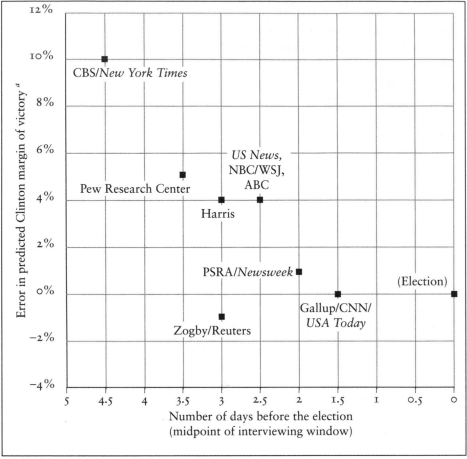

FIGURE 3.7

PREELECTION POLL FORECAST ERRORS WERE SMALLER
FOR POLLS CONDUCTED CLOSER TO THE ELECTION

SOURCE: Compiled by the author.
   a. Error = predicted Clinton margin minus actual margin.

paign topic during this period was the revelation of the Democratic Party's
extensive and possibly illegal fund-raising from foreign nationals and corporations. The stories meshed with preexisting public beliefs about Clinton's propensity for shady financial transactions and deal making, and were
made more believable by the Democratic Party's initial response, which was
to announce that fund raiser John Huang, a former Commerce Department

official, would not be available to the press, nor would the party release its interim campaign finance report before the election. The stories provided Ross Perot with a perfect issue, and he hammered Clinton and the Democrats relentlessly. On the eve of the election, in paid national telecasts and in stump speeches, Perot said the country was headed for "Watergate II" and quoted a former congressional counsel on Watergate (a Democrat) as saying that there was probable cause to indict the president and first lady as felons.[15]

Preelection polls indicated that voters were paying attention to the fund-raising scandal stories. In a Gallup/CNN/*USA Today* poll conducted 26–29 October, 53 percent of likely voters said they were closely following the story, and 57 percent thought the allegations were serious. Only 34 percent thought they were not serious.

Conclusion

The electoral outcome of four tumultuous years in U.S. politics was, surprisingly, a successful year for both presidential and congressional incumbents. In part, this outcome resulted from the traditional advantages enjoyed by incumbents, but in large measure the outcome also reflected the wishes of voters: some for the preservation of important government functions and services, others for curtailing these same functions and services. The divided government produced by the election was desired by relatively few voters, but it nevertheless mirrored the nearly equal division of the public along this deep and long-standing fault line over the appropriate scope of government.

Elections are blunt instruments for translating the public's will into public policy. But it is hard to imagine what instrument *could* provide a clear reflection of contemporary public opinion in America—a public divided over not only how much the government should do in taming the market and mitigating its effects, but also along the fault line of cultural politics, which sometimes reinforced economic divisions but just as often cut across them. In such a milieu, elections may decide who will govern but little else.

Acknowledgments

I am grateful to several colleagues and students for advice and assistance. Kim Parker, Claudia Deane, and Charmaine Thompson at the Pew Research Center provided data for several analyses; Robert Holsworth read a draft of the chapter and made useful suggestions; and Jennifer Creger, Jennifer Davis, and Bobby Pace advised me on what Shakespeare would have thought of this election. Data presented here were obtained from the Roper Center for Public Opinion Research, the Inter-university Consortium for Political and Social Research, Tom Smith at the National Opinion Research Center, and the following sites on the World Wide Web: www.politicsnow.com, www.allpolitics.com, www.gallup.com.

Notes

1. It is worth noting that one key reason for the gender gap in presidential and congressional voting is that men and women differed in their views of the role of government. By a 63–37 percent margin in the 1996 exit poll, men believed the government was doing too much, while women divided evenly on the question.

2. Data from surveys conducted by the Pew Research Center for the People and the Press, successor to the Times Mirror Center. Although these questions are similar to those in figure 3.1, they are not strictly comparable due to changes made in the response categories beginning in 1994.

3. See, e.g., Harold W. Stanley and Richard G. Niemi, *Vital Statistics on American Politics,* 5th ed. (Washington, D.C.: CQ Press, 1995), 77–80.

4. The Pew Research Center generously provided the data discussed in this section, but I am solely responsible for the analyses presented here, including the estimation of likely voters. Undecided voters were excluded from these tabulations. A similar pattern could be found in other polls. An analysis of Gallup data is described by David W. Moore, "Low Turnout Helped GOP," *Polling Report* 12, no. 22 (18 November 1996): 8.

5. See "Voter Typology: Dole Fails with Populists, GOP Moderates; Clinton Unites Dems, Gains Working Class Independents," Pew Research Center for the People and the Press, 25 October 1996. The voter typology was originally developed by the Times Mirror Center in 1987, and was updated in 1994. See "The New Political Landscape: The People, the Press, and Politics," Times Mirror Center for the People and the Press, October 1994. Figure 3.3 does not show one of the ten groups, the "Bystanders," who by definition do not participate in politics. They are approximately 10 percent of the public.

6. Alison Mitchell, "Stung by Defeats in '94, Clinton Regrouped and Co-opted G.O.P Strategies," *New York Times,* 7 November 1996, B1.

7. "Popular Programs Trump Character," *Washington Post,* 18 October 1996, A27. For a detailed discussion of the development of the Clinton strategy and the role played by campaign consultant Dick Morris, see Bob Woodward, *The Choice* (New York: Simon and Schuster, 1996).

8. Dan Balz, "A Picture of Trust, Taken Out of Focus," *Washington Post,* 26 April 1996, A14.

9. Joseph W. Doherty, "Partisanship in Political Time: Persuading Voters to

Divide Government," CSSP Data Note 2, University of California at Los Angeles, 10 October 1996. Available at http://www.sscnet.edu/issr/cssp/data2.html.

10. Reanalysis of Pew Research Center survey conducted 14–20 October 1996.

11. The 1996 survey was conducted by the Pew Research Center. Surveys from 1992 and 1988 were conducted by the Times Mirror Center.

12. See Richard Morin and Mario A. Brossard, "Many Voters Not Paying Attention," *Washington Post,* 29 September 1996, A12; "Poll: Voters Knew Early, Knew Enough; Fall Blitz Didn't Raise Awareness of Key Stands," *Washington Post,* 15 November 1996, A1. Throughout this section, I refer to the percentage of voters who "knew" a fact, but it should be kept in mind that some respondents may have guessed correctly even when they did not know the answer.

13. Everett Carll Ladd, "The Election Polls: An American Waterloo," *Chronicle of Higher Education,* 22 November 1996, A52. For a response, see David W. Moore, "Perils of Polling '96: Myth and Fallacy," *Polling Report* 12, no. 23 (9 December 1996): 1.

14. Indeed, if the poll by the John Zogby Group International is excluded, a regression line with an r^2 of .93 can be plotted through the points on the graph, indicating that 93 percent of the variation among the polls can be explained by when they were conducted. Even with the Zogby poll, the r^2 is .62. The Zogby poll was conducted for Reuters, and employed some nonstandard methodological features including the use of listed telephone numbers rather than random digit dialing. Although its forecast of the final margin in the presidential race was quite accurate, over the final weeks of the campaign it had consistently shown a much closer race than did the other polls. For a description and defense of the poll's methods, see John Zogby, "The Perils of Polling: A Look at Why Our Polls Are Different," *Polling Report* 12, no. 22 (18 November 1996): 1.

15. John Judis, "Golden Mean," *New Republic,* 25 November 1996, 17–20.

4

Financing the 1996 Elections

ANTHONY CORRADO

Now 'tis the Spring and weeds are shallow-rooted;
Suffer them now, and they'll o'ergrow the garden.
— *Henry VI, Part II* (III, i)

No race was as hotly contested in 1996 as the one for campaign dollars. Republicans and Democrats alike engaged in an unprecedented fund-raising spree, as the national party organizations, presidential candidates, and congressional contenders all solicited record amounts of money. Accordingly, an unparalleled sum was spent in conjunction with federal races. The presidential and congressional candidates, national convention committees, and national party organizations alone spent more than $2.0 billion, or approximately $650 million more than they spent in 1992.[1] In addition, tens of millions of dollars were spent in conjunction with federal races by state and local party organizations and by individuals and groups spending money independently.

Not only did the candidates and party organizations spend more money, but they also found new ways to spend it. Indeed, the most important development in the financing of the 1996 elections may prove to be the creative ways in which the available resources were used. The national party organizations and organized interest groups discovered ingenious methods of taking advantage of the opportunities created by recent court rulings and loopholes in the law to raise and spend money outside the scope of federal regulation. For example, both parties and a number of interest groups mounted national "issue advocacy" advertising campaigns designed to benefit federal candidates without violating the limits on party spending or campaign-related activity established by the Federal Election Campaign Act (FECA). For the first time, the parties also spent funds independently on behalf of their candidates. This practice, which began during the general election period, was spurred by a Supreme Court ruling issued in June[2] that left the door open to such spending.

To finance these activities, the parties had to raise larger sums than ever before. Consequently, "soft money," money raised by political parties that is exempt from federal contribution and spending limits, became a more essential part of party financing. Both parties raised record amounts of soft money, most of it in the form of contributions of $100,000 or more from wealthy individuals and corporations. The sources of these monies, as well as the increasing size of the gifts, raised new questions about the role of soft money in the political system. The Democratic Party's soft money fundraising practices, in particular, were so controversial that they became the dominant issue in the final weeks of the presidential campaign.

Thus the 1996 election cycle was characterized by an increase in political spending and a dramatic growth in the realm of financial activity that takes place beyond the purview of federal law. These activities present new problems for the regulation of political finance and raise serious questions about the ability of the current regulatory regime to exert any meaningful control over the flow of money in federal elections.

Presidential Prenomination Campaigns

The race for the Oval Office was conducted under financing laws that have changed little since they were first implemented in 1976. Candidates were allowed to accept contributions of no more than $1,000 from an individual contributor, no more than $5,000 from any political action committee (PAC), and no more than $1,000 from any other political committee. Candidates could themselves contribute unlimited amounts to their own campaigns, unless they accepted public funding. Candidates who accepted public funds were permitted to contribute a maximum of $50,000 in personal or family funds. No candidate could accept a contribution from corporations or labor union treasury funds or cash contributions in excess of $100.

Candidates therefore had to rely on limited contributions to finance their campaigns. Nevertheless, they could increase their resources and reduce their fund-raising burdens by qualifying for a voluntary program of public matching funds. To be eligible, a candidate had to raise at least $5,000 in contributions of $250 or less in at least twenty states, for a total of $100,000. Once eligible, public funds are granted on a dollar-for-dollar basis on the first $250 received from an individual, provided the contribution is received after 1 January of the year before the election.

The law also provided that those who accept public matching funds must agree to abide by spending limits. The 1974 Federal Election Campaign Act set an aggregate limit at $10 million with adjustments for inflation, plus an additional 20 percent for fund-raising expenses and unlimited legal and accounting expenses. In 1996 this ceiling had increased to $30.9 million, plus $6.2 million for fund-raising costs, for a total limit of $37.1 million. The law also set state-by-state spending limits. In 1996 these limits ranged from $618,200 in small states such as New Hampshire and Delaware to $11.3 million in California.[3]

Overall, the seventeen major candidates who ran for the presidency raised a total of approximately $244 million, almost twice the $126 million raised by the major candidates in 1992. The 1992 race was atypical, however, because the Democrats seeking to challenge then-President George Bush got off to a late start and an "open" race existed in only one party because President Bush was seeking reelection.[4] In 1988 there was an open race in both parties for the first time under the FECA and the sixteen major candidates who sought their party's nomination raised a total of $213 million.[5]

So 1996 candidate fund raising constituted an increase over that of previous elections, but not a dramatically significant increase compared to recent elections. Perhaps the best way to gauge the increase is by comparing the financial efforts of the 1996 Republican challengers with those of 1988, the last Republican field to run in an open contest for the party nomination. The six challengers in 1988 raised an aggregate $116 million in adjusted campaign receipts.[6] The eleven challengers in 1996 raised $187 million (see table 4.1). When adjusted for inflation, the 1996 figure represents a real increase of approximately $33 million, or about 27 percent. But this figure does not take into account the larger number of candidates in 1996. Nor does it account for the unique financial capacity of one 1996 challenger, Malcolm "Steve" Forbes Jr.

In fact, all of the increase in presidential fund raising in 1996 can be attributed to the deep pockets of multimillionaire publisher Steve Forbes, who followed Ross Perot's 1992 example and used his personal resources to finance a bid for the nation's highest office. But, unlike Perot, Forbes ran under the banner of one of the two major parties. Forbes loaned his campaign an extraordinary sum, $37.5 million. Only two other candidates, Senate Majority Leader Robert Dole, the Republican front-runner throughout

TABLE 4.1. FINANCIAL ACTIVITY OF 1996 PRESIDENTIAL PRENOMINATION CAMPAIGNS

Candidate	Adjusted receipts	Individual contributions	Federal matching funds	Political committee contributions	Other receipts[a]	Total disbursements
Democrats						
Clinton	$ 42,489,548	$ 28,285,108	$ 13,412,197	$ 42,441	$ 749,802	$ 38,105,490
LaRouche	3,684,253	3,058,562	624,691	1,000	0	3,706,949
Republicans						
Alexander	17,614,978	12,635,615	4,573,442	286,766	109,572	16,353,539
Buchanan	24,501,176	14,659,228	9,812,517	18,280	11,151	24,489,005
Dole	44,604,092	29,555,502	13,545,770	1,209,655	293,165	42,173,706
Dornan	346,885	297,511	0	1,000	4,374	341,718
Forbes	41,693,481	4,203,792	0	2,000	30,689	41,657,444
Gramm	28,791,502	15,880,676	7,356,218	402,866	5,151,742	28,038,313
Keyes	4,348,165	3,442,056	892,436	4,001	2,172	4,252,471

Lugar	7,769,383	2,643,477	135,265	187,029	7,631,213
Specter	3,490,295	1,010,455	158,791	36,148	3,391,843
Taylor	6,516,850	37,854	0	3,900	6,504,966
Wilson	7,363,215	1,724,254	242,349	110,723	7,219,912
Other parties					
Browne	1,147,997	1,112,482	1,244	0	1,073,600
Hagelin	1,124,318	700,085	100	0	1,117,266
Perot	8,298,527	82,781	0	0	8,031,229
Lamm	170,281	140,281	0	0	39,364
Democrat subtotal	46,173,801	14,036,888	43,441	749,802	41,812,439
Republican subtotal	187,040,022	41,558,569	2,460,973	5,940,665	182,054,130
Other subtotal	10,741,123	358,883	1,344	0	10,261,459
Grand total	$243,954,946	$55,954,340	$2,505,758	$6,690,467	$234,128,028

SOURCE: Federal Election Commission, as of 31 August 1996.
a. Loans not included.

the primaries and eventual nominee, and President Bill Clinton, managed to raise as much as Forbes spent out of his own pocket.

Forbes was not the only challenger to rely on personal resources. Fellow Republican Maurice Taylor, a leading manufacturer of tires and rims, invested almost $6.5 million of his $30 million fortune in his unsuccessful bid for the nomination.[7] In addition, Ross Perot contributed $8.2 million to fund Reform Party efforts to qualify for state ballots and to win the nomination at the party's first presidential convention.

The rise of entrepreneurial candidates and the role of personal money in the prenomination campaigns was the most significant change in presidential fund raising in 1996. Overall, these candidates spent a total of $52.3 million out of their own pockets, which equaled more than 20 percent of the aggregate amount received in the 1996 election cycle. This change suggests that presidential prenomination campaigns are now falling into line with the changes taking place in other campaigns at the federal level: personal wealth is becoming a factor in determining an individual's ability to run.[8]

This emergence of entrepreneurial candidates highlights the growing importance of money in election campaigns. In most instances, and certainly in the 1996 presidential race, these candidates have no previous political experience and are not considered to be potential contenders before their decisions to run. They gain their status as credible and potentially viable candidates solely on the basis of the resources they are able and willing to spend. It helps them gain the media coverage and name recognition that are essential elements to being competitive in the "invisible primary" that takes place before the first votes are counted.[9] While this strategy does not always work (witness Taylor), the exorbitant amounts Forbes spent helped catapult him into the thick of the Republican race.

Other than the notable influx of personal resources, fund raising in 1996 followed the patterns established in previous elections. On average, most of the money received by presidential candidates comes from individual donations and the accompanying matching funds. Individual gifts usually account for over 60 percent of all receipts, and matching funds constitute about a third. Political action committees (PACs) usually provide less than 2 percent of the total funding.[10]

As shown in table 4.1, the 1996 financing reflected these patterns. Candidates raised about $126 million of their $244 million total, or about 52 percent, from individual donors. The next largest source of funding was public matching funds, which provided almost $56 million in revenue, or about 23 percent. These percentages are lower than in previous cycles because of the preponderance of personal funding. If the figures are adjusted to exclude the monies donated by Perot and the monies loaned to their campaigns by Forbes and Taylor, then the figures rise to 65 percent for individual gifts and 29 percent for public matching funds.

EARLY MONEY

One of the principal effects of the FECA regulations is to compel candidates to begin raising money as early as possible in the election cycle. Because the spending limits are indexed for inflation, candidates have been allowed to expend more money in each successive election. The contribution limits, however, are not indexed. Consequently, with each new election cycle, candidates must spend more time building the broad base of financial support needed to solicit the tens of thousands of contributions required in a viable national campaign. Because of this imbalance in the regulation of spending and contributions, candidates begin raising money earlier and earlier in each new election cycle.

This need to raise money early has been exacerbated by the changes that have taken place in the delegate selection process (see chapter 1). The "front-loading" of the primary calendar has dramatically increased the resource demands on presidential candidates. Challengers find it much more difficult to exercise the strategic option of focusing on a few early states and trying to build a national campaign on the basis of a strong early showing. Instead, candidates must develop organizations and begin campaigning in a growing number of states well before the first votes are cast in Iowa.

These financial pressures were especially intense in the 1996 election cycle. Candidates would have to raise more money than ever before if they were going to mount viable campaigns in the sixteen states, from Arizona to New York, that would hold elections during the sixteen-day period after the New Hampshire primary (see table 1.7, pp. 49–51).

Moreover, the extremely tight timing between election days—Delaware four days after New Hampshire, Arizona and the Dakotas three days later, South Carolina four days after that, and nine states three days later—meant that candidates would have little opportunity to capitalize financially on a strong early showing, as was the case in the past with such candidates as Jimmy Carter in 1976, Ronald Reagan in 1980, and Gary Hart in 1984.[11] Simply put, there would be little time between primaries to raise a substantial amount of money, deposit it in the bank, and have it available for use during the hyper-accelerated process. As a result, most of the Republican challengers felt that they had to raise the money needed for a first strike in Iowa and New Hampshire, as well as the funds for a second-strike capability in subsequent states, before the start of the election year. The conventional wisdom among the likely front-runners was that a campaign would have to raise at least $20 million by the end of 1995 in order to meet the demands of the process.[12] The candidates thus began seeking money very early. Senator Phil Gramm began operations in November 1994, only days after the midterm election. By mid-April 1995, most of the Republican challengers (with the notable exception of Forbes) had officially announced their candidacies.[13]

By the end of 1995, Clinton and his Republican challengers had raised a total of $128.9 million, a record amount for a preelection year. This sum was more than six times the $20.9 million raised by presidential candidates in 1991, and $25 million more than the $103.5 million raised in 1987, when there was an open race in both parties. Indeed, in 1995, the Republicans alone raised $103.3 million, compared to $66.4 million for the 1987 Republican challengers and $37.1 million for the 1988 Democrats.[14]

The level of early fund raising is even more impressive when the matching funds accrued during the preelection year are considered. In total, Clinton and the seven Republicans who accepted public money earned $37 million in initial matching funds, or over $9 million more than the twelve qualifiers in 1987, a new high for initial payments.[15] When these funds are added to the candidates' other receipts, the total amount raised from private and public sources in 1995 increases to $156 million, two-thirds of the $229.5 million that Clinton and his Republican opponents received during the course of the entire 1995–96 cycle.

Still reeling from their party's defeat in the 1994 midterm elections and worried about the president's weakened popularity, the Clinton campaign made early fund raising a priority to demonstrate the president's political strength among the party faithful and to discourage any potential challengers. Clinton led all candidates in early money, generating a total of $34.6 million in combined donations and matching funds (see table 4.2). He had essentially raised the total amount he would be allowed to spend under the expenditure ceiling before the primary voting started. Dole, the Republican front-runner from the start, led all Republicans in preelection-year fund raising with $33.8 million in revenue. His closest competitors were Gramm ($27.4 million) and Forbes ($18 million).

While the Republicans raised much money, they also spent significant amounts. By the end of 1995, they had spent a total of $95.3 million, more than nine times the $10.3 million spent in 1991 and 62 percent more than the $58.7 million spent by Republicans in 1987. Moreover, only about $12 million of this total, roughly 13 percent, was spent on fund raising. Most of the money was spent on organizational efforts, travel, and early advertising.

TABLE 4.2
PRESIDENTIAL PREELECTION YEAR RECEIPTS
(IN MILLIONS)

Candidate	1995 receipts	Initial matching entitlement	Total
Clinton	$25.64 [a]	$9.01	$34.65
Dole	$24.52 [b]	9.26	$33.78
Gramm	$20.76 [c]	6.65	$27.41
Forbes	$17.97	0	$17.97
Alexander	$11.52	3.23	$14.75
Buchanan	$7.22	3.98	$11.20
Lugar	$5.90	2.28	$8.18
Wilson	$5.81	1.59	$7.40
Taylor	$4.53	0	$4.53
Specter	$3.02	.99	$4.01
Keyes	$1.70	0	$1.70
Dornan	$.28	0	$.28

SOURCE: Federal Election Commission, as of 31 August 1996.
a. Includes $250,000 transferred from Clinton's prior campaign committee.
b. Includes $242,000 transferred from Dole's senatorial campaign committee.
c. Includes $4.78 million transferred from Gramm's senatorial campaign committee.

A number of Republican candidates began extensive campaigning early in the preelection year in an effort to attract media attention, generate additional funds, and thus emerge from the pack to establish themselves as a leading alternative to Dole. As a result, 1996 witnessed the earliest television campaign in presidential primary history. Alexander and Taylor began airing ads in Iowa in the summer of 1995.[16] Alexander ran an infomercial in New Hampshire in March 1995 and began airing campaign ads in June. California Governor Pete Wilson began advertising in New Hampshire in August, and Gramm in October.[17] In addition, Gramm spent millions of dollars on preelection-year straw polls, hoping that these "victories" would launch his campaign, and he had campaign operations set up in twenty states by mid-December.[18]

So even if Forbes had not entered the race, early spending would have been greater than in previous elections. But Forbes's extraordinary willingness to spend after he entered the race in late September drove costs to unanticipated levels. Because Forbes was largely relying on his own resources, he did not have to spend millions of dollars on fund raising or need to worry about any spending limits. He thus had an open invitation to outspend his opponents, and he took advantage of it. During the last three months of 1995, Forbes spent more than $14 million, compared to $8.4 million spent by Dole and lesser amounts by Gramm, Alexander, and Buchanan. Of this $14 million total, an estimated $9.7 million went toward television and radio ads. Including advertising in September, Forbes spent an unprecedented sum—$12.5 million—on advertising in the preelection year.[19] Most of this spending was concentrated on the crucial early states. In Des Moines, Iowa, for example, Forbes had spent more on television ads by mid-December than the thirteen candidates in 1988 spent during the entire caucus campaign.[20] In contrast, Dole and Alexander each spent less than $2 million on ads in the entire preelection year.[21]

Forbes's financial assault, and his subsequent rise in the Iowa and New Hampshire polls, forced his competitors to alter their own financial strategies, especially as Forbes kept up his advertising blitz with $7 million in additional spending in January. In an effort to keep pace with the higher stakes at play, Gramm and Alexander increased their outlays and in December began to borrow money against the matching funds they expected to receive in January. This left them in the position of hoping for a strong early showing that would stimulate a fund-raising surge, since neither had a substantial surplus by the beginning of February, two weeks before the Iowa caucus. Thus, when Gramm was upset by Buchanan in the Louisiana caucuses on 6 February and then finished back in the pack in Iowa, he lacked the resources to continue and had to drop out of the race.

Alexander did better than expected in Iowa and New Hampshire, but the $1,000 contribution limit and tight schedule of events left him little time to refill his depleted campaign coffers. Even though he was receiving $100,000 a day within days of the caucuses, this money came too late to purchase additional advertising in New Hampshire.[22] After New Hampshire, the campaign estimated that it would need a minimum of $2.6 million to sustain itself through 12 March, when Alexander's home state of Tennessee and several other southern states would cast their votes.[23] But at the rate of $100,000 a day, even such a bare-bones campaign goal could never be achieved. Out of cash and out of time, Alexander took a stand in South Carolina in hopes of breathing life into his failing campaign. When he lost the state to Dole, his campaign was over.

Dole was the only candidate with the resources needed to withstand Forbes's financial assault and finance the multiple-state campaigning required by the modern nominating process. Dole entered the election year with over $4 million in the bank and $9 million in accrued matching funds. In January his campaign spent about $7 million, or around the same amount as did Forbes. By the end of January, Dole still had $8.5 million in ready cash.[24] Dole used these resources to win crucial primary victories in the first week of March. Forbes's media blitz could not overcome Dole's organizational advantage throughout the nation, and Forbes failed to win the crucial contests in Iowa, New Hampshire, South Carolina, and Georgia. Consequently, Dole had the nomination essentially won by the middle of March.

While Dole successfully fought off his challengers, the victory left him in a strategically vulnerable position. Because he had to spend so much money so quickly, by the end of March he had essentially reached the aggregate spending limit. No previous candidate had ever bumped up against the limit so early in the election year. By the end of April, the Dole campaign itself estimated that it could spend no more than $1.2 million before the Republican National Convention in August.[25] Dole had access to the money needed to continue to wage a national campaign, but the law did not allow him to spend it, even though almost a third of the delegates were yet to be selected, including those in such crucial general election states as Pennsylvania, North Carolina, Missouri, and New Jersey. As a result, the Republican nominee had to strip down his campaign; he was forced to stop advertising, cut his staff, and sell campaign assets in an effort to stay under the cap.[26] Frustrated over his inability to advertise his message, Dole declared, "I'm the only person in America who's denied my First Amendment rights."[27]

CLINTON AND THE ADVENT OF ISSUE ADVOCACY ADS

Dole's strategic quandary was compounded by the strength of Clinton's financial position. Unchallenged for his party's nomination, Clinton was able to conserve his resources, while his opponents engaged in their ferocious spending war. Consequently, in April, Clinton had $20 million left to spend, more than fourteen times the amount left for Dole.[28]

In 1995 Clinton had spent $12.3 million, one-third of which went toward fund-raising expenses. His campaign's only other major expense was an ad campaign conducted in the early summer of 1995. This ad campaign cost $2.4 million and consisted of a series of ads in over twenty major television markets in key electoral states that supported the president's position on the assault weapons ban.[29] The president's team wanted to maintain this unusual early advertising blitz by spending millions of dollars on television in the late winter and early in 1996 to bolster Clinton's popularity heading into the election year. But they faced the issue of spending limits. The president's team thus came up with an innovative strategy to achieve their objectives without using the campaign's precious, and limited, spending capabilities: they would use the resources of the Democratic National Committee and other party organizations.

Under the provisions of the FECA, any money spent by a candidate's party "for the purpose of influencing" the candidate's campaign, or made on behalf of a candidate to benefit his or her campaign, is considered "a qualified campaign expense" and is therefore subject to the contribution and spending limits.[30] But in the 1976 case of *Buckley* v. *Valeo*, the Supreme Court ruled that these limits can be applied only to expenditures that "in express terms advocate the election or defeat of a clearly identified candidate for federal office."[31] That means, the Court explained in a footnote, that the limitations therefore apply only to communications that contain express words of advocacy, such as "vote for or against," "elect," "Smith for Congress," or "defeat."[32] In other words, if an advertisement does not contain these words, if it does not expressly advocate the election or defeat of a particular candidate, then it can not be considered a campaign ad. Instead, because they are generally designed to advocate certain issue positions, such communications have come to be known as "issue advocacy" ads; they are designed to educate the public about certain issues or about a candidate's specific positions on a particular issue. They usually name or depict a particular candidate and either support or criticize that candidate's positions on specific issues such as Medicare funding, education, budget policy, or crime.

While the national party organizations had engaged in issue advocacy advertising before the 1996 election cycle (most notably during the debate over Clinton's health-care proposal in 1993 and 1994), they had never before used such advertising in a significant way to promote a presidential candidate in an election year. But the Democrats quickly recognized the potential benefits of this tactic. The ads could be used to deliver the president's basic message, policy proposals, and accomplishments and criticize Dole's views and record. As long as they avoided the "magic words" that would trigger the definition of express advocacy, none of the monies spent in this way would be considered "campaign spending" under the law. Finally, because such spending is not technically campaign spending, it could be paid for with party funds, including soft money funds that are exempt from federal contribution limits. It was a loophole in the federal regulatory scheme that the Democrats aggressively exploited.

From July 1995 to June 1996, the Democratic National Committee (DNC) and state Democratic Party organizations spent millions of dollars on ads designed to promote Clinton's reelection. These spots were mostly aired in smaller media markets where broadcast time is less expensive. The party avoided states where Clinton had won by large margins in 1992 and stayed away from states where they felt Clinton had no chance—Texas, the Great Plains states, and such southern Republican strongholds as South Carolina and Virginia.[33] In the fall of 1995 the Democrats ran ads attacking the Republican budget that covered 30 percent of the media markets in the country. By the end of December, they had run ads presenting Clinton as a leader seeking tax cuts, welfare reform, a balanced budget, and protection for Medicare and education programs. In all, the Democrats had aired pro-Clinton ads in 42 percent of the nation's media markets by 1 January 1996, at a cost of $18 million, none of which was drawn from Clinton's campaign committee accounts.[34]

According to estimates by Common Cause, the Democrats spent $34 million on pro-Clinton ads during this period. This included $12 million in federally regulated "hard money" and $22 million in soft money.[35] The DNC managed to spend such a large proportion of soft money by transferring funds to state party committees and having these committees purchase the ad time. In other words, they were able to pay for the ads mostly with soft money because the FEC has different payment regulations for national and state party organizations.[36] This perfectly legal subterfuge allowed the party to conserve its hard money, which is more difficult to raise than soft money and is the only money that can be used for direct expenditures on behalf of presidential and congressional candidates.

The Democrats focused their ad campaign on twelve key general election battleground states (see table 4.3). The party spent over $1 million in each of these states, including over $4 million in California. Combined, these twelve states represented a total of 221 electoral college votes. Clinton eventually won all of them except Colorado.

The DNC's spending and Clinton's financial advantage entering the final months of the campaign encouraged the Republican National Committee (RNC) to adopt a similar strategy as soon as its presidential nominee was determined. In May, one day after Dole decided to resign from the Senate to devote himself to full-time campaigning, RNC chairman Haley Barbour announced a $20 million issue advocacy advertising campaign that would be conducted during the period leading up to the Republican national convention in August.[37] The purpose of this campaign, said the chairman, would be "to show the differences between Dole and Clinton and between Republicans and Democrats on the issues facing our country, so we can engage full-time in one of the most consequential elections in our history."[38] In essence, the campaign was designed to fill the gap for the by-now financially tapped-out Dole committee and provide the additional resources

TABLE 4.3

PARTY ISSUE ADVOCACY SPENDING,

PRENOMINATION PERIOD 1996

Democrats		Republicans	
California	$4,156,092	California	$4,018,821
Pennsylvania	$3,809,470	Pennsylvania	$1,735,443
Florida	$3,578,159	Illinois	$1,553,663
Ohio	$2,984,535	Ohio	$1,295,910
Michigan	$2,647,529	Tennessee	$946,688
Washington	$1,910,807	Georgia	$839,699
Illinois	$1,857,482	Washington	$684,000
Wisconsin	$1,470,784	Missouri	$661,980
Minnesota	$1,401,058	Colorado	$496,485
Colorado	$1,258,217	Iowa	$420,720
Oregon	$1,115,941	Michigan	$346,260
Missouri	$1,113,584	New Mexico	$332,393

SOURCE: Common Cause, Letter to the Honorable Janet Reno, 9 October 1996.

needed to match Clinton's anticipated spending in the remaining months before the nominating conventions.

By the end of June, the RNC had already spent at least $14 million on ads promoting Dole's candidacy, including an estimated $9 million in soft money.[39] Like the Democrats, the Republicans focused their spending on key electoral college battlegrounds (see table 4.3). Indeed, the "target" list looked very similar to that of the Democrats; eight of the top twelve states were the same for both parties.

This innovative form of party spending essentially rendered the contribution and spending limits of the FECA meaningless, at least as far as the party nominees were concerned. As long as the party committees did not coordinate their efforts with the candidate or his staff, and did not use any of the "magic words" that would cause their spending to qualify as candidate support, they were free to spend as much as they wanted from monies received from unlimited sources on activities essentially geared toward influencing the outcome of the presidential race. Given the availability of polling data and other sources of political information, it was simple for the parties to develop ads that reflected their respective candidates' major themes and positions or presented the most effective attacks against the opponent.

This emphasis on issue advocacy advertising was spurred by a Supreme

Court ruling issued in June 1996 in the case of *Colorado Republican Federal Campaign Committee* v. *Federal Election Commission.*[40] The case involved a ten-year-old complaint arising from the 1986 Colorado senatorial campaign in which Representative Tim Wirth had declared his candidacy in January for the Democratic nomination. Before a Republican nominee had been chosen, the Colorado Republican Party ran radio ads and paid for two voter pamphlets criticizing Wirth's record. The FEC had ruled that these expenditures, which amounted to $15,000, should be counted against the combined party spending limit that is applied to all senatorial campaigns.[41] The Colorado Republican Party argued that the expenditures should not count against the limit, and it sought affirmation from the Court that party organizations enjoyed the same free speech liberties as PACs and other political groups and thus could engage in independent expenditures. The Republicans further challenged the notion of party spending limits, seeking a ruling that would strike down the limits as unconstitutional.

The Supreme Court produced four fragmented opinions, none of which garnered the support of more than three justices. Three justices (Breyer, O'Connor, and Souter) issued a plurality opinion stating that the FECA limits could not be applied to the Colorado ad, ruling that the spending was independent and constitutionally protected as such. Four justices (Kennedy, Thomas, Rehnquist, and Scalia) in two separate opinions were willing to strike down the FECA's restrictions on party spending coordinated with the candidates. Two justices (Stevens and Ginsburg) voted to validate the FECA's limit and enforce the FEC's suit against the Colorado party. The Court thus affirmed the right of political parties to spend money independently of a party candidate's campaign, arguing that regulations prohibiting such expenditures violate the First Amendment. It further ruled that these expenditures are not subject to FECA limits on party spending as long as they are not coordinated with a candidate or candidate's campaign. The Court, however, left open the question raised by issue advocacy ads, that is, whether the FECA's limits could be applied to speech that falls short of express advocacy but contains an "electioneering message." By virtue of the fact that four justices seemed willing to overturn party spending limits, the decision also left open the question of whether these limits could withstand constitutional scrutiny under a different set of circumstances.

The Court's decision essentially freed the parties to spend unlimited amounts of money in the general election. In addition to the limited coordinated expenditures allowed under FECA rules, the parties would now be allowed to spend money in the new and uncharted territory of independent spending.[42] They could also continue to fund issue advocacy activities. As a result, party money would play a greater role in 1996 than in any of the previous elections conducted under the FECA.

The General Election Campaign

PUBLIC FUNDING

The FECA provides a voluntary program of full public financing for presidential general election candidates. The purpose of this program is to eliminate the need to raise funds and allow the candidates to devote their time to communicating their views to the electorate. Candidates who accept this funding are required to limit their spending to the total amount of the subsidy. In 1996 the amount of the subsidy given to each of the major party nominees was $61.8 million. In addition, each of the major parties was allowed to make $12.3 million in coordinated expenditures on behalf of its nominee.

Since the first publicly financed election in 1976, no candidate other than the major-party nominees had qualified for a preelection subsidy. One non-major-party candidate, Independent John Anderson in 1980, received $4.2 million in postelection public funding by winning more than 5 percent of the vote.[43] In 1996, a non-major-party candidate received preelection funding for the first time, when Ross Perot decided to accept public money.

Although Perot ran as an independent in 1992, he ran in 1996 as the nominee of his newly established Reform Party. The FEC ruled that, despite this change, he was eligible for slightly more than $29 million in public money, or 47 percent of the total subsidy, based on his 19 percent share of the vote in the previous election.[44] Rather than fund his campaign wholly from his own resources, as he had in 1992, Perot decided to accept the public money and thereby limit his own contribution to $50,000 and his aggregate spending to $61.8 million. This choice was considered to be an important step toward institutionalizing the new party and reducing its dependence on Perot.[45] If Perot once again exceeded 5 percent of the vote, as was expected by most party supporters, the Reform Party would again qualify for public funding in 2000. The decision meant, however, that Perot would have less than half the resources available to his opponents. If he wanted to spend to the limit, he would have to raise the other $32 million in private contributions of $1,000 or less. While Perot did seek contributions early in the election period, his campaign managed to raise only $625,000 by mid-October.[46]

Perot also had trouble purchasing broadcast time early in the race. He hoped to follow the media strategy he had employed in 1992, relying on half-hour infomercials to spread his message. He aired his first such ad on 10 September and used it to introduce his vice-presidential nominee, Pat Choate. But the paid announcement drew low ratings, much like the Perot candidacy, which was mired in single digits in the polls.[47] No longer a phenomenon with strong audience potential, Perot drew little interest from network executives and found it increasingly difficult to find half-hour slots to purchase. As a result, Perot was forced to change to a media strategy based on more traditional 15–30 second advertisements. But he did not air most of these ads until the final stretch of the campaign; in fact, he had 75 percent of his $29 million still available to spend in the final stretch of the campaign.[48] Most of his spending therefore came in a final flurry at the end, but by this point Perot was far from being a decisive factor in the race.

While Perot was struggling financially, the major-party candidates were the beneficiaries of virtually unlimited campaign support. Neither Clinton or Dole relied solely on public money in waging their general election campaigns. The national party committees continued to spend tens of millions of dollars on issue ads and other activities designed to benefit their presidential nominees. This heightened level of party activity required an unprecedented level of funding. Accordingly, both parties raised record amounts of money, especially soft money, during the 1996 cycle.

SOFT MONEY IN 1996

Overall, Democratic and Republican national party committees raised over $880 million during the 1996 election cycle. By mid-November, the Republican committees (Republican National Committee, National Republican Senatorial Committee, and National Republican Congressional Committee) reported $407.5 million in federal or hard money receipts, and $400 million in expenditures. The Democratic committees (Democratic National Committee, Democratic Senatorial Campaign Committee, and Democratic Congressional Campaign Committee) reported $210 million in receipts and $198.6 million in expenditures.[49] These totals represented an increase in revenues of 53 percent for the Republicans and 35 percent for the Democrats, when compared to the similar period in the 1991–92 election cycle. The Republican expenditures were 58 percent higher than those reported by mid-November of 1992, while the Democrats registered a 35 percent increase.

Even more significant was the growth in nonfederal or soft money financing (summarized in table 4.4). As of three weeks after the election, the Republicans had raised $141 million in soft money and spent $149 million, increases of 183 percent and 224 percent respectively, when compared to a similar period in 1992. The Democrats registered even larger increases.

In all, the Democrats reported $122.3 million in soft money receipts and $117.3 million in disbursements, which represented increases of 237 percent in receipts and 257 percent in spending as compared to 1992. An illness that had plagued previous elections had developed into an epidemic.

Soft money was more important in 1996 because large amounts of this funding were needed to pay for the extensive ad campaigns in which the parties were engaged, as well as fund-raising costs and the voter mobilization drives that have become a staple of soft money financing in recent elections.[50] In general, the national party committees spent soft money on four broad kinds of political activity: (1) direct financial transfers to state and local parties; (2) joint federal and nonfederal activities, which include such items as administrative costs shared with state parties, costs of fund-raising efforts that generate hard and soft money, and voter registration and mobilization drives that benefit federal and nonfederal candidates; (3) direct contributions to state and local candidates; and (4) miscellaneous expenditures, including such items as building funds and other non-campaign-related activity.

The DNC and RNC each spent the largest share of their soft money funds on transfers to state and local party committees. The DNC trans-

TABLE 4.4

SUMMARY OF SOFT MONEY RECEIPTS AND
EXPENDITURES, 1995–96
(IN MILLIONS)[a]

	Receipts	Expenditures
Democrats		
Democratic National Committee	$99.4	$95.4
Democratic Senatorial Campaign Committee	$14.1	$13.9
Democratic Congressional Campaign Committee	$10.9	$10.3
Total Democratic[b]	$122.3	$117.5
Republicans		
Republican National Committee	$110.3	$110.7
National Republican Senatorial Committee	$26.7	$25.6
National Congressional Campaign Committee	$18.3	$27.4
Total Republican[c]	$141.2	$149.6

SOURCE: Federal Election Commission, as of 25 November reports.
  a. These figures include receipts and expenditures as of 25 November 1996.
  b. Total does not include $2.1 million that was transferred among national committees.
  c. Total does not include $14.1 million that was transferred among national committees.

ferred approximately $53.9 million, or 56 percent of its total soft money funds, to state and local party committees. In 1992 the Democrats transferred only $9.5 million, 31 percent of their total, to state and local committees. The RNC transferred $47.8 million, or 43 percent of its total, to state party organizations, compared to $5.3 million (15 percent) in 1992. The Democrats thus sent over five times more money to party affiliates in 1996 than in the previous cycle, while the Republicans sent nine times more. This sizable increase reflects the emphasis the DNC and RNC placed on issue advertising, which they maintained throughout the general election.

The parties generated these enormous sums by soliciting the kinds of large contributions from individuals, corporations, labor unions, and other organized interests that are supposed to be illegal in federal elections. In most cases, especially during the six-month period before the election, the money was raised by the same individuals who solicited funds for either the Clinton or Dole campaigns during the prenomination period. The largest gifts came from corporations or groups that faced pressing issues in Washington. For example, according to a study by the Center for Responsive Politics, Philip Morris, the embattled tobacco company that faced more stringent federal regulations on the sale of its products, donated $2 million in soft money, including more than $1.6 million to the Republicans and $400,000 to the Democrats. AT&T, a company with a great interest in telecommunications regulation, gave more than $830,000, including $450,000 to the Republicans and $381,000 to the Democrats; its competitor, MCI Telecommunications, sent at least $486,000 to the Democrats and $281,000 to the Republicans. The Association of Trial Lawyers gave $361,000 to Clinton's party and $157,000 to the Republicans. The Atlantic Richfield Oil Company contributed $695,000 to Republicans and $388,000 to Democrats.[51]

The scope of soft money fund raising, and the sources and size of the contributions it produced, reinvigorated the public controversy over the role of soft money in the election process. Once again, critics decried the use of these unlimited funds, arguing that they completely subverted the intent of the FECA, thereby rendering the regulations ineffective. They further claimed that these contributions gave undue influence to special interests, thereby corrupting the political system.[52]

None of these corporate contributions or gifts from large "fat cat" donors proved to be as controversial as a gift to the DNC made by an Indonesian landscaper and his wife. Arief and Soraya Wiriandinata, relatives of a wealthy former executive of the Lippo Group, a multibillion-dollar Singapore conglomerate, gave $452,000 to the DNC. The Wiriandinatas were legal residents in the United States, who reportedly made their gift in appreciation for a get-well card sent by President Clinton to Soraya's father, Hashim Ning, a cofounder and major shareholder of the Lippo Group, who had fallen ill on a trip to Washington.[53] This contribution raised questions about the role of foreign money in party fund raising. Although foreign nationals legally residing in the United States are allowed to make contributions under federal law, the size and source of this gift raised the question of whether it represented money that originated from a foreign source, which would be illegal. In particular, the gift raised the question of whether Mochtar Riady, the powerful head of the Lippo Group, was illegally funneling money to Clinton's campaign. The relationship between Clinton and Riady raised the question of whether these contributions might be influencing administration decision making.

The potential significance of the questions raised by the Indonesian contributions led to a feeding frenzy of media investigations and public scrutiny into the Democrats' soft money fund raising. These investigations revealed that the link between the Riady family and Wiriandinata was John Huang, a DNC fund raiser, who had worked for Lippo before joining the DNC fund-raising staff in 1992 and who had been appointed to serve in the Department of Commerce after Ron Brown, the former DNC chair, was appointed secretary of commerce.

Subsequent investigations of Huang's fund-raising activities revealed a number of suspect contributions, including a $250,000 contribution from a Korean company that was deemed illegal and had to be returned by the DNC. Huang was also linked to a $140,000 fund raiser held at a Buddhist temple in California in conjunction with an appearance by Vice-President Al Gore. The event raised additional questions about the legality of DNC efforts, since the monks and nuns listed as donors at the event had taken vows of poverty, and at least one nun reported receiving cash and being asked to donate it at the event.[54] The Democrats responded to the controversy by suspending Huang's fund-raising activities and asking the Federal Election Commission to investigate the propriety of any contributions solicited by Huang.[55]

The DNC's actions failed to stem the controversy. Dole seized on the issue, arguing that Huang was an agent of foreign influence, and made it the centerpiece of his attack on Clinton in the weeks leading up to the election.[56] Perot, too, found new life in the foreign money issue and relentlessly attacked the president over the course of the last ten days of his campaign, even going so far as to charge that Clinton would ultimately be responsible for a second Watergate crisis. These charges, however, were not enough to halt Clinton's march toward victory. After the election, the DNC laid off Huang "as part of a post-election downsizing."[57] But the questions raised by his activities were not resolved.

Congressional Election Finance

Rising costs and new forms of spending were not limited to the presidential race. Congressional elections were also more expensive in 1996 than ever before. In all, the candidates who mounted campaigns for the U.S. Senate and House raised over $659 million and spent about $626 million. Fund raising therefore rose by about 8 percent over the 1994 election cycle.[58] It is important to note, however, that the 1994 candidates raised $611 million, or 23 percent more than the $495 million raised in 1992.[59] Thus, compared to 1992, the 1996 figures represent an increase of more than 30 percent.

SENATE RECEIPTS AND EXPENDITURES

The Senate candidates in general election contests raised $220 million, spent $220.8 million, and had $8.5 million in available cash after election day (see table 4.5). The Democratic and Republican candidates raised most of this money, $219.6 million, which was almost $40 million less than the sum raised by the major-party contenders in the 1994 race. This decline primarily reflected the specific seats that were up for election: the 1996 contests included many of the smaller population states where campaigns traditionally have been less expensive; the 1994 election featured races in many of the largest, most expensive states, including a race in California in which the two major challengers spent a total of $45 million.

As is usually the case in Senate races, most of the money raised by the major-party candidates came from direct contributions from individuals. Of the $219.6 million in total receipts, $139.4 million, or 63 percent, came from individual donations. Another $40.7 million, or 18.5 percent, came from PACs, and $27.8 million, or about 12.6 percent, from the candidates' personal resources.

Most of this money was received by incumbents, who raised about $79.6 million, 41 percent more than the $56.6 million generated by their challengers. The thirteen Republican senators solicited $44.9 million, compared to $33.6 million for their Democratic challengers. Over half the Democratic total, $19.7 million, was raised by two challengers. Mark Warner of Virginia garnered $11.6 million, including $10.3 million of his own money, in his failed attempt to unseat Senator John Warner. Harvey Gantt of North Carolina received just over $8 million in his rematch with Senator Jesse

TABLE 4.5
1995–96 FINANCIAL ACTIVITY OF SENATE GENERAL ELECTION CAMPAIGNS

	Number	Receipts	Contributions from individuals	Contributions from other committees	Candidate contributions	Loans from candidate	Other loans	Disbursements
Senate	143	$220,015,348	$139,562,289	$40,711,742	$11,945,940	$16,049,054	$216,000	$220,783,542
Democrats	34	$106,537,783	$68,402,412	$14,999,382	$11,599,237	$6,140,013	$0	$106,482,406
Incumbents	7	$34,702,381	$26,820,074	$4,821,967	$0	$1,700,000	$0	$35,895,588
Challengers	14	$33,570,977	$18,108,318	$2,350,066	$11,144,581	$1,248,720	$0	$32,978,795
Open seats	13	$38,264,425	$23,474,020	$7,827,349	$454,656	$3,191,293	$0	$37,608,023
Republicans	34	$113,050,556	$70,970,893	$25,711,860	$223,755	$9,831,737	$200,000	$113,875,013
Incumbents	13	$44,892,292	$28,339,915	$13,308,721	$671	$400,000	$0	$47,226,360
Challengers	8	$23,043,064	$17,754,245	$3,690,659	$13,057	$717,664	$200,000	$22,675,263
Open seats	13	$45,115,200	$24,876,733	$8,712,480	$210,027	$8,714,073	$0	$43,973,390
Other parties	75	$427,009	$188,984	$500	$122,948	$77,304	$16,000	$426,123
Challengers	46	$254,193	$113,810	$500	$57,644	$53,692	$16,000	$252,654
Open seats	29	$172,816	$75,174	$0	$65,304	$23,612	$0	$173,469
Totals								
Incumbents	20	$79,594,673	$55,159,989	$18,130,688	$671	$2,100,000	$0,	$83,121,948
Challengers	68	$56,868,234	$35,976,373	$6,041,225	$11,215,282	$2,020,076	$216,000	$55,906,712
Open seats	55	$83,552,441	$48,425,927	$16,539,829	$729,987	$11,928,978	$0	$81,754,882

SOURCE: Federal Election Commission, as of 25 November filings.

Helms. Only one other Democrat, incumbent Representative Tim Johnson of South Dakota, had managed to raise more than $2 million by mid-October. Johnson won the race, even though Larry Pressler had a financial advantage of more than $1 million.

Likewise, the seven Democratic incumbents outraised their Republican challengers by a margin of $34.7 million to $23 million. Two Republican challengers, Governor William Weld of Massachusetts and former Senator Rudy Boschwitz of Minnesota, were responsible for more than half of their party's total. Weld raised over $8 million in his losing effort against Senator John Kerry, while Boschwitz raised close to $4.4 million in his attempt at reclaiming the seat held by Senator Paul Wellstone.

One interesting change from the patterns of previous elections was the success of Republican incumbents in soliciting PAC dollars. Having captured the Senate in 1994, Republicans now held influential committee chairmanships and positions on key committees. They thus obtained the advantage in PAC benefits that Democratic incumbents previously enjoyed. In the four election cycles between 1988 and 1994, for example, Democratic incumbents averaged about $15.9 million in PAC receipts through mid-October, compared to $3.4 million for their Republican challengers, an advantage of close to five to one.[60] In 1996 it was the Republican incumbents who enjoyed the greatest advantage in PAC gifts. The thirteen Republicans seeking reelection raised almost $13.3 million from PACs, compared to less than $2.4 million given to their Democratic challengers, an advantage of almost six to one. In contrast, the seven Democratic incumbents raised $4.8 million from PACs, compared to $3.7 million by their Republican opponents, an advantage of less than two to one.

In the races for open Senate seats, the Republicans enjoyed a noteworthy resource advantage. The Republican contenders in these contests raised $45.1 million, as opposed to $38.3 million for the Democrats. The candidates from each party raised roughly equivalent amounts from individual contributors and PACs (see table 4.5). The major difference was in the monies contributed by the candidates themselves. The Democratic candidates gave their campaigns a total of about $3.6 million, while the Republicans contributed about $8.9 million of their personal funds. This difference can be accounted for by the Georgia contest, where Republican Guy Millner contributed $6.3 million out of his own pocket in his losing effort against Democrat Max Cleland.

PARTY INDEPENDENT SPENDING

Although the amounts received by open-seat challengers were fairly equal, these funds were not the only source of spending in the open-seat contests. The national party organizations also spent significant amounts in these races, which were targeted early by both parties as crucial battlegrounds. As usual, the national senate campaign committees assisted their candidates by making coordinated expenditures on their behalf to the extent that the law allowed. Then, in a number of races, they spent money beyond the expenditure limits by taking advantage of the newest weapon in their financial arsenal: the ability to spend funds independently of their candidate.

It did not take long for the national party organizations, especially the Republicans, to act on the ruling issued in the *Colorado* decision. By August, the Republicans had a new financial operation called the "I-Team" or "independent expenditures division," that was legally distinct from the National Republican Senatorial Committee (NRSC). The party committee simply established a new office with a separate staff, separate polling and research data, and separate vendors, and charged this new agency with the task of spending monies independently on behalf of Republican candidates.[61] Because this office was a separate legal entity that had not spent funds in coordination with candidates, it could legally spend unlimited amounts of money. More important, since it was spending money independently, the new operation could broadcast ads that expressly advocated the election or defeat of a particular candidate. The brave new world of party finance had finally arrived.

The Republicans wasted little time exploiting their newest tool. By the end of August, they had spent at least $700,000 to air independent televisions ads in Rhode Island, Louisiana, and Wyoming.[62] By mid-October, partial reports filed with the FEC revealed that the committee had already funneled at least $2.8 million into open Senate races. The committee targeted open seats in Oregon, Colorado, Wyoming, Kansas, Arkansas, and Rhode Island for major ad campaigns. They also reportedly concentrated on New Hampshire and South Dakota, where Republican incumbents Bob Smith and Larry Pressler were facing strong opposition.[63]

While the Republicans started spending, the Democratic Senatorial Campaign Committee (DSCC) and Democratic Congressional Campaign Committee (DCCC) sought to clarify the rules. These committees went to court, seeking a ruling that the parties, which had already begun their coordinated spending, could not be truly independent in the 1996 election cycle. The court dismissed their claim. Party officials also sought a ruling from the FEC without success.[64] Having failed to thwart this form of spending, the Democrats joined in, organizing an independent expenditure operation of their own in October to assist some of their challengers in hotly contested races.

House Receipts and Expenditures

While Senate candidates in 1996 received less money than in the previous election cycle, the campaign finances of House candidates rose significantly. Candidates for the U.S. House of Representatives raised $439.6 million and spent $405.6 million (see table 4.6), which represented increases of 19 percent and 24 percent respectively over the record levels of 1994. This increase reflects the intensive campaigning that characterized many of the contests, as the Republicans fought to retain the narrow majority they had won in 1994 and the Democrats sought to win back the seats they needed to regain control.

Overall, two-thirds of the money raised in House campaigns went into the coffers of incumbents seeking reelection. As noted in table 4.6, the 382 members seeking another term generated $275.3 million in contributions, compared to $98.7 million by their challengers, for an average dollar advantage of almost three to one. This margin was essentially the same regardless of party: Republican members raised $169.1 million compared to $61.2 million for their opponents; Democratic members raised $105.3 million to $35.9 million for their opponents. But, as these figures indicate, the 213 Republican incumbents exceeded the fund-raising efforts of the 168 Democrats seeking reelection by nearly 62 percent.

These summary figures, however, fail to capture the extent of the advantage held by most incumbents, especially Republicans, in the 1996 cycle. As in previous elections, most incumbents faced seriously underfunded challengers who lacked the money needed to finance a competitive campaign. In general, a congressional challenger needs to raise $200,000 to $250,000 in order to be competitive.[65] While it takes more than money to win, congressional contenders failing to reach this threshold usually lack the name recognition and exposure needed to compete with an incumbent and therefore rarely win. In 1996, only 79 of the 195 Democratic general election contenders (40 percent) and 51 of the 149 Republican challengers (34 percent) had raised $200,000 by mid-October. Only about half of the Democrats (100) and Republicans (73) facing incumbents had managed to raise $100,000. As a result, most challengers were outspent by significant margins. The median receipts in races involving a Democratic incumbent were approximately $522,000 for the Democrat and $122,000 for the Republican opponent. In races involving a Republican incumbent, the median receipts were $684,000 for the Republican and $127,000 for the Democratic opponent.[66]

The best-financed challengers were those involved in hotly contested races, which in 1996 meant the races for open seats and those involving

TABLE 4.6
1995–96 FINANCIAL ACTIVITY OF HOUSE GENERAL ELECTION CAMPAIGNS

	Number	Receipts	Contributions from individuals	Contributions from other committees	Candidate contributions	Loans from candidate	Other loans	Disbursements
House	1371	$439,581,355	$242,002,479	$151,450,381	$3,620,110	$25,247,884	$741,655	$405,597,715
Democrats	431	$199,471,410	$99,601,562	$74,388,280	$1,636,483	$16,020,842	$193,373	$185,504,564
Incumbents	168	$105,248,377	$50,193,454	$49,501,990	$184,332	$514,227	$57,500	$93,746,174
Challengers	210	$61,249,544	$32,625,791	$15,811,425	$689,602	$10,003,123	$42,924	$59,399,870
Open seats	53	$32,973,489	$16,782,317	$9,074,865	$762,549	$5,503,492	$92,949	$32,358,520
Republicans	436	$236,684,518	$140,510,684	$76,333,438	$1,743,290	$8,756,078	$545,382	$216,966,619
Incumbents	213	$169,060,197	$97,318,337	$63,376,933	$98,633	$1,469,444	$398,400	$151,739,405
Challengers	172	$35,910,737	$24,699,867	$4,542,757	$685,720	$4,375,763	$138,039	$34,862,553
Open seats	51	$31,713,584	$18,492,480	$8,413,748	$958,937	$2,910,871	$8,943	$30,364,661
Other parties	504	$3,425,427	$1,890,233	$728,663	$240,337	$470,964	$2,900	$3,126,532
Incumbents	1	$1,008,998	$758,211	$225,202	$0	$0	$0	$896,549
Challengers	428	$1,527,966	$745,916	$85,028	$221,435	$450,339	$800	$1,386,065
Open seats	75	$888,463	$386,106	$418,433	$18,902	$20,625	$2,100	$843,918
Totals								
Incumbents	382	$275,317,572	$148,270,002	$113,104,125	$282,965	$1,983,671	$455,900	$246,382,128
Challengers	810	$98,688,247	$58,071,574	$20,439,210	$1,596,757	$14,829,225	$181,763	$95,648,488
Open seats	179	$65,575,536	$35,660,903	$17,907,046	$1,740,388	$8,434,988	$103,992	$63,567,099

SOURCE: Federal Election Commission, as of 25 November filings.

first-term members of Congress. In the open-seat races, the margin between Democratic and Republican challengers was relatively narrow. The Democrats raised $33 million, or less than 5 percent more than their Republican opponents, who raised $31.7 million. The Democrats therefore averaged $622,000 in receipts, the Republicans $620,000. As in the Senate open-seat races, the primary difference between the two groups was accounted for by the amount of personal money that the candidates poured into their campaigns. While in the Senate open-seat races the Republicans contributed more, in the House races the Democrats were more generous, giving $5.5 million from their own funds, compared to $2.9 million for the Republicans.

The most expensive races in 1996, however, were those involving first-term members of Congress, especially the seventy-one first-term Republicans. Because the chances of defeating an incumbent are most likely in their first bid for reelection, and many of the Republicans had won by narrow margins in the "Republican year" of 1994, these seats were targeted by both parties as the key to winning control of the House. They thus became the focal point of contributor dollars and party efforts.

While the median amount raised by all Democratic challengers running in general election contests was $127,000, the median for Democratic challengers facing first-term Republicans was over $400,000.[67] Of these sixty-nine contenders, only seventeen had failed to raise $200,000 by mid-October, while eleven had received more than $750,000, including five who had surpassed the $1 million mark. Their Republican opponents were even more successful in soliciting funds, however. The median amount received by these incumbents by mid-October was approximately $850,000, with twenty-two first-termers surpassing the $1 million mark. Moreover, only one Republican freshman, Mark Sanford of South Carolina, raised less than $350,000, and he faced no Democratic general election challenger in a safe Republican seat.

The first-term Republicans achieved this lopsided financial advantage largely as a result of their early fund-raising efforts. Upon arriving in Washington after the 1994 election, the freshmen were told by the National Republican Congressional Committee (NRCC) that if they wanted to be reelected, it would be "prudent" to begin setting fund-raising goals and resoliciting their 1994 donors immediately.[68] In addition, the Republicans, led by Speaker Gingrich and new House Majority Whip Tom DeLay, began to solicit PAC contributions very aggressively, hoping to reverse the pattern of the 1994 election cycle, in which 65 percent of the donations from the top 400 PACs had gone to Democrats.[69] These decisions led to an extraordinary emphasis on preelection-year fund raising, which provided the first-term Republicans with significant financial rewards.

By the end of 1995, the average Republican freshman had raised $272,000, including $104,000 in PAC money. By the end of March 1996, the seventy-one Republican first-termers seeking reelection had solicited an average of $384,000, including $139,000 from PACs and other nonparty committees. Their Democratic challengers, however, had received less than one-fifth of this total, averaging $68,500, including a mere $12,500 from PACs.[70]

ISSUE ADVOCACY SPENDING, CONGRESSIONAL STYLE

In a typical election year the Republicans' large war chests, especially their early financial success, would have provided most of these members with a substantial advantage, one that challengers historically would find impossible to overcome. But 1996 was not a typical election year. Any early advantage that the Republicans did achieve was more than compensated for by the issue advocacy spending that took place in these elections. As in the presidential election, issue advocacy advertising played a major role in the financing of the 1996 congressional campaigns. The congressional contests were different, however, in one important respect: much of this spending was done by groups other than party organizations.

The surge in issue advocacy money that flooded key congressional districts with political ads was stimulated by the political strategy of the nation's largest labor organization, the AFL-CIO. Early in 1996, the AFL-CIO announced that it would spend $35 million on activities designed to influence congressional elections, including roughly $20 million for advertising, and millions more for extensive organizing activities in at least seventy-five targeted congressional districts.[71] Most of these districts were open seats or seats held by freshmen Republicans. The organization's objective was to help elect a Congress more sympathetic to its legislative interests, which meant, in the best case, the restoration of a labor-friendly Democratic majority. Labor unions had already spent millions of dollars in 1995 on grassroots programs that sought to increase public opposition to an array of Republican proposals on health care, education, welfare, and education. The AFL-CIO, for example, reportedly spent $8 million on a grassroots organizational program, while the American Federation of State, County and Municipal Employees led a coalition called "Save Our Families" that ran television ads critical of Republican education and health plans.[72]

The AFL-CIO followed these initial efforts with a targeted media campaign primarily directed against freshman Republicans, particularly those who had won by close margins in 1994. The campaign consisted primarily of negative ads that attacked the Republicans' positions on health care, education, the minimum wage, and other issues in general, and named and featured specific incumbent members of Congress. They were, in short, thinly disguised campaign ads that were cast as "video voter guides." The Republicans charged that such ads blatantly violated federal law, but the unions noted that the ads did not qualify as "express advocacy"—instead of asking viewers to vote for or against a candidate, the ads urged them to contact their members of Congress. The funding for the ads came from union treasury funds, a source banned under federal law as a source of direct contributions to candidates.

The union aired ads throughout most of the election year, with most of the spending coming in two waves, one timed to coincide with primary elections, and the other concentrated in the first three weeks of October. In October, the union aired ads in twenty-one freshmen districts and in seven open-seat districts. In the two months leading up to the election, the union spent an estimated $10 million on advertising against twenty-one first-term Republicans, and about $1.1 million in districts with no incumbent.[73]

The Republicans did not allow labor's assault to go unanswered. In April the RNC responded to the labor initiative by mounting an issue advocacy ad campaign of its own. The committee launched a twenty-two-state advertising effort that focused on Republican tax cut proposals and Clinton's veto of a middle-class tax cut.[74]

The NRCC continued to broadcast such issue advocacy ads throughout the general election campaign, thus adding millions of dollars in expenditures to the total amount they spent assisting their candidates, none of which was subject to federal spending limits. In July, the NRCC announced an $8 million issue advocacy campaign that, according to NRCC chairman Bill Paxon, was "designed to build a foundation so that Republican incumbents and challengers can run credible and effective campaigns this fall."[75] In August, for example, the NRCC came to the aid of their potentially vulnerable incumbents by running a series of ads designed to defend them against charges that they had voted "to cut" Medicare. The ads ran for a ten- to twelve-day period that coincided with the Olympics and the Republican Party convention in forty media markets covering thirty congressional districts.[76] In October, the NRCC mounted an ad campaign that directly confronted the issue of AFL-CIO spending. Beginning the first week of October, the NRCC began airing an ad that attacked "big labor bosses in Washington" allegedly trying to "buy their control of Congress," and urged voters to "call the union bosses" and tell them your state "is not for sale."[77] In all, the NRCC aired ads in October that covered at least twenty-seven districts of Republican first-termers and eighteen open-seat districts.[78]

The labor unions and party organizations were not the only groups to engage in this spending free-for-all. The U.S. Chamber of Commerce also joined the fray to counter labor's spending. Under the Chamber's leadership, an association of thirty-one organizations was formed, called simply "The Coalition," to raise money to pay for ads to rebut the union arguments. The Coalition financed two issue ad campaigns, airing commercials in thirty-three congressional districts at a reported cost of $7 million.[79] In addition, the right-wing Christian Coalition spent a reported $10 million to print and distribute 46 million voter guides. The group also aired informational radio ads and mobilized thousands of volunteers to get out the vote.[80] Another Christian-based activist group, the Interfaith Alliance, mailed out its own voter guides in more than thirty House and Senate races and waged get-out-the-vote campaigns in a number of selected congressional districts.[81]

The Future of Campaign Finance

In 1974 Congress established a campaign finance system designed to limit political contributions, control campaign spending, and provide full public disclosure of the finances of candidates, national party organizations, and federal political committees. In 1996 this regulatory system, already riddled with loopholes, finally collapsed. Candidates and party organizations spent more money than ever before, including hundreds of millions of dollars from sources supposed to be banned from contributing in federal elections. Parties and organized interest groups capitalized on new opportunities to spend, rendering the expenditure limits established by federal law essentially meaningless. And tens of millions of dollars of financial activity associated with federal races went undisclosed to the public.

The 1996 election was thus characterized by an unstemmed flow of money. The legal constraints established by the FECA were more a nuisance than a hindrance. Widespread evasion of the law was possible, largely because the contours of the political finance system have radically changed. Recent decisions by the courts and FEC have greatly expanded the scope of political activity that is not considered campaign related, yet is nonetheless campaign activity. These rulings have also loosened many of the restrictions imposed on candidates and party committees under the original terms of the FECA. As a result, new methods of political finance have emerged, creating new problems for those who seek to improve the system.

Perhaps the most important lesson to be learned from the 1996 experience is that the boundaries of the campaign finance system have become increasingly blurred. The current regulatory regime was based on a system geared toward the campaign-related finances of candidates, party organizations, and PACs. Such a system is not designed for the new forms of spending that have emerged in recent elections. Consequently, when candidates or political committees find themselves constrained in one area, they simply evade the law by shifting their financial activity to another arena or by relying on some other agent, a party committee or organized interest group, to spend money on their behalf. The effect of such activity is to shift resources into less constrained and less accountable areas, making it even more difficult to trace the flow of money in federal elections.

If future efforts at campaign finance reform are to be meaningful, they must take into account the lessons of 1996. In recent Congresses, reform initiatives have primarily focused on the rising costs and sources of funding in congressional campaigns, as well as the problems associated with the unlimited contributions and spending that are possible through the the use of soft money. The major reform bills have tried to address these issues by proposing to eliminate soft money and to establish some combination of public subsidies and spending limits to control the costs of congressional campaigns. The 1996 experience highlights the limited potential efficacy of such approaches. As long as the parties and other groups can raise and spend unlimited amounts for issue advertising or independent expenditures, spending limits and public subsidies will have little regulatory effect. The lesson of 1996 is that we need to rethink our approaches to campaign finance reform and consider the broader financial context of modern political campaigns.

Most important, future efforts at reform must confront the problem of defining the realm of campaign finance activity that falls within the scope of federal regulation. Are monies spent by party organizations on party building or issue advocacy advertising forms of campaign spending? What about monies spent by labor unions and other organizations on advertising to communicate not only with their members but with the public at large about particular candidates for federal office? Or monies spent by organized interests on voter guides designed to influence the outcome of federal elections but not coordinated with any candidate or member of a campaign staff?

One step toward addressing these issues is to reconsider the current definition and regulations regarding the concept of "express advocacy." While some observers believe that the free-speech rights of party organizations, organized groups, and individuals should not be abridged by campaign finance laws, others argue that no system of regulation will be effective if the narrow definition currently used is upheld in the future. A broader definition could reduce the amount of issue advertising in the future and bring a significant share of this kind of spending under the aegis of campaign spending laws and thus effect more stringent public disclosure.

Second, the role of party financing in the political system and, in particular, the role of soft money as a source of party funds needs to be addressed. At a minimum, reform proposals must eliminate the unlimited contributions that parties can accept under current law, especially the gifts from corporations and labor unions that raise questions about the potentially corruptive influence of large donors. At the same time, reform efforts must consider how best to continue to strengthen the parties and ensure that they have the resources needed to communicate their positions to the electorate and promote fair electoral competition. In this regard, one proposal that merits particular consideration is to place all contributions to the national party organizations under federal limitations, but place a fairly high ceiling on the amount that individuals and political committees are allowed to give. Further, future reform efforts must consider the relation between the parties and their candidates. Should party organizations be allowed to spend money independently? Or should they be presumed to have a special relationship with their nominees for federal office that merits recognition in federal statutes?

The 1996 election represents a marked departure in patterns of political finance that have characterized recent elections. Many of the patterns —early fund raising by presidential candidates, the incumbent advantage in congressional races, the party emphasis on vulnerable incumbents and open seats—were similar to those of previous elections. What made 1996 notable was the emergence of new forms of spending that changed both the sources of funding and campaign tactics in wide-ranging, and possibly permanent, ways. The result was a new reality in the world of campaign finance. And with this new reality comes a more urgent need for campaign finance reform.

Acknowledgments

The author thanks Robert Biersack and Michael Dickinson of the Federal Election Commission and Katherine Charbonnier of Colby College for their assistance with the research for this chapter.

Notes

1. This figure includes only the amounts spent by presidential campaign committees, congressional campaign committees, national nominating convention committees and host committees, and the national party organizations. The figure for 1996 is based on an estimate made from FEC data available as of 15 January 1997. The 1992 estimate is based on data reported in Herbert E. Alexander and Anthony Corrado, *Financing the 1992 Election* (Armonk, N.Y.: M.E. Sharpe, 1995).

2. U.S. Supreme Court, *Colorado Republican Federal Campaign Committee* v. *Federal Election Commission,* No. 95-489, 26 June 1996.

3. Federal Election Commission, "FEC Announces 1996 Presidential Spending Limits," press release, 15 March 1996.

4. For further discussion of the financing of the 1992 contest, see Anthony Corrado, "The Changing Environment of Presidential Campaign Finance," in *In Pursuit of the White House: How We Choose Our Presidential Nominees,* ed. William G. Mayer (Chatham, N.J.: Chatham House, 1996), 224–35.

5. All figures for 1988 are based on the adjusted campaign receipts reported in Federal Election Commission, "FEC Releases Final Report on 1988 Presidential Primary Campaigns," press release, 25 August 1989.

6. The 1988 candidates were George Bush, Robert Dole, Pete duPont, Alexander Haig, Jack Kemp, and Pat Robertson.

7. William Ryberg, "Titan Chief Running for U.S. President," *Des Moines Register,* 22 April 1995, 1S.

8. Alexander and Corrado, *Financing the 1992 Election,* 188–92.

9. See Arthur Hadley, *The Invisible Primary* (Englewood Cliffs, N.J.: Prentice Hall, 1976); and Emmett Buell, "The Invisible Primary," in Mayer, *In Pursuit of the White House,* 1–43.

10. Corrado, "The Changing Environment of Presidential Campaign Finance," 226–27.

11. Dan Balz, "Pricing Themselves Out of the Presidential Race," *Washington Post National Weekly,* 20–26 February 1995, 14.

12. James A. Barnes, "Campaign Overload," *National Journal,* 13 May 1995, 1156.

13. John King, "GOP Presidential Hopefuls Jump In," Associated Press news release, 15 November 1994; Dan Balz, "Dole Formally Exploring 1996 Terrain," *Washington Post,* 13 January 1995, A7; John Milne, "Alexander Prefaces Run with Message," *Boston Globe,* 18 January 1995, 5; *Time,* 11 September 1995, 30.

14. These figures and those that follow are based on data available from the Federal Election Commission.

15. Federal Election Commission, "Initial Entitlements for 1996 Set New High," *Record* 22, no. 2 (February 1996): 3. Three of the Republican candidates in 1996 did not accept public subsidies: Dornan, Forbes, and Taylor.

16. Elizabeth Kolbert, "Ad-Heavy Race May Alter Book on Iowa," *New York Times,* 17 January 1996, A1.

17. John Milne, "Alexander Kicks Off His Run via N.H. 'Infomercial,'" *Boston Globe*, 5 March 1995, 16; Elizabeth Kolbert, "Candidates Make History with Early Ads in New Hampshire," *New York Times*, 11 October 1995, A14.

18. Michael Kranish, "Rivals Gear Up for Run at Dole," *Boston Globe*, 31 December 1995, 23.

19. Ruth Marcus and Walter Pincus, "Forbes Spent $18 Million on Race Last Year," *Washington Post*, 6 February 1996, 1; Jane Norman, "Forbes Spends $14 Million in 3 Months," *Des Moines Register*, 7 February 1996, 3A.

20. Thomas A. Fogarty, "Forbes' Ads Flood Airwaves in Iowa," *Des Moines Register*, 11 December 1995, 1A.

21. Marcus and Pincus, "Forbes Spent $18 Million."

22. Lamar Alexander, "Off With the Limits," *Campaigns & Elections*, October/November 1996, 33; Anthony Flint, "GOP Takes Stock of N.H. Lessons," *Boston Globe*, 22 February 1996, 1; Kevin Sack, "Campaign Funds Slow to Come In," *New York Times*, 19 February 1996, A11. See also Diana C. Mutz, "Media, Momentum and Money: Horse Race Spin in the 1988 Republican Primaries," in *Polls and the News Media*, ed. Paul J. Lavrakas, Michael W. Traugott, and Peter V. Miller (Boulder, Colo.: Westview Press, 1995), 229–54.

23. Ruth Marcus, "Fund Raising: Difficulty Ahead for Alexander," *Washington Post*, 21 February 1996, A14.

24. Ibid.

25. Ruth Marcus, "Spending Solution Tantalizingly Close; Dole Looks Forward to $62 Million," *Washington Post*, 21 May 1996, A6.

26. Stephen Labaton, "Limited Cash Likely to Restrict Dole's Campaign Message," *New York Times*, 16 May 1996, B11; Phil Kuntz, "Dole's Campaign May Appear Broke, but GOP Can and Will Spare a Dime," *Wall Street Journal*, 17 May 1996, A16.

27. Michael Kranish, "Dole Bemoans Preconvention Spending Limits," *Boston Globe*, 14 July 1996, 7.

28. Marcus, "Spending Solution Tantalizingly Close."

29. Bob Woodward, *The Choice* (New York: Simon and Schuster, 1996), 213.

30. 2 U.S.C. § 441a.

31. *Buckley* v. *Valeo*, 424 U.S. 1, 44.

32. Ibid., note 52.

33. Eleanor Randolph, "Clinton Camp Sows Televised Seeds of Support in Key Regions," *Los Angeles Times*, 22 May 1996, 5.

34. Woodward, *The Choice*, 344.

35. Common Cause, "Statement of Common Cause President Ann McBride at News Conference Asking for Independent Counsel to Investigate Campaign Finance Activities of Clinton, Dole Campaigns," press release, 9 October 1996, 7.

36. Current FEC regulations on party activities that benefit both federal and state candidates (and the assumption is that issue advocacy ads benefit both) require that national party organizations pay for 65 percent of the cost of such ac-

tivities with hard money. The other 35 percent can be paid for with soft money. But if a state party pays for the activity, the formula is generally reversed. For a discussion of the allocation regulations, see Federal Election Commission, "Revised Supplement on Allocation," *Record,* December 1992.

37. Republican National Committee, "RNC Announces $20 Million TV Advertising Campaign," press release, 16 May 1996, 1.

38. Ibid.

39. Common Cause, "Statement of Common Cause President Ann McBride at News Conference," 9.

40. U.S. Supreme Court, No. 95–489, 26 June 1996.

41. Under the provisions of 2 U.S.C. § 441a(d), political parties may spend a maximum of $20,000 or 2 cents multiplied by a state's voting-age population, adjusted for inflation since 1974, in a senatorial campaign in coordination with a candidate or his or her campaign committee. For a description of the facts in the case, see the Court's decision cited above or Richard Briffault, "Campaign Finance, The Parties, and The Court: A Comment on *Colorado Republican Federal Campaign Committee* v. *Federal Election Commission*" (paper presented at the American Political Science Association annual meeting, 29 August–1 September 1996).

42. Ruth Marcus, "Party Spending Unleashed," *Washington Post,* 27 June 1996, A1.

43. Federal Election Commission, "Dole, Clinton, Perot Receive Public Funds," *Record* 22, no. 10 (October 1996): 3. Under the public funding law, a new party or independent candidate running for the first time is eligible for a proportionate share of public money after the election if he or she receives more than 5 percent of the vote. If that candidate receives the nomination of the party and abides by the other requirements of the program, he or she is eligible for a proportionate share of the public subsidy before the election in the next cycle. This preelection entitlement is based on the ratio of votes received by the non-major-party candidate in the previous election compared to the average share of the vote received by the major-party candidates. Any candidate who receives over 25 percent of the vote in the previous election is entitled to the full subsidy. In 1980 Anderson received 6.6 percent of the vote.

44. Ibid.

45. Mimi Hall, "Perot Accepts Taxpayer Funding," *USA Today,* 20 August 1996, 4A.

46. Figure based on the amount reported to the FEC in the preelection filing of the Perot '96 Committee.

47. Peter S. Canellos, "Perot Ad Announcement Is Also-Ran Against Reruns," *Boston Globe,* 13 September 1996, A24.

48. "Perot Spending Millions on TV Commercials," *New York Times,* 3 November 1996, 37.

49. Federal Election Commission, "Political Parties' Fundraising Hits $881 Million," press release, 10 January 1997. The figures include monies received as

of 25 November 1996. All the figures on party spending that follow, unless otherwise noted, are based on the data contained in this release.

50. On the uses of soft money in 1992, see Alexander and Corrado, *Financing the 1992 Election*, 147–75.

51. Center for Responsive Politics, "Soft Money Contributions: 1996 Elections," press release, 17 October 1996. See also Jill Lawrence and Judi Hasson, "Donations to Both Parties Skirt Limits Set by Reform," *USA Today*, 28 October 1996, 1A and 8A.

52. See, among others, R.A. Dyer, "Clinton Helps Democrats Cash In on 'Soft Money,' " *Houston Chronicle*, 29 September 1996; Robert Kuttner, "Why a Campaign Finance Loophole Must Be Closed," *Boston Globe*, 23 September 1996, A15; and John H. Fund, "The Department of Political Favors," *Wall Street Journal*, 29 October 1996, A22.

53. Peter Waldman, "By Courting Clinton, Lippo Gains Stature at Home in Indonesia," *Wall Street Journal*, 16 October 1996, A1.

54. Howard Fineman and Mark Hosenball, "The Asian Connection," *Newsweek*, 28 October 1996, 26–27; "Who Is Mochtar Riady-II?" *Wall Street Journal*, 10 October 1996, A18; Jeff Gerth and Stephen Labaton, "Wealthy Indonesian Businessman Has Strong Ties to Clinton," *New York Times*, 11 October 1996, A20.

55. Stephen Labaton, "Democrats Curb Raising of Funds by a Top Official," *New York Times*, 19 October 1996, A1.

56. Jill Abramson and Glenn R. Simpson, "Lippo Issue Remains at Center of Presidential Race," *Wall Street Journal*, 21 October 1996, A24; David E. Sanger and James Sterngold, "Fund Raiser for Democrats Now Faces Harsh Spotlight," *New York Times*, 21 October 1996, A1.

57. Ruth Marcus, "DNC Lays Off Fund-Raiser Huang, a Figure in Foreign Donors Dispute," *Washington Post*, 18 November 1996, A12.

58. Federal Election Commission, "1996 Congressional Financial Activity Continues Climb," press release, 31 December 1996. All the data on Senate and House campaign finances are based on the information contained in this release, which reports receipts and expenditures as of 25 November.

59. Federal Election Commission, "1994 Congressional Spending Sets Record," press release, 22 December 1994, 1.

60. Based on the historical data reported in Federal Election Commission, "1996 Congressional Financial Activity Continues Climb."

61. Walter Shapiro, "The Hard Truth: Soft Money Has Bought This Campaign," *USA Today*, 4 October 1996, 9A.

62. Based on the data reported in Federal Election Commission, Independent Expenditures Index by Committee/Person Expending, 1995–96.

63. David Rogers, "GOP's New TV Attack Ads Take Aim at Democratic Candidates for Senate," *Wall Street Journal*, 21 October 1996, A24.

64. Eliza Newlin Carney, "Party Time," *National Journal*, 19 October 1996, 2217.

65. See Michael J. Malbin, "Campaign Finance Reform: Some Lessons from the Data," *Rockefeller Institute Bulletin*, 1993, 49; Jonathan S. Krasno and Donald Philip Green, "Stopping the Buck Here: The Case for Campaign Spending Limits," *Brookings Review*, Spring 1993, 17–21.

66. Based on the data reported in Federal Election Commission, "1996 Congressional Financial Activity Continues Climb."

67. This figure is based on the receipts of sixty-nine Democratic general election candidates running against first-term Republicans. It does not include challengers in races in Texas in the thirteen districts affected by a Supreme Court redistricting decision. In these districts, an open primary was held on 5 November with a runoff election, if necessary, to be held between the top two finishers, regardless of party, on 10 December 1996.

68. Adam Clymer, "Contract with America Includes Cash Bonuses," *New York Times*, 18 February 1996, E4; and "For Freshmen, Fund Raising Has Yielded Big Results," *New York Times*, 6 May 1996, A13.

69. Richard L. Berke, "Republicans Rule Lobbyists' World with Strong Arm," *New York Times*, 20 March 1995, A1; David Maraniss and Michael Weisskopf, "Speaker and His Directors Make the Cash Flow Right," *Washington Post*, 27 November 1995, A1; "The New Beneficiaries of the Top 400," *Washington Post*, 27 November 1995, A9.

70. Clymer, "For Freshmen, Fund Raising Has Yielded Big Results."

71. Julie Kosterlitz, "Laboring Uphill," *National Journal*, 2 March 1996, 476.

72. Ibid.

73. Figures based on NRCC estimates provided to the author in a data set prepared by the NRCC on 20 November 1996.

74. Republican National Committee, "Statement by RNC Chairman Haley Barbour," press release, 9 April 1996; Sandy Hume and Doug Obey, "RNC Returns Union Fire with Ad Campaign," *The Hill*, 10 April 1996, 7.

75. Carney, "Party Time," 2218.

76. Tim Curran, "NRCC Launches Medicare Ad Campaign for At-Risk Incumbents in 30 Districts," www.rollcall.com/newsscoops/5thscoop.html, 22 August 1996.

77. National Republican Congressional Committee, "Republicans Counter Big Labor's Big Lies and Big Money," press release, 4 October 1996.

78. Figure based on information provided to the author by the NRCC.

79. Jonathan D. Salant, "Finances Take Priority In This Year's Races," *Congressional Quarterly Weekly Report*, 26 October 1996, 3083; Eliza Newlin Carney, "Reform Could Strike Out Over Labor," *National Journal*, 30 November 1996, 2617.

80. Richard Benedetto, "Christian Coalition Saving Its Strength for Local Races," *USA Today*, 18 October 1996, 9A.

81. Ibid.

5

The Presidential Election

GERALD M. POMPER

What need the bridge much broader than the flood?
The fairest grant is the necessity.
Look what will serve is fit.
— *Much Ado About Nothing* (I, i)

William Jefferson Clinton constructed a broad "bridge to the twenty-first century" in the 1996 presidential election. Along with Vice-President Albert Gore, he gained the approval of essentially half of America's 96 million voters and won 379 of the nation's 538 electoral votes. But will the bridge prove too broad, or too narrow, or too weak, to serve the future needs of the United States?

Clinton's success is remarkable. He became the first Democrat since Franklin Roosevelt to win consecutive presidential elections and only the fourth candidate of his party (also emulating Andrew Jackson and Woodrow Wilson)[1] in American history to turn the trick. The president rebounded from opinion ratings that found disapproval outnumbering approval by as much as three to two. He overcame the 1994 landslide congressional elections that brought Republicans to power in both houses of Congress for the first time in forty years. He survived the defeat of ambitious programs such as health-care reform, a cascade of investigations and allegations about his personal conduct, foreign policy embarrassments, and an often maladroit administration of the executive branch. And by 5 November 1996 he made it look easy, even inevitable.

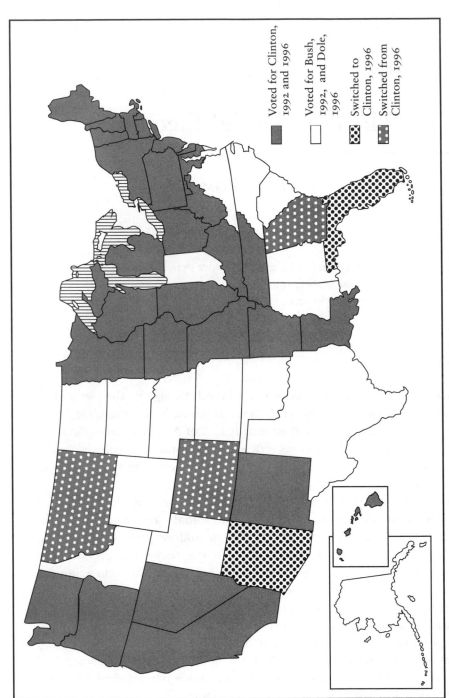

Voted for Clinton, 1992 and 1996

Voted for Bush, 1992, and Dole, 1996

Switched to Clinton, 1996

Switched from Clinton, 1996

FIGURE 5.1. THE 1996 ELECTORAL MAP

The Democratic Bridge

THE ELECTORAL MAP

Clinton's victory is impressive, politically and even visually. As seen in figure 5.1, the president carried states in all regions of the nation, in effect marching down both coasts and through most of the major states across the continent with the exception of Texas. He held twenty-nine of the states (and the District of Columbia) that he had won in 1992 and added the previous Republican redoubts of Florida and Arizona, while losing closely his 1992 majorities in Colorado, Georgia, and Montana. The president won a national victory, with the vote in most states approximating the national figures.[2] (The state-by-state figures can be seen in table 5.1.)

As he laid away his Republican challenger, former Senator Robert Dole, Clinton also interred past clichés of American electoral history. The old Democratic "solid South" is now the Republicans' strongest area. In contrast, the "Grand Old Party" lost decisively in its historical homelands of New England and the Midwest. Defeated across the nation, the Republicans no longer can boast of a presumed "electoral lock" on presidential elections. The most common political pattern for forty years—Republican presidents and Democratic control of Congress—has been reversed, as a two-term Democratic president faces a Congress where Republicans maintain the majority they won in 1994.

The state pattern also shows remarkable stability in the vote. There was an average change in the two-party vote of only 1.2 percent from one state to another, and little variation. Clinton gained in thirty-two states and lost ground in eighteen, but almost all changes were small. (The standard deviation, a common statistical measure, was 3.2 points.) Clinton did well in 1996 in precisely those areas where he had run successfully in 1992, and his strength is based on the same geographical coalition as that of other recent Democratic candidates. There is a remarkably high correlation of .91 between the 1992 and 1996 results, and a similarly high correlation of .85 between the results of 1996 and of the four previous presidential elections.[3]

DEMOGRAPHY OF THE VOTE

The Clinton vote also parallels the Democratic coalition among social groups in previous presidential elections. As in 1992, the president won his greatest support among those of lesser income and education (as well as those with more than a college education), Catholics and Jews, urban residents, and blacks and Hispanics (see table 5.2). This pattern suggests that the election reflected short-term forces moving all groups in a Democratic direction, not fundamental change in the parties' electoral foundations.

TABLE 5.I
THE 1996 PRESIDENTIAL VOTE

	Electoral vote		Percentage, 3-party vote			Percentage, 2-party vote		Popular vote (in thousands)		
	Clinton	Dole	Clinton	Dole	Perot	Clinton	Dole	Clinton	Dole	Perot
Alabama		9	43.5	50.5	6.0	46.3	53.7	662.2	769.0	92.1
Alaska		3	35.0	53.5	11.5	39.6	60.4	80.4	122.7	26.3
Arizona	8		47.1	44.8	8.1	51.2	48.8	653.3	622.1	112.1
Arkansas	6		54.6	37.4	8.0	59.4	40.6	475.2	325.4	69.9
California	54		53.1	39.7	7.2	57.2	42.8	5,119.8	3,828.4	697.8
Colorado		8	45.9	47.3	6.8	49.2	50.8	671.2	691.8	99.6
Connecticut	8		54.2	35.6	10.3	60.4	39.6	735.7	483.1	139.5
Delaware	3		52.3	37.0	10.7	58.6	41.4	140.4	99.1	28.7
District of Columbia	3		88.3	9.7	2.0	90.1	9.9	158.2	17.3	3.6
Florida	25		48.3	42.5	9.2	53.2	46.8	2,546.0	2,243.3	483.8
Georgia		13	46.2	47.4	6.4	49.4	50.6	1,053.8	1,080.8	146.3
Hawaii	4		59.2	32.9	7.9	64.3	35.7	205.0	113.9	27.4
Idaho		4	34.1	53.0	12.9	39.2	60.8	165.4	256.6	62.5
Illinois	22		54.8	37.1	8.1	59.6	40.4	2,341.7	1,587.0	346.4
Indiana		12	41.9	47.5	10.6	46.9	53.1	887.4	1,006.7	224.3
Iowa	7		50.9	40.4	8.6	55.7	44.3	620.3	492.6	105.2
Kansas		6	36.5	54.8	8.7	39.9	60.1	387.7	583.2	92.6

State									
Kentucky	8	46.1	45.2	8.7	50.5	49.5	636.6	623.3	120.4
Louisiana	9	52.6	40.4	7.0	56.6	43.4	927.8	712.6	123.3
Maine	4	53.5	31.9	14.7	62.7	37.3	312.8	186.4	86.0
Maryland	10	54.8	38.6	6.6	58.6	41.4	966.2	681.5	115.8
Massachusetts	12	62.4	28.5	9.0	68.6	31.4	1,571.5	718.1	227.2
Michigan	18	52.3	38.9	8.8	57.3	42.7	1,989.7	1,481.2	336.7
Minnesota	10	52.2	35.7	12.0	59.4	40.6	1,120.4	766.5	257.7
Mississippi	7	44.5	49.6	5.9	47.3	52.7	394.0	439.8	52.2
Missouri	11	48.1	41.7	10.2	53.5	46.5	1,025.9	890.0	217.2
Montana	3	41.7	44.6	13.7	48.3	51.7	167.9	179.7	55.2
Nebraska	5	35.3	54.1	10.6	39.4	60.6	236.8	363.5	71.3
Nevada	4	45.6	44.5	9.8	50.6	49.4	204.0	199.2	44.0
New Hampshire	4	50.1	40.0	9.9	55.6	44.4	246.2	196.5	48.4
New Jersey	15	54.8	36.6	8.7	60.0	40.0	1,652.4	1,103.1	262.1
New Mexico	5	50.8	43.2	6.0	54.0	46.0	273.5	232.8	32.3
New York	33	60.7	31.2	8.1	66.0	34.0	3,756.2	1,933.5	503.5
North Carolina	14	44.3	49.0	6.7	47.5	52.5	1,107.8	1,225.9	168.1
North Dakota	3	40.4	47.3	12.3	46.1	53.9	106.9	125.1	32.5
Ohio	21	47.8	41.4	10.8	53.6	46.4	2,148.2	1,859.9	483.2
Oklahoma	8	40.6	48.5	10.9	45.6	54.4	488.1	582.3	130.8

Continued....

TABLE 5.1. — Continued

	Electoral vote		Percentage, 3-party vote			Percentage, 2-party vote		Popular vote (in thousands)		
	Clinton	Dole	Clinton	Dole	Perot	Clinton	Dole	Clinton	Dole	Perot
Oregon	7		49.6	41.1	9.3	54.7	45.3	649.6	538.2	121.2
Pennsylvania	23		49.8	40.5	9.7	55.2	44.8	2,215.8	1,801.2	431.0
Rhode Island	4		61.1	27.4	11.5	69.0	31.0	233.1	104.7	43.7
South Carolina		8	44.3	50.1	5.6	46.9	53.1	506.2	573.3	64.4
South Dakota		3	43.4	46.9	9.7	48.1	51.9	139.3	150.5	31.3
Tennessee	11		48.4	46.0	5.6	51.3	48.7	909.1	863.5	105.9
Texas		32	44.1	49.1	6.8	47.3	52.7	2,459.7	2,736.2	378.5
Utah		5	34.1	55.7	10.2	38.0	62.0	221.6	361.9	66.5
Vermont	3		55.3	32.3	12.4	63.2	36.8	137.9	80.4	31.0
Virginia		13	45.7	47.6	6.7	48.9	51.1	1,091.1	1,138.4	159.9
Washington	11		51.9	38.8	9.3	57.2	42.8	1,123.3	840.7	201.0
West Virginia	5		51.8	36.9	11.3	58.4	41.6	327.8	233.9	71.6
Wisconsin	11		50.0	39.4	10.6	55.9	44.1	1,072.0	845.0	227.3
Wyoming		3	37.3	50.4	12.4	42.5	57.5	77.9	105.4	25.9
Totals	379	159	50.1	41.4	8.5	54.7	45.3	47,401.1	39,197.4	8,085.3

SOURCE: *Congressional Quarterly Weekly Report*, 55 (18 January 1997), 188, updated through www.politicsnow.com.
NOTE: Calculations by the author. The total national vote was 96.3 million. Minor candidates are omitted.

TABLE 5.2

THE PRESIDENTIAL VOTE IN SOCIAL GROUPS (IN PERCENTAGES)

% of 1996 total vote	Social group	1992 Clinton	1992 Bush	1992 Perot	1996 Clinton	1996 Dole	1996 Perot	2-party vote 1996 Clinton	2-party vote 1996 Dole
	Total vote	43	38	19	49	41	8	54	45
	Party and ideology								
2	Liberal Republicans	17	54	30	44	48	9	48	52
13	Moderate Republicans	15	63	21	20	72	7	22	78
21	Conservative Republicans	5	82	13	6	88	5	7	93
4	Liberal Independents	54	17	30	58	15	18	79	21
15	Moderate Independents	43	28	30	50	30	17	62	38
7	Conservative Independents	17	53	30	19	60	19	24	76
13	Liberal Democrats	85	5	11	89	5	4	95	5
20	Moderate Democrats	76	9	15	84	10	5	89	11
6	Conservative Democrats	61	23	16	69	23	7	75	25
	Gender and marital status								
33	Married men	38	42	21	40	48	10	45	55
33	Married women	41	40	19	48	43	7	53	47
15	Unmarried men	48	29	22	49	35	12	58	42
20	Unmarried women	53	31	15	62	28	7	69	31

Continued....

TABLE 5.2 — Continued

% of 1996 total vote	Social group	3-party vote						2-party vote 1996	
		1992			1996				
		Clinton	Bush	Perot	Clinton	Dole	Perot	Clinton	Dole
	Race								
83	White	39	40	20	43	46	9	48	52
10	Black	83	10	7	84	12	4	88	12
5	Hispanic	61	25	14	72	21	6	77	23
1	Asian	31	55	15	43	48	8	47	53
	Religion								
46	White Protestant	33	47	21	36	53	10	40	60
29	Catholic	44	35	20	53	37	9	59	41
3	Jewish	80	11	9	78	16	3	83	17
17	Born Again, religious right	23	61	15	26	65	8	29	71
	Age								
17	18–29 years old	43	34	22	53	34	10	61	39
33	30–44 years old	41	38	21	48	41	9	54	46
26	45–59 years old	41	40	19	48	41	9	54	46
24	60 and older	50	38	12	48	44	7	52	48

	C1	C2	C3	C4	C5	C6	C7	C8	C9
Education									
Not a high school graduate	6	54	28	18	59	28	11	68	32
High school graduate	24	43	36	21	51	35	13	59	41
Some college education	27	41	37	21	48	40	10	54	46
College graduate	26	39	41	20	44	46	8	49	51
Post graduate education	17	50	36	14	52	40	5	56	44
Family income									
Under $15,000	11	58	23	19	59	28	11	68	32
$15,000–$29,999	23	45	35	20	53	36	9	60	40
$30,000–$49,999	27	41	38	21	48	40	10	54	46
Over $50,000	39	39	44	17	44	48	7	48	52
Over $75,000	18	36	48	16	41	51	7	44	56
Over $100,000	9	—	—	—	38	54	6	41	59
Region									
East	23	47	35	18	55	34	9	62	38
Midwest	26	42	37	21	48	41	10	54	46
South	30	41	43	16	46	46	7	50	50
West	20	43	34	23	48	40	8	54	46
Community size									
Population over 500,000	10	58	28	13	68	25	6	73	27
Population 50,000 to 500,000	21	50	33	16	50	39	8	56	44
Suburbs	39	41	39	21	47	42	8	53	47
Rural areas, towns	30	39	40	20	45	44	10	51	49

SOURCE: Voter News Service exit poll, reported in *New York Times*, 10 November 1996, 28.

An emphasis on short-term influences is underlined by the great stability of the vote in Clinton's two victories. Overall, the Democratic candidate added about 6 percent to his vote, from under 44 percent in 1992 to the even split of 1996. Leaving Perot aside, the shift toward Clinton from 1992 to 1996 was even less impressive, barely over 1 percent of the total two-party vote (53.5 percent in 1992, 54.7 percent in 1996). Most social groups paralleled the overall change in the vote.[4] Clinton did gain a plurality among the young, but lost some of his previous edge among seniors. He also benefited from both an increased vote and a stronger showing among union households.[5]

While most shifts were modest, some significant differences from the past may presage more long-lasting changes. Religion provides one notable indication of change. As in the past, Protestants were the relatively strongest Republicans and Jews the most reliable Democrats. But Catholics moved nine percentage points toward the Democrats, altering more recent loyalties, and fundamentalist Christians probably evidenced a smaller shift in this direction.[6]

Catholics had once been a mainstay of the Democratic Party, providing large majorities from the time of the New Deal through the election of John Kennedy in 1960. Their loyalties had been based on the economic programs of the Democratic Party, directed toward the urban working class, where Catholics were concentrated. Over time, however, these loyalties eroded. One cause was the social mobility of Catholics, who left their Democratic allegiances behind as they moved from factory gates to office suites. Probably more significant was the changing character of the Democratic Party. As the party placed less emphasis on economic and class issues, and more on matters of race, gender, and individual expression, it began to lose support among Catholics, who have always been relatively conservative on social issues such as personal morality, sexuality, and patriotism.

A vivid exemplar is Tim Carey, the descendant of Irish American domestics, gravediggers, waitresses, and butchers. Carey began abandoning his inherited Democratic loyalties when, as an army draftee, he faced a Vietnam protest.

> Tim remembered not the peaceable mass but the abusive and violent fringe, the ones who taunted him, the ones he clubbed, the ones who returned to college dormitories while he returned to Fort Bragg. He had not yet heard the phrase "liberal elite." For the first time, however, he understood the concept and recognized its face.[7]

More recently, fundamentalist Christians have become politically significant. Historically, fundamentalists have emphasized individual salvation and the rewards of the afterlife, rather than political mobilization for secular purposes. In the past two decades, however, a succession of conservative religious leaders have emphasized the politics of this world, culminating in the contributions of the Christian right to the Republicans' 1994 congressional landslide.[8] By adopting more conservative social attitudes on such questions as school uniforms, the death penalty, and homosexual marriage, Clinton may have enabled the Democrats to regain support among these religious groups, particularly Catholics. But their long-term loyalties remain uncertain.

Another change, among Hispanics, carries considerable import for the future. Clinton gained considerably among Latin Americans, increasing his vote by ten points, a partial explanation of the change among Catholics. A larger significance may be found in the size of the group, which expanded to 5 percent of the electorate between the two presidential elections. The Hispanic proportion of the electorate expanded because of the simplification of registration under the National Voter Registration (Motor-Voter) Act and because of the naturalization of immigrants, which reached historic highs in 1996.

The mobilization of this group came partially in reaction to Republican-sponsored initiatives such as the denial of welfare services even to legal immigrants, denial of public education to the children of illegal immigrants, an end to affirmative action, and a drive to establish English as the official language of the United States. The new Hispanic voters helped Clinton win Florida, Arizona, and California in 1996. Their long-term impact is likely to grow. With high birthrates and easy access across national borders, this group eventually will be the largest minority in the United States.[9] Numbers count in elections.

The most significant change in past voting patterns is the enormous "gender gap" evident in the presidential vote. Women and men took different political paths: women voted strongly for Clinton, but Dole won a bare plurality among men. Moreover, the sexes voted more distinctly in this election than ever in the past, with women giving Clinton 54 percent of their vote, 11 percent more than men. By comparison, the gender gap was but three points in 1992 and seven points in 1988.

Gender differences in the vote are real, not the result of other social influences. The gender gap remained stable among both blacks and whites, among all age groups and in suburbs, and across levels of education and in-

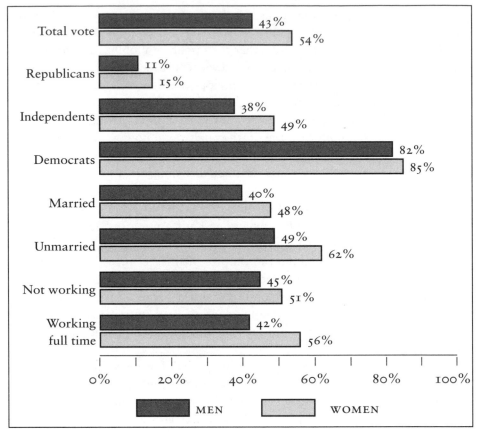

FIGURE 5.2
VARIATIONS IN THE GENDER GAP
(% VOTING FOR CLINTON)

come. As illustrated in figure 5.2, however, a more distinct sexual slant appears among two groups. Working women and unmarried women were particularly likely to vote for Clinton, and they were most different from their male counterparts. These women were most independent of men, and their vote reflected their personal autonomy. Yet Clinton won a distinctive vote even among married women, a change from his performance four years earlier.

"Women's issues," in a narrow sense, cannot explain the gender gap (see chapter 3). The 1996 campaign did not emphasize any matters unique to women, such as the defunct Equal Rights Amendment, while on another issue vital to women the candidates totally agreed on the need for more research on breast cancer. Abortion sharply differentiated the presidential candidates, but this issue, while obviously of particular relevance to women, divides the public on ideological, not sexual lines: men are as likely as women to take "pro-life" or "pro-choice" positions.

The electorate did see an important difference in the general stances of the parties. Democrats were perceived as caring far more about "the needs and problems of women" (by a 55 to 24 percent margin), and the Republicans were more narrowly seen as dealing better with "the needs and problems of men" (42 to 33 percent).[10] Generally, women were more likely to emphasize the protective aspects of government, men more likely to emphasize its restrictions. Consequently, half the women surveyed believed "government should do more to solve problems," while almost two-thirds of men believed "government is doing too many things better left to business and individuals."

The protective aspects of government framed the particular issues of the 1996 campaign: the economy, education, Medicare, Social Security, and health care. Matching gender stereotypes, men were more likely to emphasize foreign policy, taxes, and the deficit; women gave higher priority to Medicare and education. Men were more likely to focus on the candidates' general "view of government," women on whether or not the candidate "cares about people like you." These differences are grounded in real-world experiences. Women are more likely to be involved in their children's education or in the care of elderly parents or in their families' health. More aware of these problems, "women are more likely to feel that it's important to preserve the social safety net in this country."[11] Clinton's emphasis on these issues, and his perceived concern for their solution, brought him the unusual degree of support from women.

The Campaign and the Vote

In the heat of a presidential election, observers are likely to emphasize campaign effects and attribute the results to the clever strategies of the winners and the faults of the losers. Bill Clinton is now seen as a consummate campaigner. Bob Dole will bear the onus of the Republican loss for the rest of his life, denigrated even by his closest advisers as "Noble. But . . . his clock stopped in the late 1950s or early 1960s. He is not a man of this time."[12]

The reality of politics is less exciting. The outcome of a presidential election depends on longer-term forces, extending back at least over the four years of an administration, as well as over longer historical periods. Indeed, predictions made in June of the election year based on political science models are more accurate than those based on the election polls during most of the actual campaign.[13] One analyst, for example, safely ignored campaign events in closely predicting Clinton's percentage of the two-party vote, using only data on past elections and the current level of economic growth and inflation.[14]

In 1996 the campaign particularly lacked apparent significance. Although Clinton had appeared vulnerable after the Republicans won control of Congress,[15] he later bested the opposition in the budget showdown and governmental shutdown. As early as October 1995, more than a year before the election, Clinton held a lead over Dole of 48 to 35 percent. Little changed over the next year. The poll standings of the candidates in the campaign itself, as seen in figure 5.3, resembled the flat-line electrocardiograms of dead patients, reflecting none of the liveliness of an energetic contest.

Certainly the candidates tried to breathe life into their political bodies. Senator Dole defeated a fistful of active opponents to win the Republican nomination. At several points during the year, he attempted to create political drama. In a moving speech in June, he resigned from the Senate after

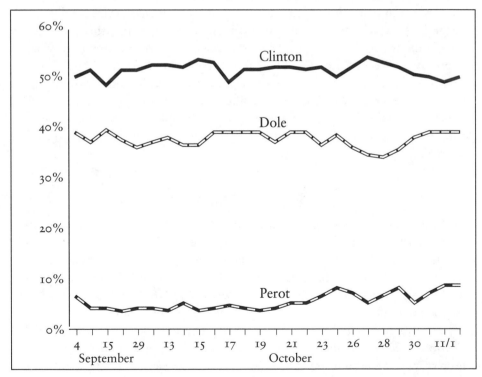

FIGURE 5.3
ABC TRACKING POLL RESULTS (1996)

thirty-five years in national office and a record ten years as his party's Senate leader. Before the Republican convention, he selected Jack Kemp, a former ideological opponent, as his running mate. Dole reversed a long-held skepticism about "supply-side economics" and advocated a 15 percent cut in income taxes and a halving of capital gains taxes. When this economic program failed to change the poll standings, Dole concentrated on the "character issue," a series of attacks on the alleged moral failures of the Clinton administration. Electoral strategy was continually revised, from an initial emphasis on the Midwest and South to a later effort to win the electoral prize of California, as well as a futile effort to persuade Ross Perot to withdraw from the contest. In the final days, the Republican candidate sought to demonstrate his vitality and commitment through ninety-six hours of nonstop campaigning. But nothing worked.

President Clinton, too, exercised his political muscles, moving purposefully toward the political center. Proclaiming in the State of the Union address that "the era of big government is over," he adopted the Republican goal of a balanced budget, signed a moderate welfare reform bill, and pointed to personal attitudes different from Democratic Party tradition, such as support of school prayer and the death penalty. Clinton also endorsed steps in keeping with more traditionalist sentiments, such as mandatory school uniforms, nonsmoking, opposition to homosexual marriage, and control of television pornography. He adeptly became "the most powerful representative of old fashioned liberal Republicanism in America" just at the time when "the liberal Republican tradition is so close to collapse in its party of origin."[16]

Further, Clinton seized credit for bipartisan accomplishments in Congress, such as a partial health-care reform, tighter controls on illegal immigration, and extension of the Safe Drinking Water Act. Like any incumbent president, he used the powers and aura of the White House to enhance his personal standing, including ceremonial bill signings and foreign policy initiatives, such as a bombing raid in Iraq or a peace effort among the nations of the Mideast.

Although the president moved to the center, he maintained significant differences from Senator Dole and the Republicans. As demonstrated in the 1995 winter budget showdown, Clinton continued the more traditional Democratic defense of active government. Throughout the year, he repeatedly emphasized government's role in Social Security, the health programs of Medicare and Medicaid, education, and protection of the environment, while touting such actions as guaranteed family leave for illness and child care, a rise in the minimum wage, increased federal spending on police, and gun control. Despite a reputation for inconstancy, the president consistently endorsed women's access to abortion, the continuation of most affirmative action efforts, and a focus on targeted, not general, tax reductions. The combined effect of these actions was to raise Clinton's popularity rating to the highest levels he had achieved since his brief inaugural honeymoon.

SOURCES OF THE VOTE: PARTY LOYALTY

Clinton and Dole ran the presidential race within the boundaries set by these previous actions and on a track constructed on other, often older foundations. The most important footing was the existing party loyalties of the voters. Although partisanship is of declining importance in electoral behavior, voters "continue to perceive candidates, issues, and elections in partisan terms and often vote accordingly."[17] For two generations, the Democrats have held a lead among voters identifying with one or another of the major parties. Despite considerable weakening of the hold of these loyalties, and despite some drift toward the Republicans, the Democrats entered the 1996 election with a small advantage, 36 to 33 percent, and they maintained that advantage in the actual vote.[18]

The effect of these party loyalties is seen in the 1996 vote. Clinton secured five of every six votes cast by self-identified Democrats. Dole was less successful, but still won support from four out of five Republicans. To a considerable extent, these partisan leanings explain the differing votes of men and women. Both sexes voted strongly along party lines, as seen earlier in figure 5.2. The decisive vote, as is typical, was among the Independents, who cast a plurality for Clinton and evidenced a sharp gender gap. In similar fashion, Clinton consolidated his base among self-identified liberals and expanded his support among moderates, regardless of party identification. While Clinton benefited from a public perception that he was more moderate than Dole,[19] partisanship affected the vote more than ideology.

Beyond identification, the Democrats had gained an advantage for the election in perceptions of the parties (see figure 5.4). Asked their views of the character of the parties, "regardless of how you usually vote," Americans thought better of the Democrats in general, as well as in their ability "to insure a strong economy," "to make sure the tax system is fair," and to help people "achieve the American dream," while also giving the Democrats better marks for understanding "the needs and problems of families" and having "better ideas for leading the country into the 21st century."[20]

The favorable attitude toward the Democrats may not last, to be sure. For the moment of the 1996 election, however, it marked both an immediate advantage and a reversal of past perceptions. In most recent years, Re-

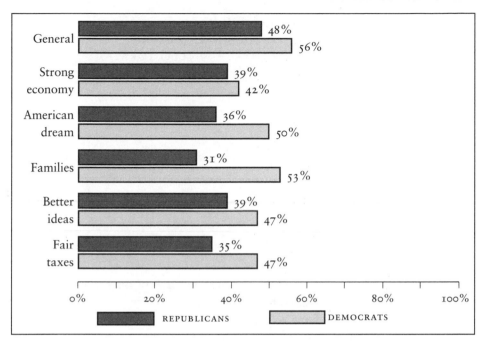

FIGURE 5.4

FAVORABLE PERCEPTIONS OF THE PARTIES, 1996

SOURCE: CBS News polls.

publicans have been considered better as managers of the economy and more likely to provide tax relief; Dole's tax plan attempted to build on these memories. Now, at least for a time, the Republican advantage has been lost. Another Republican loss came in foreign policy, an area of party strength for most of the Cold War.[21] With the end of open international conflict, this attributed ability of the party became irrelevant for the 1996 election.

Within the boundaries of party loyalty, there was considerable movement by voters, although the net effect of these changes was overall stability. Three of every ten ballots represented either a change from 1992 or the decisions of new voters (see table 5.3). Clinton held his vote much better than Dole kept the 1992 Bush base, and the president did slightly better among partisan defectors and new voters. It was enough to give him an increased margin of victory.

Ross Perot had threatened to diminish the effect of party loyalty for both Democrats and Republicans. In 1992 he had won nearly a fifth of the national vote, and that achievement underlay some pundits' prediction of a major change in American politics.[22] By 1996, however, Perot's own appeal

TABLE 5.3

DYNAMICS OF THE VOTE, 1992–96

(PERCENTAGES OF TOTAL 1996 ELECTORATE)

Clinton loyalist	37%
Republican loyalist	29
Perot loyalist	4
Bush to Clinton	5
Perot to Clinton	3
Clinton to Dole	4
Perot to Dole	5
Clinton/Dole to Perot	3
New voter for Clinton	5
New voter for Dole	3
New voter for Perot	1

SOURCE: Calculations by the author from exit poll data of Voter News Service.

had lessened considerably, and he lost more than half of his earlier vote under the label of his self-centered Reform Party.

In the intervening four years, the Texas businessman had revealed many personal faults: a lack of understanding of public policy, egotism verging on paranoia, and a reluctance or inability to build a broader political movement.[23] His claim of disinterested patriotism paled when he manipulated the nominating process of his new party to defeat a new claimant to its leadership, former Colorado Governor Richard Lamm. The claim virtually vanished as he held his considerable fortune out of politics and accepted federal money for his campaign. By election day, a majority of Americans regarded him unfavorably, three times the number of those who still held a positive opinion.[24]

Even in 1992 Perot had had no effect on the election outcome, since his support came equally from potential Clinton and Bush voters. In 1996 his impact was still smaller, although he may have hurt Dole more than Clinton because he presented another alternative for voters unhappy with the president.[25] Perot's four-year erosion certainly benefited the Republican candidate. Of those who remembered voting for Perot earlier, close to half changed to Dole, twice as many as defected to Clinton. Had he retained these votes, a stronger Perot would probably have shrunk Dole's vote. This pattern explains the senator's efforts to keep Perot out of the television debates and his futile plea for the Texan's withdrawal from the race.

While Perot himself may have a questionable political future, his candidacy may still carry important implications for the future. The Reform Party, despite its emaciated vote, will continue, having won a place on most state ballots and being assured of significant federal funding in the future. The bonds of traditional loyalty have obviously weakened, and as many as half of Americans vaguely support the emergence of a new political party.[26] Even if Perot and his party follow the patterns of American history and soon disappear, this underlying discontent can result in a different party system in the next century.

The Reform Party, and possibly other alternatives, will reappear in the next election, but there is no clear direction to these movements. Those disaffected from the existing parties "divide into two distinct and incompatible camps: the moderate middle and the radical center." The first group combines opposition to governmental programs with a liberal outlook on social issues such as abortion. The second group, conservative socially, favors populist governmental activity, such as protectionism. The prospect of a common party uniting these groups is as unlikely, Michael Lind suggests, as the staid budget balancer "Warren Rudman joining Pat Buchanan in summoning the country to 'religious war.' "[27]

SOURCES OF THE VOTE: LOOKING BACK AND LOOKING FORWARD

Beyond established loyalties, a more immediate influence on any election is the voters' retrospective judgment on the people and party currently in power.[28] Particularly when an incumbent such as Clinton is on the ballot, voters respond to the question famously put by Ronald Reagan, "Are you better off than you were four years ago?" Although Senator Dole dourly disagreed, the voters were satisfied that the Clinton administration, for all its faults, merited a second term.

This satisfaction was particularly evident in the most critical area, the economic record. Clinton persuasively took credit for a series of successes during his term: the creation of over 10 million new jobs, a steady 2.5 percent growth rate, unemployment at a seven-year low, inflation at a thirty-year nadir, and a reduction by two-thirds in the federal budget deficit. By the last weeks of the campaign, the voters shared his optimism, in contrast to their sour mood in the previous election. By a five-to-four margin, they thought the national economy was in a good, not bad, condition (compared to a one-to-five ratio in 1992). By more than three to two, voters also thought their personal economic situation was better, rather than worse, over the past four years (vs. a two-to-three ratio in 1992). The electorate's cheer was not a partisan distortion; Republicans joined Democrats and Independents in these upbeat assessments.[29] Clinton's vote, as can be seen in table 5.4, strongly reflected this economic enthusiasm. The effect of opti-

TABLE 5.4

ECONOMIC EFFECTS ON THE PRESIDENTIAL VOTE
(% VOTING FOR CLINTON)

	Change in personal finances in past four years			
	Better off	About the same	Worse off	Total
View of the national economy	(33%)	(45%)	(20%)	
Excellent (4%)	87	79	58	78
Good (51%)	73	61	50	62
Not so good (36%)	54	35	28	34
Poor (7%)	45	19	20	23
Total	66	46	27	

SOURCE: Calculations by the author from exit poll data of Voter News Service.

mism about the national economy was apparent even among the small numbers who felt personally dissatisfied.

Economic approval strongly affected Clinton's overall evaluation. On the eve of the election, the president won approval of the "way he is handling his job" from 56 percent of the electorate, virtually the same as both the approval of his economic performance and his ultimate proportion of the two-party vote.[30] Before the campaign, the voters' commendation of Clinton varied considerably, with disapprovals often more common than approvals. From June 1995, when the president began his move to the political center with the acceptance of a balanced budget, his positive rating rose steadily (see chapter 3).

Clinton's support depended not only on evaluations of the past record but also on voter preferences for the future. On virtually every issue in dispute between the major candidates, voters preferred Clinton over Dole. While abortion, for example, was hardly discussed, the voters favored Clinton's pro-choice position over Dole's pro-life stance. When asked to select among six issues, voters preferred Clinton on the three issues they considered of greatest significance: the economy, Medicare, and education. Dole did better on issues the voters considered less significant: taxes, the budget deficit, and welfare.[31] Even on these issues, Dole's position was regarded skeptically; most voters preferred reducing the deficit to cutting taxes, and only 30 percent believed he would carry through on his program of tax cuts.

SOURCES OF THE VOTE: THE CANDIDATES

Ultimately, the presidential election of 1996, like all others, came down to a choice of a man. The voters approved the Clinton record but gave no clear vote of confidence to the president himself. Voters continued to have questions about his personal and official conduct, including his involvement in the Whitewater resort development in Arkansas, possible adulterous relationships, the misuse of the powers of the White House to investigate political opponents, and questionable campaign contributions. Even as they decided to cast the ballots on his behalf, only a minority (46 percent) held a "favorable opinion" of him, while a majority of voters held the unflattering positions that Clinton was not honest and trustworthy and that he had "not told the truth" about matters under investigation. Even endowed with the majesty of the presidency, Clinton had not gained greatly over four years in the affections of his citizens.

But Clinton, if not well liked, was liked better than his opponent, who gained the favor of only 30 percent of the electorate. Dole had considerable merits—sponsorship of major legislation, an ability to achieve reasonable compromise, tolerance of diversity, a long-term perspective on national needs. Hiding these qualities, he devoted the latter part of his campaign to an advertisement of his own character and solipsistic narratives about his war wounds. But reciting military experiences half a century in the past —before most voters were born—only reminded voters of his age, viewed as a problem by a third of the electorate.

In 1996, the candidates ran very different campaigns; they argued but did not engage. Their different emphases were highlighted in the first television debate:[32]

DOLE: The best thing going for Bob Dole is that Bob Dole keeps his word. It's a question between trust and fear. . . . People will tell you who served with Bob Dole, agree or disagree, he kept his word. That's what this race is all about.

CLINTON: I'd like the American people to know that I have worked very hard to be on their side and to move this country forward. And we're better off than we were four years ago. But the most important thing is my plan for the twenty-first century is a better plan.

The language became more pointed in their second debate, but the contestants still avoided a direct confrontation:

CLINTON: I hope we can talk about what we're going to do in the future. No attack ever created a job or educated a child or helped a family make ends meet. No insult ever cleaned up a toxic waste dump or helped an elderly person.

DOLE: When it comes to public ethics, [the president] has a responsibility. And when you have thirty or some in your administration who have either left or [are] being investigated or in jail or whatever, you've got an ethical problem.

Outside the television studio as well, the candidates failed to conduct a true political debate. In table 5.5 we see the major topics presented each day of the campaign by the major candidates.[33] Clinton and Dole did cover a lot of ground, but few substantive topics received sustained attention. Moreover, aside from the economy, the candidates generally did not deal with the same topics. The electorate could not select a particular recipe for its political food; it could only choose among vague "specials of the day."

Dole's attacks on the president's character, however, did succeed in shaping some popular perceptions: voters did believe that the senator was notably more moral and honest than the president. But, to Dole's chagrin, it didn't matter enough. The electorate preferred political to personal virtues. With the former senator disguising his own governmental abilities, voters emphasized Clinton's attributed qualities: understanding the problems of average people, vision for the future, standing up for his beliefs. Dole won seven out of ten votes from those who decided on the basis of "personal character and values," but he was matched by Clinton's 70 percent among those more numerous voters who emphasized the candidates' "position on the issues."

Dole's effort to center the election on questions of "character" and "trust" was inherently flawed. A career politician, he was in no position to mobilize the country's anger toward Washington. He inconsistently attacked Clinton both as an ideological liberal and as a person without a coherent philosophy. Personal criticism of the president was restrained by Dole's own record, which also exemplified some of Clinton's presumed faults. Dole too had received campaign contributions from special-interest groups. He too had changed policy positions to win favor, as in his surrender on the Republicans' abortion plank and his sudden conversion to supply-side economics.

Ultimately, Dole could not make a convincing attack because of his own character, for he either lacked the passion or had too much honor to turn the presidential election into a direct assault. "I don't like to get into personal matters," Dole admitted in the first debate, and his running mate eschewed such attacks, declaring it would be "beneath Bob Dole to go after anyone personally." Before Dole did turn to a critique of Clinton, he openly discussed its electoral utility among reporters and even with campaign

TABLE 5.5

DAILY ISSUES OF THE CAMPAIGN

	Clinton	Dole
Foreign policy		
Mideast/Iraq	6	1
General/defense	3	2
Terrorism	2	
Particular issues		
Economy	7	8
Taxes/deficit	4	10
Crime/drugs/guns	5	5
Health	3	4
Medicare		2
Welfare	4	
Education	6	1
Environment	3	
Civil rights/immigration		3
Government	1	1
Family/women	1	
Morality, general		
Campaign finance	1	7
Moral values		3
Clinton/ethics		10
"The Future"/unity	6	
Politics		
Campaign/turnout	3	4
Debate/preparation	5	2
No activity	4	1
Total days	64	64

SOURCE: Calculated by the author from *New York Times*, 3 September–5 November 1996.

crowds. His criticism was openly tactical, an effort to win votes more than the expression of moral indignation.

When Dole did change course, he berated voters for their passivity. "Where's the outrage, wake up America!" he hectored. Voters took it badly: Dole was more widely seen as conducting a negative campaign, and his poll standings fell. Unlike the benevolent president, Dole was seen as spending more time attacking his opponent than explaining his positions, and he damaged his own reputation for honesty and integrity.[34] It was hardly convincing for Dole to assess his supposed indignation by tracking polls, or hardly wise for him to disparage the very people he was courting.

Neither Savanarola nor Prince Charming, Dole became only a scolding grandparent.

THE FINAL RESULTS

As Americans entered their voting booths, they ended a campaign that had created little interest but had provided sufficient information for a reasoned decision. They did not know everything about the candidates and their issue positions, but they knew enough.[35] Table 5.6 apportions the 1996 vote among six individual traits and seven issues. The table lists the traits and issues in the order of importance mentioned by voters and the division of the vote among each group. In the last columns, we calculate the contribution of each trait or issue to the final vote for Clinton, Bush, and Perot.[36]

Clinton's most attractive features to the electorate were his "vision of the future" and their belief that he was more "in touch with the 1990s" and that he "cares about people like you." Dole was vastly preferred on the personal characteristic of "honest and trustworthy," but this preference was insufficient to overcome the president's more programmatic appeals. Clinton also led decisively on the most important issues. (Perot showed no distinctive attractions of either traits or issues.) In short, Clinton had achieved both attention and agreement. He successfully both set the election agenda and convinced the electorate that he could better handle that agenda. He had to win.

The electoral verdict of 1996, however, conveys no clear message. The voters were not called on to decide between clear alternatives of philosophy or policy. Dole and Clinton sought the moderate center and gave little attention to their ideological purists, the Republican religious right or the Democratic liberal left. Their model voter was the "soccer mom," a woman too distracted by the demands of children, jobs, and suburbia to devote her flagging energy and limited time to politics. Rather than realistically consider the true issues facing the nation, they fantasized about a golden age, Dole evoking a nostalgic arcadia, Clinton summoning a futuristic utopia.

After this campaign without substance, Clinton's victory may have only limited meaning beyond the White House. As in most years, the election conveyed a mood more than a message. In the previous presidential election, the voters expressed hope for improvement, not endorsement of a liberal program. In the congressional upheaval of 1994, the voters' anger was directed against unproductive government, not in favor of a conservative counterrevolution.[37] In 1996 the electorate's mood was one of skepticism, neither hope nor anger. "Americans have become restive about the status quo, even though they also regard change as a suspicious thing."[38]

TABLE 5.6. SOURCES OF THE PRESIDENTIAL VOTE

	% mention	Percentage voting for			Contribution to vote for		
		Clinton	Dole	Perot	Clinton	Dole	Ferot
Trait							
Government view	20	41	46	10	9	10	2
Honest/trustworthy	20	8	84	7	2	19	2
Vision for future	16	77	13	9	14	2	2
Stand up for beliefs	13	42	40	16	6	5	2
In touch with 1990s	10	89	8	4	10	1	0
Cares about you	9	72	17	9	7	2	1
Totals					49	40	9
Issue							
Economy/jobs	21	61	27	10	16	7	3
Medicare	15	67	26	6	12	5	1
Education	12	78	16	4	11	2	1
Deficit	12	27	52	19	4	8	3
Taxes	11	19	73	7	3	10	1
Crime/drugs	7	40	50	8	3	4	1
Foreign policy	4	35	56	8	2	3	0
Totals					51	38	9

SOURCE: Calculated by the author from exit poll data of Voter News Service. See note 36.

The voters never became excited about the election of 1996. They expressed little interest in the campaign generally, and television audiences dwindled for all major events, including the nominating conventions, the presidential and vice-presidential debates, rallies, and even the ballot count on election night. Fewer than half of American adults came to the polls, the second-lowest turnout in American electoral history, despite the new simplicity of voter registration and record naturalization of immigrants.

When they did vote, Americans dispassionately returned most incumbents to office, in the Oval Office, the Senate, and the House (see chapter 6). They seemed to expect little from their new government. By the same two-thirds margin, voters doubted the fundamental premises of both campaigns: Clinton's promise to reduce the deficit while paying for new programs and Dole's vow to reduce the deficit while cutting taxes. "Gullibility has its off years," Alan Ehrenhalt rejoices, "and 1996 is one of them. Voters are disinclined to listen to easy answers from either party's candidate."[39]

In this sober frame of mind, majorities casting ballots for each candidate admitted that they voted for their man "with reservations," and only a minority of the nation found itself "excited" or optimistic" about a second Clinton term. In this lukewarm mood, voters were already thinking of other possibilities. In a hypothetical contest, Colin Powell defeated Clinton overwhelmingly, and even in the partisan heat of election day, Powell won the support of a quarter of the Democrats.

The president provided little basis for enthusiasm. Even on election eve, two-fifths of voters were unclear "what he wants to accomplish in the next four years" and consequently only about a fourth were fully behind this vague program.[40] The president himself must bear responsibility for this limited support. He never openly advocated the election of a Democratic Congress to promote his programs. Never asking for a specific mandate, it was inevitable that he would not receive one, regardless of his popular vote. At best, his programs were only incremental, such as tax deductions for college tuition. More commonly, they were trivial, such as mandated family leave for school conferences, or irrelevant to the federal government, such as teenage curfews. The Clinton bridge to the future was built on weak, shifting foundations.

The Political Future

Whatever its condition, the bridge still exists; it remains true that America will soon enter the twenty-first century. Evading the need for leadership, however, the candidates neglected major issues of the new era. At least three require attention.

1. The American dream of equality and achievement, which Tocqueville saw as the essence of the national experience, is threatened. In the past two decades, there has been no real increase (aside from inflation) in average personal income. Moreover, the gains from overall economic growth have widened class differences. In terms of what people own, the very rich doubled their share of wealth, bringing the nation "back to where it was in the late 1920s, before the introduction of progressive taxation."[41] While the most affluent Americans (the top 5 percent) have seen a real growth of 38 percent in their incomes since 1979, most Americans (the bottom 60 percent) have endured a decrease of 2.5 percent in their paychecks.[42]

As Labor Secretary Robert Reich put it, "The rising economic tide used to lift all boats. Now it's only lifting the yachts. Most Americans are treading water. Some are sinking." Appropriately voters remain cautious, even in today's good economic times. They misperceive the state of the economic realities, estimating both inflation and unemployment as four times greater than the reality.[43] They find it difficult to get a good job, fear that they may be laid off, and question whether the next generation will have a better life than their parents.[44]

2. The federal budget may soon collapse under the burden of entitlements for senior citizens. Social Security, Medicare, and Medicaid (which is used far more for elderly nursing than for the poor) already constitute nearly half of total federal expenditures. With the aging of baby boomers and the increase in life expectancy, these costs, along with interest on the national debt, will grow in only fifteen years to consume virtually *all* of the federal government's budget, "leaving a choice between deep cuts in defense and domestic spending or ruinously high taxes on working families."[45] As the elderly become a fourth of the electorate, with a clear self-interest, it will become ever more difficult to repair this imbalance in national commitments.

3. America's role in the world is inescapable but undefined. For over fifty years, the United States had a clear national mission, first the defeat of Nazism, then engagement with Soviet communism. With the end of the Cold War, the United States is the dominant military power in the world, but a power without any clear purpose for its massive armed strength. It has old friends but no meaningful enemies, general interests but no specific policies.

The 1996 campaign hardly touched on these issues, and the election therefore could not set a course for the new administration, much less the new century. To Republicans, class inequality was not even a problem, but only a benign result of individualist enterprise. To Clinton, if not to all Democrats, it was an inconvenience that should not disturb a centrist appeal.[46] Both presidential candidates, conscious of the political strength of the elderly, ignored or exploited the problem of senior entitlements, agreeing only to appoint a commission to take the issue out of politics. The basic issues of foreign policy were shunted aside by recourse to unspecified "national interests." A presidential election is the single greatest opportunity for national dialogue and democratic decision. The opportunity was sadly lost in 1996.

This election campaign also carries important implications for the future of American government. Whoever was elected president—Dole or Perot as much as Clinton—would occupy a diminished office. He might, like Clinton, be forced to remove himself from partisan leadership, "triangulating" the White House between congressional Democrats and Republicans. He could only follow the model of a patriotic but detached chief of state, as created by George Washington and prescribed in The Federalist: "to guard the community against the effects of faction, precipitancy, or of any impulse unfriendly to the public good."[47]

In keeping with this restrictive model, Clinton became less involved in controversial issues, newly emphasizing the less partisan area of foreign policy while appealing to consensual attitudes such as "family values" and school achievement. He adopted Republican programs, even changing previous positions on many issues, most prominently the balanced budget and welfare reform. He won reelection, but at the cost of the loss of policy initiative.

Clinton, like any contemporary chief executive, cannot rely on a strong political party to support his programs. He will face a Congress sharply divided ideologically, where partisans will cooperate only when necessary, even as they uncivilly compete for television audiences, financial contributions, and rhetorical triumphs. The Republican opposition, while tactically united, is riven between acolytes of puritanical morality and laissez-faire capitalists "dedicated to the worship of flat taxes and dead Hapsburgs."[48] Clinton's own Democratic Party is uncertain of its program, prepared neither to abandon its proud New Deal heritage nor to commit to a vague "New Democrat" alternative nor to build a new progressive coalition.[49]

Bill Clinton did not energize the power of the White House, but he does illustrate its contemporary limits. The presidency is already a diminished office because the end of the Cold War has removed a principal support of its power, the predominance of foreign and defense policy. The constraints on federal funds, created by the emphasis on budget balancing and the burden of middle-class entitlements, restrict the energy of the executive. Public opinion is distrustful of politicians, and most voters still would prefer a smaller government, even if it provides fewer services.

The candidates did little in 1996 to lessen these constraints and made no effort to enlist the voters in any ennobling public effort. Clinton's pieties on children, Dole's denunciation of drugs, and both candidates' condemnation of pornography provide no basis for substantial future advances. Who, then, will guide the republic?

Notes

1. On election night, Vice-President Gore included Thomas Jefferson, James Madison, and James Monroe as previous Democratic winners of consecutive terms. Although there is some lineage, these early presidents represented a different heritage and were titled Republicans. The modern Democratic Party began with Jackson. Grover Cleveland won two nonconsecutive terms.

2. On a state-by-state basis, the president won an average two-party vote of 53 percent; two-thirds (one standard deviation) were within a narrow range of 7.6 percent above or below this average. The mean vote for the three-party vote = 48 percent, the standard deviation = 6.9.

3. For the three-party vote in 1992 and 1996, the mean of shifts in the vote = 6.6, the standard deviation = 3.4. The correlation of 1996 and 1992 on a three-party basis = .87. The correlation of the three-party vote in 1996 with the four-election average of 1980–92 (using the three-party vote for 1992) = .85. The relevant Democratic percentage is the variable in all calculations. Because its extremely high value would distort the results, the District of Columbia is excluded in these calculations. For comparison, the correlation of 1988 and 1992 = .79 for the two-party vote, .65 for the three-party vote.

4. Data are derived from the national exit poll of Voter News Service, reported in the *New York Times,* 10 November 1996, 28, and through CNN on the World Wide Web site, www.allpolitics.com, 7 November 1996. All data not otherwise cited are from this poll.

5. Union households provided 23 percent of the total vote, an increase from 19 percent in 1992, while Clinton support rose from 55 percent to 59 percent. Together, these changes meant that Clinton received about 2 million more votes in 1996 from union families.

6. The change among fundamentalists is less certain because of changes in question wording. Clinton won 23 percent in 1992 among "white born-again Christians," and 26 percent in 1996 among self-identified white members of "the

conservative Christian political movement, also known as the religious right." In both years, the identified group was 17 percent of the electorate.

7. Samuel Freedman, *The Inheritance* (New York: Simon and Schuster, 1996), 322.

8. See Mark J. Rozell and Clyde Wilcox, *God at the Grass Roots* (Lanham, Md.: Rowman & Littlefield, 1995).

9. R. Drummond Ayres, "The Expanding Hispanic Vote Shakes Republican Strongholds," *New York Times,* 10 November 1996, 1. See also David M. Kennedy, "Can We Still Afford to Be a Nation of Immigrants?" *Atlantic Monthly* 278 (November 1996): 46–68.

10. CBS News poll, 12–13 August 1996. Interestingly, this poll was conducted in the middle of the Republican convention, when the party was making a concerted effort to demonstrate its concern for women.

11. Susan Carroll, "The '96 Vote and the Gender Gap," ABC News *Nightline,* 21 October 1996. On women's vote generally, see Susan Carroll, "Women's Autonomy and the Gender Gap," in *Politics of the Gender Gap,* ed. Carol Mueller (Beverly Hills, Calif.: Sage, 1988), 236–57.

12. Don Sipple, dismissed as Dole's communications director, quoted by Jonathan Alter, " 'A Man Not of This Time,' " *Newsweek,* www.politicsnow.com, 4 November 1996. Campaign manager Scott Reed made similar preelection criticisms to Michael Kelly, "Ire in the Belly," *New Yorker,* 11 November 1996, 59–62.

13. Andrew Gelman and Gary King, "Party Competition and Media Messages in U.S. Presidential Elections," in *The Parties Respond,* 2d ed., ed. Sandy Maisel (Boulder, Colo.: Westview Press, 1994), 255–95.

14. Helmut Norpoth, "Of Time and Candidates: A Forecast for 1996," special issue, *American Politics Quarterly* 24 (October 1996): 443–67. Without inclusion of the primary elections as a variable, this model predicted a Clinton vote of 53.1 percent; adding this variable increased the predicted Clinton vote to 57.1 percent.

15. Dole led Clinton in a March 1995 poll, when less than a fourth "believes that Clinton deserves to be reelected." Richard Morin, "Like It or Not, the Race for '96 Is On," *Washington Post National Weekly,* 6–12 March 1996, 37.

16. E.J. Dionne Jr., "Clinton Swipes the GOP's Lyrics," *Washington Post National Weekly,* 29 July–4 August 1996, 22.

17. Paul A. Beck, *Party Politics in America,* 8th ed. (New York: Longman, 1997), 167.

18. "Partisan Instability in the 1996 Campaign," *Public Perspective* 7 (October/November 1996): 53. The data, however, show considerable variability with a different question wording and over short periods of time. In the actual vote, 39 percent identified as Democrats, 35 percent as Republicans.

19. Almost as many voters considered Clinton a moderate (44 percent) as characterized him as liberal (37 percent), and Independents were equally split. Dole was more sharply defined as a conservative (58 percent) rather than a mod-

erate (23 percent), and Independents used the same descriptions (CBS News/*New York Times* poll, 10–13 October 1996).

20. The data are from the CBS News/*New York Times* poll of 2–4 September 1996, except for the figures on "fair taxes," derived from a poll of 12–14 August.

21. See Byron Shafer, "The Notion of an Electoral Order," in *The End of Realignment?* (Madison: University of Wisconsin Press, 1991), chap. 3.

22. For example, see Kevin Phillips, "The Champagne's Gone Flat," *Washington Post National Weekly,* 14–20 August 1995, 23; and Michael Kelly, "Uninvited Guests," *New Yorker,* 11 March 1996, 58–60.

23. The deficiencies of the Perot candidacy in 1992 are illuminated by James Ceaser and Andrew Busch, *Upside Down and Inside Out* (Lanham, Md.: Rowman & Littlefield, 1993), chap. 4.

24. CBS News/*New York Times* poll, 4 November 1996.

25. Equal proportions (30 percent) of Perot voters said they would vote for Clinton or Dole in a two-man race. The remainder said they would not vote in this hypothetical situation.

26. Times Mirror (now Pew Research) Center for the People & the Press, *New York Times,* 21 September 1994, A21. The diminished impact of partisanship on the vote is analyzed in "Unanchored Voters," *Public Perspective* 7 (October/November 1996): 47–54.

27. Michael Lind, "The Radical Center or the Moderate Middle?" *New York Times Magazine,* 3 December 1995, 72.

28. For the definitive theoretical explanation, see Morris Fiorina, *Retrospective Voting in American National Elections* (New Haven: Yale University Press, 1981).

29. Preelection polls showed even greater optimism, a 3–1 favorable assessment of the national economy (see CBS News/*New York Times* poll, 10–13 October 1996). Changes in question wording may explain the different assessments. The 1992 data, also originally from CBS News polls, are presented in Gerald Pomper, ed., *The Election of 1992* (Chatham, N.J.: Chatham House, 1993), 147.

30. Kathleen Frankovic, "The Final Weekend" (CBS News/*New York Times* poll, 3 November 1996).

31. Gary Langer, "Clinton Keeps Winning the Battleground Issues," ABC News poll, 21 October 1996. CBS News found a similar ranking of issues in " 'Where I Stand': CBS News Issues Survey," CBS News poll, 17 October 1996.

32. Transcripts of the debates may be found at www.allpolitics.com.

33. The topics are the leading item in the published coverage of each candidate in the *New York Times,* from the beginning of the formal campaign on Labor Day, 3 September, to the day of the election.

34. CBS News/*New York Times* poll, 3 November 1996.

35. On the process of voter decision, see Samuel Popkin, *The Reasoning Voter* (Chicago: University of Chicago Press, 1991).

36. The calculation for the last columns is a simple multiplication of the per-

centage of all responses citing the specific trait or issue by the percentage in that group voting for a particular candidate. Since all respondents did not answer these questions, the resulting figures are then normalized on a base of 100. For example, 20 percent cited "his view of government" as the most important individual trait, 41 percent of this group voted for Clinton, and all responses summed to 88 percent. The contribution to Clinton vote = $.20 \times .41 / .88 = .09$.

37. Soon after the "revolutionary" Congress convened, public opposition to its program was evident in the CBS News/*New York Times* poll reported in the *New York Times,* 28 February 1995, A1.

38. Tony Snow, "What Did It All Mean?" www.intellectualcapital.com, 8 November 1996, 1.

39. "The Voters Sober Up," *New York Times,* 20 October 1996, E15.

40. CBS News/*New York Times* poll, 3 November 1996.

41. Lester Thurow, "Why Their World Might Crumble," *New York Times Magazine,* 19 November 1995, 78.

42. Gary Langer, "For the Roots of Economic Anxiety Look at Paychecks, not Pink Slips" (ABC News poll, April 1996).

43. "Economic Anxieties," *Washington Post National Weekly,* 4–10 November 1996, 6.

44. CBS News/*New York Times* poll, 10–13 October 1996. The percentages expressing these attitudes are, respectively, 71 percent, 56 percent, and 46 percent.

45. David Broder, "Is the Party Over?" *Washington Post National Weekly,* 19–25 August 1996, 31f.

46. See Ruy Teixeira, "The Democrats' Losing Strategy," *Newsday,* 25 August 1996, A41.

47. *The Federalist,* No. 73 (New York: Modern Library, 1941), 477.

48. Kevin Phillips, "Can Bob Dole Pull a Truman?" *Washington Post National Weekly,* 27 May–2 June 1996, 21.

49. E.J. Dionne Jr. argues persuasively for this alternative in *They Only Look Dead* (New York: Simon and Schuster, 1996). William Mayer describes the difficulty of achieving party unity in *The Divided Democrats* (Boulder, Colo.: Westview Press, 1996).

6

The Congressional Elections

MARJORIE RANDON HERSHEY

> We are born to do benefits: and what better or properer can
> we call our own than the riches of our friends? O, what a
> precious comfort 'tis to have so many, like brothers, com-
> manding one another's fortunes!
>
> — *Timon of Athens* (I, i)

The 1994 congressional election produced such dramatic change that reporters reached into the vocabulary of natural disasters to describe it:
"avalanche," "tidal wave," "earthquake," "landslide." On that election day,
Republicans gained a net of fifty-two seats in the U.S. House of Representatives and seven in the Senate. It was the first time the Republican Party had
controlled both branches of the national legislature since the Congress
elected in 1952. The average American in 1994 had never lived under Republican congressional control. Only one House Republican elected in 1994
could claim to have served in the House under Republican leadership—and
he was a teenage page at the time.

Democrats, long accustomed to their status as masters of the House,
were stunned by the breadth of their defeat. The congressional Republicans
did not lose a single incumbent who ran for reelection. Republican House
candidates got 5.5 million more votes in 1994 than in the midterm election
in 1990. Even Democratic Speaker of the House Thomas S. Foley was defeated—the first Speaker denied reelection in almost a century and a half.

It was true that the actual voting returns showed something less than a
landslide. The Republican share of the national congressional vote increased from 46 percent in 1992 to 52 percent—a majority, but not by
much. Almost two-thirds of the new Republican House members (43 of the

73 elected in November) had won their seats by less than 55 percent of the vote.

Nevertheless, the gavel had been passed, and journalists as well as political scientists were eager to explain why.[1] Many saw it as a conservative rejection of Bill Clinton and his liberal stances on health care, gays in the military, and other initiatives. Others argued that it was a repudiation of big government in general, which had been symbolized for decades by the Democratic congressional majority. "Angry white males," upset about such issues as affirmative action, high taxes, and illegal immigrants, figured prominently in some analyses. Still others saw a more lasting shift in the voting public toward conservatism and the Republican Party.[2]

The explanations raised questions about the long-term meaning of the results. Would the Republicans be able to consolidate their hold on Congress in the 1996 elections, or was 1994 just a quick sneeze by a voting public temporarily irritated, but addicted to the tangible benefits that Democratic legislatures provided? How fast would campaign money move to the Republican side once Republicans were in control of Congress, and how would that affect the 1996 election results? In the near term, how would the Republican majority interpret the reasons for its victory, and thus how substantial would be the changes it attempted in public policy? The answers begin with the 1994 congressional campaign.

The 1994 Campaign: Not All Politics Is Local

The dictum that "all politics is local" has been the eleventh commandment in congressional races. These contests, especially for House seats, have traditionally been fought as local elections writ large. Typically, an incumbent emphasizes a record of service to the district and individual constituents and at the same time criticizes that distant institution called "Congress" whose members inexplicably waste so much public money.[3] Democrats, long the party of government, won House majorities for two generations under these conditions (see figure 6.1).

Newt Gingrich set out to change that pattern. In his quick climb through the House Republican leadership to the position of minority whip, Gingrich sought to alter the political environment and set the stage for long-term Republican dominance of Capitol Hill. He found his opportunity in 1994. Gingrich was convinced that the conservative Republican philosophy resonated better with the public mood than did the Democratic philosophy. If the party's House campaigns could be clearly focused on a series of popular national Republican themes as opposed to local concerns, Ging-

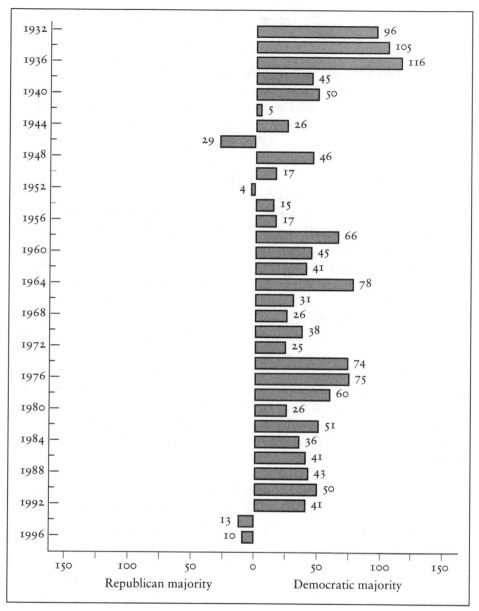

FIGURE 6.1

PARTY MAJORITIES IN THE HOUSE OF REPRESENTATIVES,

1932–96

SOURCE: Calculated from Norman J. Ornstein, Thomas E. Mann, and Michael J. Malbin, *Vital Statistics on Congress 1995–1996* (Washington, D.C.: CQ Press, 1996), 41–42.
NOTE: Numbers reflect the immediate election results.

rich believed, then the Democrats would no longer be able to dominate congressional elections.

Working with pollsters, Gingrich and Representative Dick Armey (R-Tex.) drew up a list of ten broad pledges, each ostensibly supported by at least 60 percent of the public. They termed this the Republicans' Contract with America. Its centerpiece was a promise to balance the federal budget within seven years; the Contract also included provisions on congressional term limits, tax cuts, property rights, and other presumably popular measures. On a September day in 1994, the Contract was signed by more than 350 Republican House challengers and incumbents. They included almost all the Republicans who won election to the House six weeks later.

Did the Contract with America, then, produce the Republican sweep? It was a tempting conclusion; the Contract was frequently mentioned among political activists and in the media. But some data suggested caution; both pre- and postelection polling in 1994 found that the great majority of voters, even Republican supporters, had not heard of it.[4] In a CBS/*New York Times* preelection survey, only 7 percent of respondents said that the Contract would make them more likely to vote Republican for Congress, 5 percent said it would make them *less* likely to do so, and another 71 percent hadn't heard of the Contract at all.[5]

These poll findings may not be a fair measure of the Contract's real influence. The publicity surrounding it may have communicated Republican themes effectively even if voters did not remember the document itself. Regardless of its real impact, a lot of House Republicans came to Washington in 1995 convinced of the Contract's electoral potency and prepared to write it into law.

THE REPUBLICAN ASCENT INTO LEADERSHIP

That, as it turned out, was harder than it looked. The new majority was determined to leave its mark; there had been a strong ideological tone to many of the House Republican campaigns. But their leaders were inexperienced in organizing and running Congress. Forty years of exile in the political wilderness is not optimal training for a party suddenly thrust into national leadership. At the same time, Republican House leaders had both internal and external challenges. The external problems would prove to be the Senate and the president; internally, it was the large and obstreperous freshman class.

In some ways, the new Republican House members were the caboose that drove the train. The seventy-three Republican freshmen elected in 1994 were more inclined toward far-reaching change, more hard-line and intransigent, than were most of those with greater seniority. One observer suggested, "They see themselves as the conscience of the Republican conference, the guardians of [the 1994] historic election results. And to the dismay of veteran lawmakers and House leaders, the freshmen have proved willing to block compromise and upend protocol to achieve their ends. With evangelical intensity, the newcomers believe they must change government before it changes them."[6] Freshman "class" vice-president Mark E. Souder (R-Ind.) was more concise: "We are not going to be housebroken, period."[7]

It wasn't that the freshmen's views differed dramatically from those of other House Republicans. The two congressional parties had become more internally homogeneous, and more distinct from one another, as the result of elections during the 1980s, and especially in 1992 and 1994. It was disproportionately the more moderate Democrats who lost or retired in 1994 and the more conservative Republicans who won.[8] But the Republican freshmen became more of a force within Congress than is usually the case, not just because they were cohesively conservative but because they were numerous, and unwilling to compromise. Together with the forty-four Republican freshmen elected in 1992, they constituted more than half of all House Republicans.

That permitted them to set their own agenda, independent of the Republican leadership. For example, a large number of the freshmen had emphasized campaign finance and lobbying reform in their 1994 campaigns. Republican House leaders had no incentive to act on such reform; having finally become the majority party in Congress, Republicans were the grateful recipients of increasing quantities of political money. So it was the freshmen who were later pivotal in the passage of a gift ban and lobbying regulations in the fall of 1995. It was the freshmen, too, who tried to hold their leadership to the demand for a balanced budget in seven years. Speaker Gingrich soon began to look like someone trying to walk a Great Dane: "Gingrich has been able to harness [the freshmen] with varying degrees of success, and it has sometimes been difficult to tell who is leading whom."[9]

Generally, however, the Republican freshmen were steadfast allies of their party leadership, especially on issues related to the Contract with America. Many felt they owed their election to Newt Gingrich's fund raising and his strategy of nationalizing the Republican House campaign. And their intransigence enabled House leaders to use them as the business end of a "good cop, bad cop" routine through which House leaders warned Republican moderates and other recalcitrants: if you think the option we're pushing is bad, you should see what the freshmen would prefer.

The situation was quite different in the Senate. The eleven Republican

Senate freshmen—there were no freshman Democrats— found their side of the Capitol harder to sway. Their majority was slim: fifty-two votes (fifty-four by the end of 1995), far short of the sixty needed to stop a Democratic filibuster. Republican House leaders, then, found a formidable challenge awaiting them when House-passed bills had to meet with Senate approval.

REPUBLICAN INITIATIVES, DEMOCRATIC DESPERATION

Senate approval was not needed, however, for changes in the way the House worked. One of the first tasks chosen by the new Republican House majority was to reform the institution they had captured. Several reforms shifted power to the Speaker of the House, often by chipping away at committee and subcommittee independence. Committee chairs were limited to six-year terms. Three committees—those without a likely Republican constituency—were eliminated, as were twenty-five subcommittees. Remaining committees were renamed and restructured. Committee staffs were cut—a blow felt primarily by Democrats, who had to downsize even more as the new minority. And as the Contract promised, Congress agreed to apply a variety of workplace and other laws to itself as well as to the larger society.

Passage of these reforms and other early votes made the House Republicans look like a well-oiled machine. Party unity, which had not been ever-present under Democratic rule, came with a vengeance in the early days of the 104th Congress. On ten of the major House bills carrying provisions of the Contract with America, on which there were 2,300 possible Republican votes, only fourteen were cast opposing the Republican leadership's position.[10] House Republicans cast unanimous votes on more than half of the first 139 roll-call votes taken in 1995; Republicans in the Senate were unanimous on almost three-quarters of their first 73 roll-call votes.[11] With that record of party loyalty, the House not only voted on all ten major planks of the Contract within the first hundred days of the session as promised, but passed nine of them (all but the constitutional amendment to limit congressional terms).

The Republican united front triggered more unified behavior among House Democrats as well. The conservatism of the Republican agenda was so pronounced that it led moderate and conservative Democrats to close ranks with their party. "Congressional Democrats, whose distinguishing trait used to be their propensity to battle one another, recoiled almost in unison from the House Republican agenda."[12] In short, congressional activity and partisanship climbed hand in hand.

The early Republican successes strained the chastened Democrats to their limit. Coping with minority status was a difficult adjustment for many

Democrats—and for some, an impossible one. Voting machines had barely cooled when Democratic Senator Richard C. Shelby of Alabama switched parties, increasing the Republican majority in the Senate by one. He was joined in 1995 by a less predictable colleague: Senator Ben Nighthorse Campbell of Colorado. In the House, five southern Democrats crossed the aisle to become Republicans during 1995.[13]

The frustration of many congressional Democrats peaked during the 1995 budget fight. House and Senate Democrats had concentrated on attacking the Republicans' push for a balanced federal budget, rather than on offering a Democratic alternative. But President Bill Clinton, in a move unexpected by many in his party, chose to sign on to the idea of a balanced budget and promote his own version. Many Democrats felt that Clinton's effort to get back to the safety of moderate ground had left them out on a limb.

POLITICAL MONEY MOVES TO THE REPUBLICANS

Moreover, the newly disempowered Democrats quickly saw an important source of campaign money slip away. Through the 1994 elections, most special-interest money in the form of political action committee (PAC) contributions, even those from business and trade association PACs, had gone to incumbents, most of whom were Democrats. The tendency became more pronounced from 1978 to 1994.[14] Philosophically, most business and trade association PACs undoubtedly preferred Republican representatives. But they needed access to likely winners, and given the reelection rate of incumbents in the House and Senate (most of whom were Democrats), most of the PAC money had gone to Democratic incumbents.

What happens when these two impulses—maintaining access to a winner and helping elect a representative who is ideologically compatible—coincide? Republicans began to get the majority of PAC money. The trend was encouraged by warnings from Republican congressional leaders that PACs that did not acknowledge the new majority should expect two very chilly years in Washington. PAC contributions to Republicans increased substantially, while Democrats got less (see chapter 4). By June 1996 the Center for Responsive Politics found that Republican candidates were pulling in $3 in PAC money for every $1 received by Democrats.[15]

The PAC money, as well as other funding sources, was actively pursued by Republican freshmen. Many had been elected in swing or Democratic-leaning districts and knew that they would have to work hard for reelection. Raising money, and raising it early, became a top priority. By late 1996, the freshmen were raising almost as much of their campaign money from PACs and out-of-state donors as were their more senior colleagues. As the president of Common Cause put it, "They came to Washington to shake it up and they stayed to shake it down."[16]

The strategy paid quick returns. By raising campaign funds early, several Republican freshmen were able to keep potentially strong opponents from deciding to run, in both the primary and the general election. In Nevada, for example, freshman Republican John Ensign raised $1.3 million between January 1995 and June 1996—a formidable sum. "That's intimidating, certainly, facing that much money," said the state Senate's minority leader, explaining why she declined to run. The eventual Democratic nominee came out of the primary with less than a tenth of the money the incumbent had raised. " 'It's one of the reasons we did it and did it early,' Ensign said. 'You want to scare as many opponents as you can out of the race.' "[17]

THE PARTIES' FORTUNES CHANGE

To Gingrich, the Republican ascendancy must have seemed too good to be true. In fact, it was. The juggernaut began to slow in the summer of 1995. Once the central Contract votes were over, disagreements began to surface among House Republicans on other issues, particularly between the twenty to thirty moderates and their more conservative brethren. During that summer, for instance, the House Republican leadership used the unusual method of attaching several policy riders to appropriations bills in an attempt to roll back or gut environmental laws. These efforts were pushed heavily by Republican freshmen, but a group of moderate Republicans broke with their party's leadership and voted with the Democrats to protect the regulations, sensing that their party's public image was in jeopardy.

Government Shutdown.—As the year wore on, the harsh partisan conflicts took a serious toll on the legislative process. The new fiscal year began on 1 October 1995, before Congress had succeeded in passing its budget. Twice, when President Clinton refused to accept the Republican balanced-budget plan, the Republican majority countered by refusing to pass stopgap spending bills that would have kept government agencies open. The result was two partial government shutdowns in which several hundred thousand federal workers were furloughed, and even more worked without pay. The second shutdown lasted twenty-one days, the longest in U.S. history. The 1995 budget process did not end until late April 1996.

Although Republicans had expected the public to blame Clinton for the shutdown, it was the president who was able to get his definition of the situation accepted. He contended that the Republicans were using the budget to cut programs such as Medicare and education and had forced the shutdowns to blackmail Clinton into accepting the cuts. The congressional

Republicans appeared, by turns, heartless and reckless. Media coverage showed popular tourist attractions closed and told of federal workers trying to feed their families without being paid. In his 1996 State of the Union address, Clinton introduced a courageous government worker from Oklahoma City who had helped in the rescue effort after the April 1995 bombing of a federal building—and had then lost his salary because of the government shutdown. By the time the second shutdown ended, Clinton, who had seemed stunned and silenced during much of 1995, was again in charge of his administration.

Newt Gingrich, Lightning Rod. —In particular, the negative fallout from the new majority's missteps landed on its leader, Speaker Gingrich. In the wake of the 1994 elections, the media had portrayed him as a larger-than-life figure. Reporters paid homage to his vision and power. *Time* magazine named him "Man of the Year" for 1995, explaining, "Leaders make things possible. Exceptional leaders make them inevitable. Newt Gingrich belongs in the category of the exceptional.... Gingrich has changed the center of gravity."[18] Gingrich himself, managing to put modesty aside, promised to " 'shift the entire planet'—and then added: 'and I'm doing it.' "[19]

Gingrich, however, proved to be his own undoing. His verbal indiscipline made him seem less than engaging, for example, complaining that he had been snubbed by the president on *Air Force One* on the way home from Israeli Prime Minister Yitzhak Rabin's funeral and threatening to take his revenge in talks to end the government shutdown. His push for sweeping policy change, most notably in attempting to cut the rate of growth in Medicare, gave Clinton an opening to mischaracterize the Republicans' goal as cutting benefits for older people. Gingrich's personal history provided additional fuel for his detractors, including tales of ruthlessness related to his divorce. He had made himself a lightning rod, and the rain came.

These problems left their mark on public opinion in short order, and especially among women. As figure 6.2 shows, the initial uptick in public approval of Congress at the time of the 1994 election and in the early months of 1995 did not survive the remainder of the year. Throughout this time, women's reactions were consistently more negative than men's. The programs Congress targeted for cuts were those of particular concern to women: education, environmental protection, and social services for the young and the old.[20]

But the gender gap in approval of Congress was minor compared to the gap between men's and women's opinions of Newt Gingrich. Women's reactions to Gingrich (see figure 6.3) were highly negative and dramatically different from men's. By 1996, Gingrich had become one of the most dis-

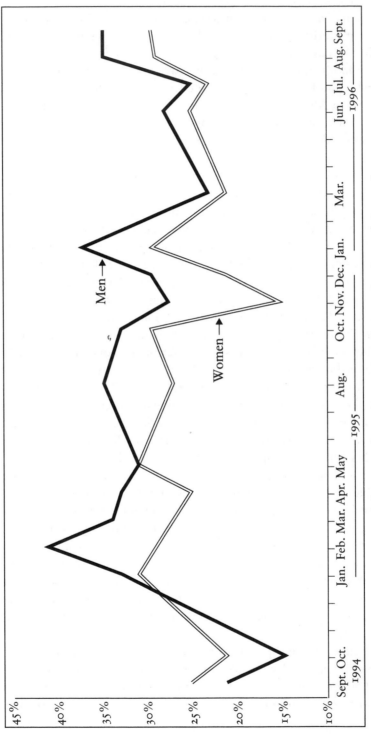

FIGURE 6.2. APPROVAL OF CONGRESS BY GENDER, 1994–96

SOURCE: CBS News/*New York Times* monthly polls. The question: "Do you approve or disapprove of the way Congress is handling its job?" Lines indicate the perecentage of men and women who "approve."

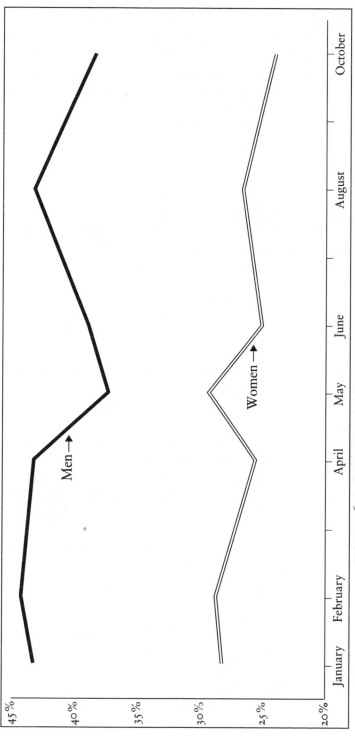

FIGURE 6.3. APPROVAL OF NEWT GINGRICH BY GENDER, 1995

SOURCE: CBS News/*New York Times* monthly polls. The question: "Is your opinion of Newt Gingrich favorable, not favorable, undecided, or haven't you heard enough about Newt Gingrich yet to have an opinion?" (Percentage favorable, after "undecideds" were given a second chance to express an opinion.)

liked public figures in the nation. Because he had made himself a prominent symbol of the Republican majority, his low rating among women contributed to a gender gap that appeared in a number of House and Senate races.

The boldness of the conservative Republican agenda, regarded by Gingrich as his party's greatest strength, had been effectively reinterpreted by Democrats as extremism. Indeed, some of the Republican initiatives —cutting taxes for the wealthy while slowing the rate of increase in supports for senior citizens—could have been scripted by the Democrats to play into traditional public concerns about Republicans as the party of privilege. As Representative Jim Chapman put it, "the Republicans so dramatically overreached, it would have been almost impossible for Democrats not to take advantage of that and regain some ground."[21]

Did the Republican Majority Make a Difference?—By the end of their first year of congressional control, Republicans had precious little to show for their revolutionary zeal. Republicans in the Senate slowed the pace and cooled the temperature of much of the legislation pushed through the House by their fellow partisans. For instance, although House Republicans passed a constitutional amendment in January 1995 requiring a balanced federal budget, the Senate narrowly failed to concur a month later. Most of the other changes promised by the House Republican majority—including tax cuts and property rights legislation—were left on the cutting-room floor because of conflicts with the Senate or the president.

The 104th Congress saved itself from a "do nothing" label in its waning days. After the negative public reaction to the government shutdowns, congressional Republicans moved reluctantly toward compromise, led by the small group of moderates. Substantial achievements were put together in a short time, by congressional standards. Legislation was passed to raise the minimum wage, make health insurance more portable from job to job, amend safe drinking water rules, and, most notably, greatly change the welfare system to eliminate the New Deal guarantee of a minimum level of federal support for poor parents and children. These achievements came at a cost to the Republicans; to ward off another government shutdown, they had to restore billions in federal spending that the Republican leadership had hoped to cut.

Even in the light of so many disappointments, the Republican majority left a substantial imprint on American politics. Most important, it set the political agenda for most of the 104th Congress—no mean feat, given the many advantages presidents have in directing congressional attention. Republicans did force substantial cuts in domestic programs: about 9 percent from 1995 to 1996.[22] Further, some federal agencies scaled down their own activities, in order to ward off the congressional budget ax. The Republican majority had clearly changed the terms of congressional debate. The question was whether most voters liked the change.

THE SETTING OF THE CAMPAIGN

In short, both parties had experienced a dizzying ride in public opinion since the start of 1995. Because the congressional Democrats had come out of the 1994 election looking like roadkill, dozens of Democratic incumbents chose to retire rather than face the butchery they anticipated in the 1996 elections. They were joined by several Republicans. In all, thirteen senators retired voluntarily—the most since 1896. One involuntary retirement occurred as well when the appointed replacement for Majority Leader Robert Dole lost her race for renomination. There were fifty voluntary retirements from the House,[23] two members defeated for renomination, and one death.

A large number of retirements has been characteristic of congressional elections in the 1990s, though markedly different from the pattern that had existed in the previous four decades. In the House, forty-eight incumbents had retired in time for the 1994 election, and sixty-five in 1992, in contrast to an average of only thirty-two from 1946 to 1990. Nine senators had retired in 1994 and seven in 1992, compared with an average of five from 1946 to 1990. And although Democrats and Republicans had retired at equal rates between 1946 and 1990 (an average of sixteen from each party per election), almost two-thirds of the retirees in 1992 and 1994 were Democrats, as were about 60 percent in 1996. For some, the decision reflected distaste for the harsh realities of minority status in Congress. For others, it showed frustration with bitter partisan divisions and incivility in an institution once known for elaborate restraint.[24]

There might have been fewer Democratic retirements if the retirees' decisions could have been delayed until the fall of 1996. By that time, the Democrats' agony seemed to be at an end. With a Democratic president all but assured of reelection, Democrats began to speak openly about a possibility that only a year earlier would have sounded like whistling past the graveyard: regaining control of Capitol Hill.

The Fate of the Freshmen. —As Democratic representatives climbed out of the abyss, concern increased among Republicans. How many of the Republican freshmen would survive? Freshmen might be expected to be especially vulnerable to defeat. They are not as experienced in running successful campaigns or in managing effective constituent relations as are more senior members. Some have probably been elected as the result of unusual circumstances.

But in fact, since the 1970s, House freshmen have become more skilled at using the resources of office to improve their chances of reelection. The result has been called "sophomore surge"—the tendency for members of Congress to increase their margin of victory between their first and second elections.[25] From 1980 to 1992, freshmen were less likely to be defeated for reelection than were House members who had served for at least ten years.[26] Even in the Republican sweep of 1994, most of the freshman Democratic House members who sought reelection survived.

Incumbents at all levels of seniority still hold most of the cards in congressional races, relative to their challengers.[27] Adding to the incumbents' advantage in 1996, the media spotlight did not shine on congressional races. Challengers normally need to attract as much public attention as possible in order to raise money, gain name recognition, and otherwise compensate for the many advantages held by incumbents. But local newscasts, the only source of news for millions of Americans, focused the vast majority of their political coverage on the presidential race. One study of fifty-two local television stations' newscasts found that only thirty-seven carried any election coverage on a particular evening, of which only 1 percent of the reports dealt with House races and 9 percent with Senate contests.[28] Many congressional challengers might be justified in feeling that they would have received more coverage from their local stations if they had been campaigning in Bosnia.

But such advantages of incumbency may not have seemed obvious to Republican freshmen in 1996. In the nationalized House elections of 1994, Republican newcomers had pinned their hopes on the sweeping ideological vision of Newt Gingrich. As that vision became more controversial, so did they. It was a marked change that so many of the Republican freshmen, so stalwart in their support of Gingrich during the 104th Congress, avoided association with him in their 1996 campaigning. One reporter described Gingrich as having been "downsized" for the 1996 campaign.[29] Like Hillary Clinton, the Speaker spent much of the race flying below the media's radar, giving pep talks to and raising funds from groups of party faithful.

He was a much more substantial presence in Democratic House campaigns. If the proverbial visitor from Mars had learned about House elections solely by viewing Democratic candidates' media ads, it would probably conclude that most Democrats were running against the same candidate, a glowering presence named Newt who was intent on harming senior citizens. The observer might note that many Republicans had an opponent in common as well: an embarrassingly ultraliberal captive of big labor bosses. Like Godzilla and the Smog Monster, the specters of Ted Kennedy and Newt Gingrich seemed to clash nightly on every television channel.

Pork Redux. — In addition to distancing themselves from Gingrich, a number of the Republican freshmen learned a lesson that many others in their position had previously absorbed. Even many of those who had expressed the most fervent support for government spending cuts came to understand the need for targeted government spending, which their opponents might prefer to term constituent service or pork barrel. A reporter noted that "conservative Republican House freshmen seeking reelection brag about the highway, water and research projects they have brought home to their states and districts."[30] As election day drew nearer and the prospects for Republican congressional candidates grew more uncertain, even some local projects that had not been authorized by Congress nevertheless received federal funds.

Democratic candidates had another advantage leading up to the November election. The 1994 Republican sweep had been a painful way of reducing Democratic vulnerabilities in 1996. Republicans had held the presidency during most of the period of Democratic congressional dominance. As a result, a number of House and Senate Democrats had been elected from districts that voted Republican for president.

In 1994, however, Republican congressional candidates took most of those districts. Almost 90 percent of the remaining Democratic seats, then — 89 percent of Democratic House seats and 87 percent of Democratic Senate seats — were in districts and states President Clinton won in the last presidential election. This time it was the Republicans who had more seats to defend in territory at least potentially friendly to the other party. Only 67 percent of Republican House seats and 63 percent of Republican Senate seats in 1996 were in districts won by Bush in 1992.[31]

Democratic Weakness in the South. — But Democrats still had to defend the few Democratic seats remaining in Bush territory, several of which would be very difficult to protect. Of the twenty-one Democratic House seats in districts that had voted for Bush in 1992, fourteen were in the South, and four of these were open seats, where a Democratic incumbent had retired. The erosion of Democratic strength in the South in 1994 continued a trend that had been building for a generation. In 1975, 92 of the 121 House seats in the South, or 76 percent, were held by Democrats.[32] After the 1994 elections, there were only 64 Democrats out of 137 (47 percent)—the first time since Reconstruction that Democrats have been the minority party in the South. After the party switches in 1995, Democrats were down to fifty-nine seats (43 percent) (see figure 6.4).

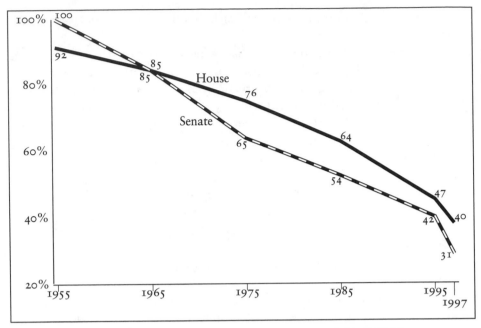

FIGURE 6.4. DEMOCRATIC STRENGTH IN THE SOUTH:
U.S. HOUSE AND SENATE SEATS, 1955–97

SOURCE: Calculated from Rhodes Cook, "Dixie Voters Look Away: South Shifts to the GOP," *Congressional Quarterly Weekly Report,* 12 November 1994, 3231 (for 1955–95); and *New York Times,* 7 November and 11 December 1996 (for 1997).
NOTE: Points are the percentage of southern U.S. House and Senate seats in a given year held by Democrats. "Southern" is defined as the 11 states of the Confederacy plus Kentucky and Oklahoma.

The pivotal years were 1992–94. Before the 1992 elections, Republicans held only one of Georgia's House seats; the incumbent in question was Newt Gingrich. By 1995, the Georgia delegation consisted of eight Republicans and three Democrats. The latter were all African Americans; the creation of "minority-majority districts" to improve the representation of blacks and Hispanics in Congress had contributed to the swing by concentrating African Americans, overwhelmingly Democratic voters, in a few districts. So, as one writer pointed out, "for the rest of the 1990s, the 'party of Lincoln' will increasingly draw its life from the land of Jefferson Davis."[33]

In the Senate, Democrats had only fifteen seats to defend. But because of retirements, eight of those were open-seat races, and four of the eight were in the South. In the House, the Democrats had thirty open seats to defend, nineteen of those in the South. Democrats needed to regain a net of only nineteen seats to retake the House majority, and three seats in the Senate.[34] If Democratic campaigners lost a number of the southern open seats, however, those relatively small numbers would grow to insurmountable size.

A Flood of Fund Raising and Interest-Group Activity

The engine that sustained this campaign activity was a major escalation in the raising and spending of campaign money. Ever since government began to regulate campaign spending, innovative minds have worked to "interpret" the regulations so as to advantage their causes. In 1996 they went into overdrive. The political party organizations greatly expanded their use of two means of funneling money into competitive congressional races: independent spending and the use of "soft money" to fund issue ads (see chapter 4).

LIFTING RESTRAINTS ON PARTY SPENDING

Five months before the election, a Supreme Court ruling took the ceiling off the amounts that political parties could spend on federal campaigns. It gave parties the right to make "independent expenditures," just as interest groups and individuals had long been permitted to do. Party organizations could thus buy unlimited amounts of advertising in a congressional election as long as their efforts were not coordinated with a candidate's campaign. That, the Court said, was part of their right to free speech.

To take advantage of this new opportunity for party spending, the national parties needed to raise as much money as possible, as fast as possible. They turned to "soft money"—the contributions from businesses, labor unions, other groups, and individuals that the national parties can raise for themselves to fund party-building activities. The money cannot be used legally to advocate a vote for or against a candidate, but both parties in 1996 experimented with using soft money for "issues ads."

Because of their new ability to spend independently, the parties put several times as much money into congressional races as they would otherwise have been permitted to do. The results were not always edifying. A Democratic Party official commented that "the independent expenditure is one that basically permits you to run any kinds of ads you want in the most personal and direct way and it suits negative advertising to a tee."[35] Consider one NRSC ad run in the Louisiana Senate race: "Mary Landrieu. A real tax-and-spend liberal who just can't wait to spend more of our money."

In all, by election day, parties, PACs, and candidates for federal office managed to raise a total of $1.7 *billion,* not including a variety of other groups' independent expenditures.[36] The figures were staggering—though it is worth noting, in comparison, that the Philip Morris corporation spent $2.6 billion in 1995 alone to advertise its cigarettes and other products.[37]

INTEREST GROUPS WITH DEEP POCKETS

A variety of interest groups also mounted an unprecedented effort to unseat or protect the new Republican majority. After congressional Republicans threatened (though unsuccessfully) to pass antiunion legislation, the AFL-CIO began a series of media campaigns in spring 1995 against Republicans perceived to be vulnerable. Most of the money was targeted for about two dozen House districts represented by Republican freshmen. In Representative J.D. Hayworth's race in Arizona, for example, an AFL-CIO ad ran up to fifty times a day on district television stations.[38]

The AFL-CIO ad blitz ran unopposed for months. National Republican committees held their fire until the summer and fall of 1996, when they began a counterattack along with the U.S. Chamber of Commerce and other industry groups. This response was regarded by many Republican activists as too little, too late. Even so, the Republican Party spent at least $8 million in the six weeks before the election on ads accusing "union bosses" of a variety of political sins.[39]

CHRISTIAN RIGHT EFFORTS

Christian right organizations added to the activity on behalf of Republican candidates. For two decades, the Christian right had been expanding its influence within the Republican Party. Negative public reaction to a series of hard-line speeches at the 1992 Republican convention convinced party leaders to keep the Christian right in the background during the 1996 convention, but the movement's handiwork could be seen clearly in the party's platform. That in turn reflected evangelical support for the Republican slate; in 1994, evangelicals constituted 29 percent of the total Republican vote, and 75 percent of all evangelicals voted for Republican congressional candidates.[40]

In 1996, the Christian Coalition funded contacts with an estimated 3 million voters and distributed about 46 million voter guides, typically at churches on the Sunday before election day. Its executive director, Ralph Reed, explained that "it would be the end of the world to core religious conservatives if Dick Gephardt became Speaker or Tom Daschle became majority leader. It would make it impossible to move any pro-family legislation through Congress for the foreseeable future."[41]

THE DEMOCRATS PEAK TOO SOON

The Democratic momentum that had built during the fall may have peaked about ten days before the election. The national Democratic Party, embarrassed by news accounts that it had neglected to file a required preelection campaign finance report, was further hit by charges that it had unlawfully accepted large contributions from foreign businesses.

Republican ads, acknowledging the unbudgeable Clinton lead, warned voters not to give the president a "blank check," but to give Republicans control of Congress as a means of counterbalancing Clinton initiatives. Democratic ads turned the focus around, threatening that "Newt Gingrich isn't done. He wants to keep his Republican Congress so they can try again." Facing both the frying pan and the fire, voters decided whether to go to the polls.

Election Day: It Ain't Over Till Texas Sings

The dust didn't settle for more than a month after the congressional elections. A Supreme Court decision overturning minority-majority districts in Texas meant that the November election had to become a rerun of the primaries for thirteen House seats, three of which required a runoff in early December.[42]

But even before those last districts were decided, it was apparent that neither the Democrats nor the Republicans had done as well as they had hoped, nor as badly as they had feared. Republicans held control of both houses of Congress—the first time since the 1920s that the party had managed to win consecutive majorities in the House and the Senate. The upper house was a little more Republican and clearly more conservative in 1997 than it had been in 1996. But Speaker Gingrich led a thinner majority in the House—the slimmest in four decades (see table 6.1).

In the Senate, Republicans picked up three of the eight open seats formerly held by Democrats, including two of the four in the South, and lost none of their own open seats. Only one incumbent senator was defeated for reelection: Republican Larry Pressler of South Dakota. The result was a net gain for the Republicans of two, boosting their Senate majority from fifty-three to fifty-five.[43] In thirty of the thirty-four Senate races up for election, there was no party change.

The limited party turnover hid a much more substantial ideological change. There are fifteen freshman senators in the 105th Congress, an unusually large number. Many of the retiring Republicans were moderates and compromise brokers, such as William Cohen of Maine, Nancy Landon

TABLE 6.1

WINNERS, LOSERS, AND PARTY CHANGE:

1996 GENERAL ELECTION

	House	Senate
Democrats elected	207	45
Republicans elected[a]	227	55
Democratic incumbents defeated	3[b]	0
Republican incumbents defeated	18[b]	1[b]
Open seats won by Democrats	24	5
Open seats won by Republicans	29	9
Democratic freshmen	42[c]	6
Republican freshmen	32[d]	9
Seats changing parties:	35	4
Democrat to Republican	13	3
Republican to Democrat	22	1

a. The remaining House seat is held by Bernard Sanders of Vermont, an independent who caucuses with the Democrats.

b. Plus another incumbent who was defeated in the primary.

c. Includes Ted Strickland (Ohio) and David Price (N.C.), who had also served in the House prior to 1995.

d. Includes Jo Ann Emerson, who was elected on 5 November both to a seat in the 105th Congress and to fill a vacant seat for the remainder of the 104th Congress; and Ron Paul (Tex.), Bob Smith (Ore.), and Wes Watkins (Okla.), who had also served in the House prior to 1995.

Kassebaum of Kansas, and Mark Hatfield of Oregon. With the exception of Cohen, who was replaced by a like-minded former staffer, they were succeeded by hard-line conservatives, many of them more confrontation oriented.

Similarly, centrist Democrats who retired, such as Howell Heflin of Alabama and David Pryor of Arkansas, gave way to strongly conservative Republicans. Only one of the thirty-four elections produced a markedly more liberal senator: South Dakota's, where Democratic Representative Tim Johnson beat the conservative Pressler. Further, the new majority leader was Trent Lott of Mississippi, a Gingrich ally when he served in the House. The Senate, then, is likely to be more partisan and polarized than it was in the 104th Congress. Because the Senate must confirm the president's cabinet and Supreme Court nominations, its rightward movement will limit the president's ability to nominate liberals to these positions.

The results in the House were more mixed. Altogether, thirty-five House seats changed parties; fourteen of these were open seats and twenty-one were districts in which the incumbent was defeated. Republicans more than held their own in the open-seat races. Twenty-three of the open seats had belonged to Republicans in the 104th Congress. Republican candidates were successful in keeping nineteen of those seats, turning only four over to the Democrats, while winning ten of the thirty open seats formerly held by Democrats. Most of the open seats captured by Republicans were in the South.

Democrats made their gains primarily by defeating first-term incumbents. Only 17 percent of the seventy Republican freshmen who ran for reelection lost—a smaller toll than had been taken in 1994 among Democratic freshmen. But the twelve defeated Republican freshmen in 1996 were a full two-thirds of the losing Republican incumbents. In addition, almost twice as many Republican freshmen won reelection with 53 percent or less of the total vote.

The Democratic victories broke no new ground for the party; in most cases, Democratic challengers simply picked off the ripest fruit. Ten of the twelve losing Republican freshmen had won their last races by 52 percent of the vote or less. Four other losing incumbents were second-term Republicans, most of whom had won narrowly in 1994. Another was a third termer with a similarly marginal victory his last time out. Combative nine-term Republican Bob Dornan of California was the last loser, and he had taken a time-consuming (and unsuccessful) run at the Republican presidential nomination earlier in 1996. Only three Democratic incumbents were defeated.

What accounted for the relatively small change in the House? First, it attested that incumbents still bring powerful advantages into House races. Even in the Republican sweep of 1994, when media accounts suggested that incumbency could be hazardous to a candidate's electoral health, 90 percent of the incumbents who ran for reelection won their primary and general election races. The winning percentage of those who sought reelection has dropped below 90 percent only once since 1974. The exception was 1992, when a postwar record of nineteen incumbents went down in the primaries, many as the result of the House bank scandal and redistricting.

In 1996, all but twenty-three incumbents who ran for reelection won both their races, the fewest losses since 1990. That was a reelection rate of 94 percent. Many Americans would consider that a desirable level of job security over a two-year period (though few would probably want to raise the hundreds of thousands of dollars and spend the innumerable hours necessary to keep it that way). In the Senate, the reelection rate has ranged much more widely, from 55 percent in 1980 to 97 percent in 1990. It was an impressively high 90.5 percent in 1996.

Yet recall that in figure 6.2, most Americans disapproved of the way

Congress was doing its job. The irony of these results was noted by one analyst: "dissatisfied with their political leadership, American voters opted for the status quo."[44] As in 1990 and 1992, the main route out of Congress was retirement (or the desire for advancement to a higher office) rather than defeat at the polls.

The movement to limit the number of terms incumbents could serve in Congress had been a popular cause in the early 1990s. Yet if they chose to run again, most long-term incumbents were elected easily in 1996. So the term-limit movement might best be interpreted as a means for voters to say, "Stop us before we reelect them again!" Incumbents normally have ample opportunities for reaching voters, and most have the money and the experience to use those opportunities effectively. The result was that even though most Americans held a negative opinion of Congress, most congressional incumbents, including most of the Republican freshmen, were able to preserve their seats in 1996 by tending to their districts' local needs.

What, then, kept the losing Republicans from reaping the benefits of incumbency? Did they bear the brunt of their support for the Republican leadership's initiatives and the Contract with America? Out of sixty-six important recorded votes in 1995 on Contract issues, the average House Republican voted in favor on 97 percent, an amazing level of unity. Sixty-three of the 230 members elected as Republicans in 1994 (27 percent) supported the Contract on every one of those votes. Of the eighteen Republicans who lost in the general election in 1996, seven (39 percent) had voted in favor of the Contract every time, and six others were at or above the House Republican average. So the "hundred percenters" were defeated at a higher rate than were Republicans as a whole. These seven losing "hundred percenters" refused to trim their sails, at least for the first session of the 104th Congress; they voted with the majority of their party an average of 96 percent of the time during 1995, compared with 91 percent for all Republicans.[45]

It is plausible, in short, that some of these Republicans lost because they were voting their party rather than their district, forgetting that it would be their district, not their party, that voted on their reelection. On the other hand, five of the defeated Republicans scored below the Republican average on Contract votes, and two—Representatives Peter Blute and Peter Torkildsen of Massachusetts—had among the lowest Contract support scores of all House Republicans. The 1995 party unity scores for these five averaged only 84 percent.

The defeats of the freshmen were often interpreted as a warning that representatives should not act like clones of their party leadership and that extremism would be punished at the polls. Moderate after moderate argued that the voters were asking for moderation in 1996. But in fact, although some highly conservative freshmen lost, others won, and several equally right-wing candidates were sent to Congress for the first time. And several Republicans who had voted to support environmental legislation and controls on assault weapons still lost their races. What constitutes "extremism" in one district is mainstream in another.

Blute, Torkildsen, and the three other relative moderates among the Republican losers, as well as most of their conservative colleagues, had all been targeted by the AFL-CIO in 1996. Did organized labor's electioneering cause their defeats? Four of the five represented northeastern districts, where labor may have had some influence. But in all, the AFL had targeted more than sixty potentially vulnerable Republicans in 1996, and all but fifteen of them won.

In the end, the bottom line for organized labor was this: after the AFL spent $35 million on highly confrontational ad campaigns and grass-roots mobilization, Republicans still controlled both houses of Congress. Labor could cite a variety of silver linings. Most of the losing Republican incumbents had been targets of the AFL's advertising. That advertising, especially because of its early start and clear message, helped set the agenda of many House campaigns. And in contrast to organized labor's poor showing in 1994, union households accounted for almost one-fourth of the total House vote in 1996 (up from 14 percent in 1994). According to exit polling, 63 percent of these voters cast Democratic ballots in House races.[46] Organized labor, suspected by many of being a paper tiger in politics, was back.

The downside for labor came out of its efforts to portray even relatively moderate Republicans as Gingrich clones. As one moderate Republican, Representative Christopher Shays, argued, "The national labor movement basically carpetbombed a lot of good Republicans. They went for broke, they went for the whole thing, and they've made a number of enemies in the process."[47]

Why didn't the Democrats win more of the marginal Republican seats? A major reason—a powerful force keeping the Democrats from regaining control of Congress—was the relatively large number of Democratic retirements in the South. As they had in recent decades, Republican candidates were especially likely to win southern open seats. Of the nineteen southern House seats left open by Democratic retirements, seven moved into the Republican column.

THE SOLID REPUBLICAN SOUTH
The magnitude of the party shift in the South is apparent in a comparison

of two maps (see figures 6.5 and 6.6). In 1953–54, as figure 6.5 indicates, Republican strength could be seen in congressional delegations all across the northern tier of the United States. The Pacific Coast, the Plains states, the rest of the Midwest, and the Northeast were all Republican dominated. The South was the most dependably Democratic region of the country; to be openly Republican was a form of deviance.

By 1997, only about a generation and a half later, there had been an almost complete reversal of regional party strength. Before the 1994 elections, Republicans held a majority of House seats in only one southern state: Florida. After the 1994 vote, the party had a majority in seven of the thirteen states: Florida, Georgia, Kentucky, North and South Carolina, Oklahoma, and Tennessee. The trend continued in 1996, when the South was the only region in which Republicans gained House seats. Although Arkansas's and North Carolina's delegations were evenly split between the parties, Republicans held six other states and picked up House majorities in Alabama, Louisiana, and Mississippi as well. So in the 105th Congress, only Texas and Virginia had Democratic dominated state delegations.

Regional distinctiveness in the two parties' strength, then, can still be

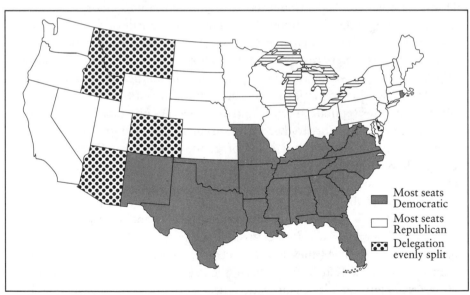

Most seats Democratic

Most seats Republican

Delegation evenly split

FIGURE 6.5

PARTY DOMINANCE IN HOUSE STATE DELEGATIONS
IN THE 83D CONGRESS (1953–54)

SOURCE: *Congressional Quarterly Weekly Report,* 12 November 1994, 3231.

seen in American politics; the regions have simply switched sides. The Northeast, the upper Midwest, and most of the Pacific Coast were dependably Democratic in the 1996 congressional races. The backbone of the Republican Party has become the South, as well as the states of the mountain West and much of the Plains. It has been an issue-driven switch; as cultural issues have come to rival the economy in public concern, the parties' coalitions have changed in significant ways.[48]

The change has profound implications. As southern representatives become a larger percentage of the Republican Party in government, issues of particular concern to southern states, from race to welfare to military bases to "traditional values," become more prominent in Republican campaigns and the party platform. As southern conservatives move out of the Democratic Party, Democratic liberals no longer feel as much internal pressure to move to the center (though external pressure from election losses often does the trick). As many other nations can attest, party conflicts with a regional base can cause serious challenges to a democratic government, even one with a federal structure.

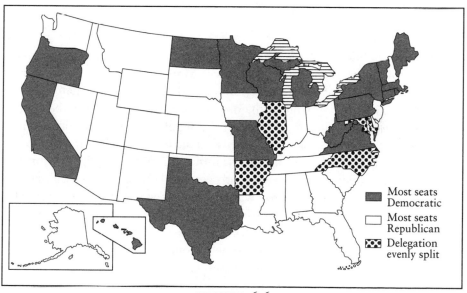

FIGURE 6.6

PARTY DOMINANCE IN THE HOUSE STATE DELEGATIONS
IN THE 105TH CONGRESS (1997–98)

SOURCE: Calculated from *New York Times*, 7 November 1996, B8–B9, as updated.
NOTE: Vermont is shown as a Democratic state in 1997. Its sole House member is an independent who caucuses with the Democrats.

Turnout data confirm that southern support for Republicans in 1996 congressional elections increased by 2 percent over 1994 levels, and southern turnout was up. In contrast, the other regions of the nation all became more Democratic in their House voting, according to exit polls.[49] In addition to their southern gains, there were other bright spots for the Republicans in these data. The white religious right gave a full 73 percent of its votes to Republican House candidates, compared with 63 percent in 1994. Interestingly, black voters more than doubled their support for Republican House candidates, even while white voters moved more toward the Democrats. (Black voters, nevertheless, remain overwhelmingly Democratic.) Finally, those who supported Ross Perot for president in 1992 were more likely to vote for Republican than for Democratic House candidates, which helped save several Republican seats.

Democratic candidates improved their standing with other groups, including young people (those 18–29 years old) and the less educated. And although both women and men were more likely to vote Democratic in 1996 than in 1994, there was a substantial gender gap, with women choosing Democratic House candidates by a 55–45 percent margin, and men supporting Republicans by 54–46 percent (see chapter 5).

WOMEN IN CONGRESS

As women's political preferences become somewhat more distinctive, larger numbers of women are running for office. More women than ever ran in congressional primaries in 1996: 215 House and more than 50 Senate candidates.[50] There were 115 women major-party candidates in November. But there was no proportionate increase in the number of women winning in the general election. The last big increase came in 1992, when the number of women voting members of the House jumped from twenty-eight to forty-seven, and up to six in the Senate (with a seventh added in a special election). One more woman senator was added in 1994, and another served briefly in 1996 as the replacement for Bob Dole after he resigned from the Senate, but the number of women House members remained constant.

In 1996, Congress gained thirteen new women members. Maine elected a second female Republican senator, Susan Collins, and Louisiana chose its first, Democrat Mary Landrieu. Because of the retirement of Nancy Kassebaum of Kansas and a primary defeat, however, there was no net increase in women senators. In the House, eleven women were elected as freshmen, and another who had won a special election in 1996 was reelected. But eight women incumbents had either retired or lost. In consequence, women remain much more underrepresented, in relation to their proportion of the

U.S. population, than do black and Hispanic Americans (see table 6.2).

Why should that be? The numbers of blacks and Hispanics in the House improved markedly due to the creation of minority-majority districts in time for the 1992 election. Because blacks and Hispanics tend to be concentrated residentially, it is feasible to draw congressional districts in which they form clear majorities, and thus to increase their numbers in the House.[51] Leaving aside some college dormitories, women tend not to be

TABLE 6.2

REPRESENTATION OF WOMEN, BLACKS, AND HISPANICS

IN CONGRESS, 1973–97

	Women		Blacks		Hispanics	
	%	N	%	N	%	N
1973						
% of population (1970)	51.3		11.1		4.6	
% of House membership	3.7	16[b]	3.4	15	1.1	5
% of Senate membership	0.0	0	1.0	1	1.0	1
Representation ratio[a]		.06		.27		.24
1983						
% of population (1980)	51.4		11.7		6.4	
% of House membership	5.1	22[c]	4.6	20	2.1	9
% of Senate membership	2.0	2	0.0	0	0.0	0
Representation ratio		.09		.32		.26
1993						
% of population (1990)	51.2		12.3		9.0	
% of House membership	10.8	47	8.7	38	3.9	17
% of Senate membership	6.0	6	1.0	1	0.0	0
Representation ratio		.19		.59		.35
1997						
% of population (1996)	51.2		12.7		10.6	
% of House membership	11.7	51	8.5	37	4.4	19
% of Senate membership	9.0	9	1.0	1	0.0	0
Representation ratio		.22		.56		.34

SOURCES: U.S. Bureau of the Census; *Congressional Quarterly Weekly Report*, 11 November 1972, pp. 2990–91; 6 November 1982, p. 2805; 7 November 1992 (Special Report), p. 8; *New York Times*, 7 November and 11 December 1996. Data refer only to voting members; nonvoting delegates are excluded.

a. The ratio of the percentage of women (or blacks or Hispanics) in Congress (both House and Senate) to the percentage of that group in the general population.

b. Includes two women members elected in special elections.

c. Includes one woman member elected in a special election.

concentrated residentially. In addition, women in the United States are considerably more diverse in terms of income and education than are American Hispanics and blacks and thus perhaps are less likely to feel an intense need to be represented by someone of their gender.

Like men who seek congressional seats, women have their best chance of winning when an incumbent retires or there is a national trend in favor of their party. Most voters tend not to discriminate against women candidates,[52] and whatever disadvantage women have faced in attracting campaign money has been in part erased by groups (the pro-choice EMILY's List and Women in the Senate and House, or WISH, and the pro-life Susan B. Anthony List) that dedicate themselves solely to the financial support of women candidates.

In 1992, the large number of congressional retirements made possible a big gain in the number of Democratic women, most of them liberals. (The Republican wave in 1994, although it did not expand the female contingent in the House, did replace several incumbent Democrats with conservative Republican women.) In 1996 House retirements—this time among women members—held women's gains to a handful. But for the first time, most of the women newcomers beat incumbents, normally a tougher task than winning an open seat.

A NOT-SO-REVOLUTIONARY FRESHMAN CLASS

The resulting freshman class of 1997 had a very different character from that of 1995.[53] Most significantly, there were Democrats in it. In 1995, every one of the newly elected senators was a Republican, as were 85 percent of the new House members. In contrast, 40 percent of the Senate class of 1997 were Democrats, and 57 percent in the House.

The main differences between the two groups of freshmen—their ages and occupations—suggest a more politically experienced, more diverse collection of representatives. In the House, the 1997 freshmen were older than their 1995 counterparts (only 35 percent were under forty-five, compared with 59 percent in 1995). In both houses, the freshmen in 1997 were more likely to have previously held elective office and much less likely to have had careers in business or banking. The political newcomers of 1995 had not paved the way for squads of others like themselves. If the revolution wasn't over, then it was at least taking a long lunch break. Its foot soldiers had learned, as so many did before them, that voters tend to reward their House members and senators on the basis of their performance as representatives of individual districts, not as representatives of their party's leadership or its philosophy.

Polarization or Common Ground?

Newt Gingrich and the freshman Republicans of the 104th Congress tried, with limited success, to put into action a vision of a leaner, less intrusive government. It was the vision passionately expressed, but largely not implemented, by President Reagan in the 1980s. After two years of effort, "there are ... signs that the whole antigovernment mythology that has energized and galvanized the conservative movement since Ronald Reagan ran for president in 1980 may be losing its edge." The reason, says the writer, is that "Americans like the services, subsidies, programs and protections that government provides."[54]

This more differentiated view of government—that it provides valued services such as national parks and passports as well as taxes and waste—may have been prompted by the government shutdowns that called attention to the range of federal services. It may have been furthered by the bombing of the Oklahoma City federal building, which put a human face on government agencies as victims, not as perpetrators. Or perhaps it was there all along; as an election post-mortem noted, Newt Gingrich "had mistaken the election returns of 1994 for a revolution, when only 19 percent of the eligible electorate had actually voted Republican for Congress."[55]

Given the mixed results of 1996, there are two possible paths for the Republican majority. Many of the winners expressed a hope for the long-sought common ground. Senate Majority Leader Trent Lott, in his postelection news conference, seemed to underscore the desire to get away from the bulldozer approach of the Gingrich ascension: "We're not going to rush out there Jan. 8 and start trying to pass x number of bills in the first 100 days.... Let's see what [Clinton] has to say and what he proposes. We will consider that. And where we can, we will work with him."[56] Similarly, House Minority Leader Richard Gephardt (D-Mo.) pledged during the campaign that if Democrats regained the House majority, they would return with a more modest and moderate agenda.[57]

Yet there are better reasons to predict that the party polarization that has been developing during the last decade will continue into the 105th Congress.[58] The two congressional parties are as internally cohesive and divergent from one another as they were in 1995. Further, the coalition that elected the Republican congressional majority in 1996 differed markedly from the coalition that voted to reelect Clinton. In a *Washington Post* poll, Clinton's voters tended to be female, Catholic, single, and moderate to liberal, whereas those who voted for Republicans for Congress tended to be more male, Protestant, conservative, pessimistic, and wealthy. Only about one in seven voters were found in both coalitions.[59]

Almost two-thirds of Clinton voters in the poll said government should do more to solve problems, while three-quarters of Republican congressional voters said government is doing too much now. The highest priorities for the Clinton supporters were education, Social Security, and Medicare. For the Republican congressional coalition, taxes and the deficit mattered most. The differences between the two coalitions suggest two opposing viewpoints in the electorate rather than a widespread desire for moderation that leads individuals to hedge their vote for Clinton by selecting a Republican for Congress. To satisfy their differing constituencies, Clinton and the congressional Republicans have every reason to remain at odds.

The poisonous atmosphere of many close House and Senate races in 1996 is not likely to help bridge the gap between the parties. A number of Republicans felt unfairly tarred by the charges made in the AFL-CIO's ad campaign that they were trying to cut Medicare rather than reduce its rate of growth. And if the majority Republicans choose to express their resentment legislatively, they have ample opportunity to do so. In addition to the investigation industry that has already been built on Capitol Hill, ranging from Arkansas real estate deals to the firings of White House travel office workers to the unauthorized acquisition of FBI files by Clinton administration workers, there were now charges of illegal foreign contributions to the Democratic Party.

Nor is any relief in sight for the Democrats in 1998. The off-year election in a president's second term takes an inevitable and often substantial toll on his co-partisans in Congress. By 1998, four years in the minority will probably have convinced many Democrats that the House and Senate are not places where they can fulfill their dreams. And because it was widely believed that the Democrats gave the 1996 elections their best shot and still failed to regain a majority in Congress, it will be more difficult for the party to find experienced candidates to replace the retirees, and money to fund their campaigns.

Even more difficult will be the achievement of a policy change whose need was so clearly underlined by the closing weeks of the 1996 race: campaign finance reform. The flood of legal, quasi-legal, and probably illegal contributions dwarfed that of previous election years. A single tobacco company donated almost $2 million to Republican Party committees in the 1995–96 election cycle, plus more than one-third of a million to the Democrats, at a time when the regulation of smoking remains a major national issue.[60] If this corporation were motivated solely by a desire to be charitable, the United Way might have been a more appropriate choice. It is difficult to prove that interest-group money buys votes in Congress.[61] But it is equally hard to imagine why big givers—corporations, unions, wealthy individuals—contribute so much to parties or candidates if they believe that their money gets them nothing in return.

Reform legislation was introduced in the 104th Congress, with provisions ranging from a ban on PAC contributions and incentives to comply with campaign spending limits to an end to soft money. But like most reform bills that threatened to take away funding from the people who would have to vote on it, the bills failed. As has always been the case with political money, it takes very exceptional conditions to encourage successful politicians to turn off their own financial spigot, particularly at a time when campaign costs are rising and the number of competitive campaigns is increasing.

The problem of political money goes beyond the threat that big givers can get big favors. It is the perennial dilemma of balancing the right of narrow interests to organize and act politically with the obligation of government to meet broader societal needs.[62] Some groups, those with narrow interests and a clear stake in government policy, are relatively easy to organize. Broader interests—consumers as opposed to producers, insurance buyers as opposed to insurance providers—are much harder to bring together for political activity. The system of political action committees, private contributions, soft money, and independent spending provides the narrower, more affluent producer groups a clear channel of influence. It does not offer a comparable means of access for the broader interests.[63]

The Supreme Court's decision to let political parties make independent expenditures could help restore this balance. It gives the parties, which, as majoritarian institutions, have an incentive to speak for broader interests, a chance to counterbalance interest-group spending more fully. But when the parties raise the money for their independent spending from narrow interests, that balance is lost.

The serious threat posed by the present system of campaign finance may have something to do with the final and perhaps the most important statistic of the 1996 elections. The average voter didn't go to the polls; fewer than 50 percent of eligible voters participated. There are a lot of possible explanations for this decline in turnout. Some undoubtedly relate to the weaknesses of politics as a spectator sport. In 1992, when Ross Perot's quirky independent campaign hit the airwaves, voter turnout hit a recent high of 55 percent. The elections of 1996 were not as engaging.

One might argue that voters stayed home in large numbers because they were satisfied with the record of their presidential and congressional leadership. This is a time, one might suggest, of social rest. Voting takes time; why vote if you like things the way they are? And in fact, surveys in 1996 reported public satisfaction with the state of the nation's economy.[64]

But there is an alternative argument. It may be that the hundreds of millions of dollars of "interested money" collected by candidates, the wave of negative ads, and the sensationalized reporting have made political campaigns the electoral equivalent of professional wrestling. They are entertaining to some, distasteful to many others, and regarded by most as little more than a sham. Effective reform is rare. But in this context, the case for thoroughgoing reform is all the more compelling.

Acknowledgments

I am most grateful to Howard V. Hershey and David Holian for their help.

Notes

1. See, for example, Gary C. Jacobson, *The Politics of Congressional Elections*, 4th ed. (New York: Longman, 1997), 159–68; and Clyde Wilcox, *The Latest American Revolution?* (New York: St. Martin's Press, 1995).

2. Alan I. Abramowitz and Suzie Ishikawa, "Explaining the Republican Takeover of the House of Representatives" (paper presented at the 1995 American Political Science Association annual meeting, Chicago).

3. Richard F. Fenno Jr., "If, as Ralph Nader Says, Congress Is the 'Broken Branch,' How Come We Love Our Congressmen So Much?" in *Congress in Change: Evolution and Reform,* ed. Norman J. Ornstein (New York: Praeger, 1975).

4. Wilcox, *The Latest American Revolution?* 21.

5. Jacobson, *Politics of Congressional Elections,* 162.

6. Jackie Koszczuk, "Freshmen: New, Powerful Voice," *Congressional Quarterly Weekly Report,* 28 October 1995, 3251.

7. Ibid., 3254.

8. John H. Aldrich and David W. Rohde, "Theories of the Party in the Legislature and the Transition to Republican Rule in the House" (Political Institutions and Public Choice working paper, Michigan State University, 1995), 16–18.

9. Jackie Koszczuk and David S. Cloud, "GOP Leaders Tell the Troops, It's Time to Lock Hands," *Congressional Quarterly Weekly Report,* 16 September 1995, 2770.

10. The votes were on the balanced-budget amendment, unfunded mandates, the line-item veto, requiring a three-fifths vote to impose new taxes, congressional compliance with workplace laws, two crime provisions (on the exclusionary rule and death penalty appeals), and three internal reforms to transfer power from committee chairs to the party leadership (cuts in committee staff, term limits for

committee chairs, and a ban on proxy voting). The possible total of 2,300 votes reflects the opportunity for each of the 230 Republicans serving in the House in February 1995 to vote on each of these ten bills.

11. Janet Hook, "Republicans Vote in Lock Step, but Unity May Not Last Long," *Congressional Quarterly Weekly Report,* 18 February 1995, 495.

12. Jeffrey L. Katz, "A Record-Setting Year," *Congressional Quarterly Weekly Report,* 27 January 1996, 195.

13. One, Representative Greg Laughlin of Texas, was later defeated in the 1996 Republican primary.

14. Jeffrey M. Berry, *The Interest Group Society,* 3d ed. (New York: Longman, 1997), 151–53.

15. Leslie Wayne, "Business Is Biggest Campaign Spender, Study Says," *New York Times,* 18 October 1996, A1.

16. Associated Press, "PAC Money Is Fund-Raising as Usual for House Freshmen," *Herald-Times* (Bloomington, Ind.), 17 October 1996, A3.

17. Jonathan D. Salant, "Freshman's War Chest Deters Challengers," *Congressional Quarterly Weekly Report,* 24 August 1996, 2363.

18. Lance Morrow, "Newt's World," *Time,* 25 December 1995–1 January 1996, 50, overleaf. This *Time* paean goes on to warn that "the Gingrich Republicans, however, may be in danger of exercising their party's perverse talent for throwing away its advantages with both hands."

19. Dale Russakoff, "On the Stump, Gingrich Adjusts to Reduced Stature," *Washington Post,* 24 October 1996, A1.

20. On gender differences in policy attitudes, see Robert S. Erikson and Kent L. Tedin, *American Public Opinion,* 5th ed. (Boston: Allyn and Bacon, 1995), 208–11.

21. Quoted in Jackie Koszczuk, "Democrats' Resurgence Fueled by Pragmatism," *Congressional Quarterly Weekly Report,* 4 May 1996, 1205.

22. George Hager, "Congress, Clinton Yield Enough to Close the Book on Fiscal '96," *Congressional Quarterly Weekly Report,* 27 April 1996, 1156.

23. As retiring Representative Mel Hancock of Missouri put it, it's time to leave Congress "when the debate on the House floor starts making sense," and "when you cannot remember whether it costs millions or billions." *Congressional Record—House,* 104th Cong., 2d sess., #136, p. H11573 (27 September 1996).

24. See Eric M. Uslaner, *The Decline of Comity* (Ann Arbor: University of Michigan Press, 1993).

25. See Robert S. Erikson, "Malapportionment, Gerrymandering, and Party Fortunes in Congressional Elections," *American Political Science Review* 66 (December 1972): 1234–45.

26. This was not the case in 1994, when seventeen of the thirty-eight defeated House members were in their first terms, and eight more had served two or three terms. See Norman J. Ornstein, Thomas E. Mann, and Michael J. Malbin, *Vital Statistics on Congress 1995–96* (Washington, D.C.: CQ Press, 1996), 63–64.

27. See Marjorie Randon Hershey, "The Congressional Elections," in *The*

Election of 1992, ed. Gerald M. Pomper (Chatham, N.J.: Chatham House, 1993), 158–62.

28. Steven A. Holmes, "Local TV Focusing on Presidential Race," *New York Times,* 24 September 1996, A14.

29. Russakoff, "On the Stump," 1.

30. Dan Morgan, "A Revolution Derailed," *Washington Post,* 20 October 1996, C1.

31. Rhodes Cook, "In White House and Hill Races, Democrats Keep Advantage," *Congressional Quarterly Weekly Report,* 29 June 1996, 1804.

32. The South is defined here as the eleven states of the Confederacy plus Oklahoma and Kentucky.

33. Ronald D. Elving, "Southern Republicans: A National Outlook," *Congressional Quarterly Weekly Report,* 15 June 1996, 1730.

34. This presumes the reelection of a Democratic vice-president, who could break a tie Senate vote.

35. Ruth Marcus, "Reinterpreting the Rules," *Washington Post,* 26 October 1996, A1.

36. Ruth Marcus, "GOP Keeps Fund-Raising Lead Despite Trade Groups' Shift in Giving," *Washington Post,* 3 November 1996, A31–33.

37. Philip Morris Co., November 1996.

38. B. Drummond Ayres Jr., "Where Labor and Business Overshadow a House Race," *New York Times,* 11 October 1996, A12.

39. Robin Toner, "In Final Rounds, Parties Wield Bare-Knuckle Ads," *New York Times,* 21 October 1996, A1.

40. Lyman Kellstedt, James Guth, and Clyde Wilcox, "Religion and Politics Workshop" (Paper presented at the 1995 American Political Science Association annual meeting, Chicago).

41. Robin Toner, "Parties Pressing to Raise Turnout as Election Nears," *New York Times,* 27 October 1996, A1.

42. In June 1996 the Supreme Court ruled that three Texas House districts had to be redrawn because they had been created primarily to produce black-and/or Hispanic-majority constituencies. Three federal judges redrew district lines to meet the Court's objections and in early August invalidated the primary results in thirteen congressional districts altered by the remapping. These races would have to be run again on election day, in a combined two-party primary. Some of the earlier primary losers filed again, as did all the winners and several new candidates. A candidate would need a majority of the vote to win. Ten of these districts did produce a winner on election day. The other three held runoffs on 10 December.

43. Recall that there were fifty-four Republicans by the end of 1995, after two senators switched to the Republican Party. But the Republican majority was reduced to fifty-three before the 1996 election when Senator Robert Packwood (R-Ore.) resigned and was replaced by Democrat Ron Wyden.

44. R.W. Apple Jr., "Despite Some Words of Bipartisanship, More Political

Storms Are Likely," *New York Times,* 7 November 1996, B6.

45. Data on support for the Contract with America come from *Congressional Quarterly Weekly Report,* 24 February 1996, 502–3. Party unity scores for 1995 are from *Congressional Quarterly Weekly Report,* 27 January 1996, 246–47.

46. Robin Toner, "G.O.P. Leaders Proclaim Victory Over Labor," *New York Times,* 7 November 1996, B3.

47. Ibid.

48. See Edward G. Carmines and James A. Stimson, *Issue Evolution: Race and the Transformation of American Politics* (Princeton: Princeton University Press, 1989).

49. "Who Voted for Whom in the House," *New York Times,* 7 November 1996, B3.

50. Michael Janofsky, "Women Make Only Moderate Gains Despite the Many Contenders," *New York Times,* 7 November 1996, B2.

51. The Supreme Court has ruled many of these districts unconstitutional, but their black and Hispanic representatives, drawing on the benefits of incumbency, have often been reelected in redrawn, white-majority districts.

52. R. Darcy, Susan Welch, and Janet Clark, *Women, Elections, and Representation* (New York: Longman, 1987), 70–71, 75–77.

53. Data are drawn from new member profiles in *Congressional Quarterly Weekly Report,* 12 November 1994, 13–20; 7 January 1995, 48–105; and 9 November 1996, 13–54, supplemented by www.politicsnow.com.

54. Morgan, "A Revolution Derailed," C1, C5.

55. "The Small Deal," *Newsweek,* 18 November 1996, 127.

56. Quoted in Adam Clymer, "Top Republicans Say They Seek 'Common Ground' with Clinton," *New York Times,* 7 November 1996, 1.

57. Dan Balz, "The New 'New Democrats,'" *Washington Post National Weekly Edition,* 23–29 September 1996, 6.

58. See Aldrich and Rohde, "Theories of the Party," for a discussion of the development of this polarization.

59. Thomas B. Edsall and Mario A. Brossard, "Clashing Coalitions Produce Split in Government Power," *Washington Post,* 7 November 1996, A1.

60. Rebecca Carr, "As Soft Money Grows, So Does Controversy," *Congressional Quarterly Weekly Report,* 16 November 1996, 3273.

61. John R. Wright, "PACs, Contributions, and Roll Calls: An Organizational Perspective," *American Political Science Review* 79 (June 1985): 400–414.

62. For an excellent summary, see Berry, *Interest Group Society,* chap. 1.

63. See Thomas L. Gais, *Improper Influence: Campaign Finance Law, Political Interest Groups, and the Problem of Equality* (Ann Arbor: University of Michigan Press, 1996).

64. Eric Schmitt, "Half the Electorate, Perhaps Satisfied or Bored, Sat Out Voting," *New York Times,* 7 November 1996, B6.

CONCLUSION

The Meaning of the Election

WILSON CAREY McWILLIAMS

> Shall we their fond pageant see?
> Lord, what fools these mortals be!
> — *A Midsummer-Night's Dream* (III, ii)

In the election of 1996 the tumult and shouting were mostly contrived. There were no great captains and certainly no kings, and the parties' over-funded armies fought out the campaign on the dreary edges of political life.

The result amounted to a decision not to decide, dividing government between bitterly partisan rivals but issuing what Garry Wills called a "man-date to get along."[1] Uneasy about the direction of things, most Americans were unready for big changes, balanced, like a vampire's lover, between fas-cination and dread.[2]

Not much inclined to cheer, the voters found even fewer reasons for doing so. They didn't like the Congress or trust the president, but they re-elected both, and the percentage of Americans who even made it to the polls was the lowest since 1924, the second lowest in the history of mass democratic politics.[3] It didn't help that the race was one-sided—Clinton's victory was predictable from the end of the primary season, if not ear-lier—or that both candidates, whatever their defects, were safe and sane, so that staying home was unlikely to do damage.[4] But more ominously, mil-lions of Americans believe or suspect that democratic politics, even at its best, has become largely irrelevant; in America's developing postindustrial-ism, economics and technology seem to call the tune even where govern-ment plays the fiddle.

Conservatives have profited from and encouraged this mood, linking it

241

to their own critique of government, and neoliberals have embraced it, albeit with less enthusiasm. But the conviction that politics is impotent rests on a relativism that, while it deprecates government and law in the first instance, goes on to devalue all institutions, all promises and choices, and even the idea of human freedom and responsibility.[5] Ultimately, that logic is bound to provoke contradiction. Human beings are creatures, but they are also made to be creative; the products of a society, they are also its shapers.[6] And it bears remembering that many, if not most, of us would rather be governed by someone than be subjected, voicelessly, to the ordeal of change. Jean Bethke Elshtain is right: democracy is "on trial," challenged to demonstrate that its politics is equal to the time.[7]

Americans have been there before. Back in 1896, during our transition to industrialism, intellectual orthodoxy held that government should not meddle with socioeconomic evolution; William Graham Sumner had proclaimed, more than a decade earlier, that the "inadequacy of the State to regulative tasks is agreed upon, as a matter of fact, by all."[8] The incumbent president was Grover Cleveland, the first Democrat to be reelected since Andrew Jackson (though for nonconsecutive terms), as Bill Clinton was the first since FDR, and also like Clinton, Cleveland practiced "third-way" politics, cracking the GOP majority by adopting large parts of respectable Republicanism—sound money, internationalism, and a frugal government suspicious of welfare.[9]

Discontent divided both parties. The old distinctions, defined largely by the tariff and memories of the antislavery struggle, were coming to seem outmoded, and the third-party Populists had won significant support in 1892 and 1894. In 1896, the minority Democrats took the gamble: their convention was dominated by a large majority—a little fast footwork provided the two-thirds then needed to nominate a candidate—dedicated to the repudiation of Cleveland's policies. In the process, they redefined and revived American party politics and signaled the advent of the age of reform.

In the short term, however, the nomination of William Jennings Bryan on a "free silver" platform was a political flop. The accents of the campaign were agrarian and Protestant, and while Bryan added a number of Plains and western states to the then-Solid South, he lost the East and the Midwest.[10] But Bryan's oratory formulated what, ever since, has been the Democrats' ruling image: a rejection of "trickle-down" economics in favor of the proposition that "if you legislate to make the masses prosperous," their well-being "will find its way up through every class which rests upon them."[11] Bryan's rhetoric pointed beyond free silver and the gold standard, ranging the Democrats as partisans of a government active in the pursuit of civic equality.[12]

There were no Bryans, however, in 1996.[13] In fact, it is tempting to regard the election as the revenge of the Cleveland Democrats: Bill Clinton, like Cleveland, played down the claims of government, urging a moderate social liberalism informed by internationalism, and his areas of electoral strength paralleled those of McKinley and the Republicans a century ago.[14] But where Cleveland's party was fractious, Clinton's was surly but willing to check its discontent in the interest of checking or reversing 1994's swing to the right.[15] Democrats are less likely to be compliant, four years down the road. For that matter, Republicans cannot expect much serenity in their own future. In the shallows and silences of 1996, it is possible to make out signs of a political redefinition waiting for its season. Half postponement and half prelude, the election of 1996 let Americans off the hook for a while longer, and they were happy to be spared.

Clinton's Victory: The Uncertain Economy

To most observers, Clinton's victory was easily explained. In the first place, the economy was prosperous, the country was at peace, and most Americans were enjoying a decent level of well-being: R.W. Apple's postelection column was subtitled "Good Times Lead to Second Term."[16] Second, Clinton had the good fortune to be opposed by Bob Dole, a candidate who was famously inarticulate and startlingly out of touch.[17] In both respects, however, this account is only the beginning of the story, and each of its parts —the economy and the opponents—deserves exploration.

By all accounts, the economy was doing reasonably well in 1996, but prosperity hadn't saved the Democrats in 1994, when economic conditions were so good that Fred Greenstein could only describe the voters' discontents as "iatrogenic," produced by the diagnoses of gloomy economic experts and would-be healers.[18] Politically, immediate economic circumstances are apt to matter less than judgments about the economy as a whole, and especially, about its future.[19] In politics, economic questions are not narrowly material; our reactions are affected by loyalties and memories and by culture generally, and the crucial issue is less dollars than dignity, the hope of winning and preserving a socially honorable station.[20] And Americans, so long confidently expectant, are showing long-term uncertainties and even fears of decline.[21]

It seemed logical that when the voters' estimates of the direction of the economy turned down in June 1995—47 percent said things were "getting worse," as against 34 percent the year before—Richard Morin counted it as "disturbing news for Clinton's reelection team," and by May 1996, the figures, if anything, were a little worse.[22] The public's feeling was more than subjective: economic growth was slow, as Bob Dole repeatedly pointed out, often in rather shrill hyperbole, but the fact did Dole very little good.[23] Economic expectations proved to have an unexpected effect: by July, the economy was getting fairly good marks, but those who thought its direction "good" divided the credit almost evenly between Clinton and Congress, while those who said conditions were "bad" were more than twice as likely to blame Congress.[24] Those who experienced things as not going well, in other words, tended to regard the president (and probably his party) as on their side. Clinton benefited from a combination of economic well-being and worry.

Battered by technological change and globalization, most Americans are living with a sense of vulnerability, most immediately in relation to their jobs. In 1996, "downsizing"—and "outsourcing," a parallel term in economic Newspeak—became something like the economic rule; in March, the *New York Times* ran a seven-part series on "the downsizing of America."[25] It is cold consolation that the problem is international and that conditions elsewhere are generally worse than they are in the United States; misery, in this respect, does not love company.[26] Even where there are jobs, the quality of work is, to put it generously, unreliable: wages edged up a little in the late summer of 1996, but the long-term tendency of real wages has been down, and more and more Americans are working as temporary workers in the "contingent economy," with volatile wages and few benefits.[27]

The problem, of course, is most severe among the urban poor, but it gnaws at the people E.J. Dionne calls the "anxious middle"—older workers threatened by technology (which includes virtually anyone over thirty-five), white-collar families whose precarious prosperity rests on debt, retail small businesses facing competition from category-busting superstores, and younger people, comfortable in the "information age" but facing a future shaped by the "hollowing out" of labor.[28]

Americans do tend to exaggerate the country's economic woes, but they are on the mark in seeing an increase in inequality, now more extreme than in any other industrial nation.[29] Russell Baker called it "disgusting": the affluent are virtually rushing away from middle- and working-class Americans.[30] Upward mobility is slower, and elite incomes are exploding, so that the average corporate CEO, who earned 35 times the salary of the average production worker in 1974, now earns 120 times as much.[31]

Too many Americans feel stalked by indignity, and the very idea of civic community is more open to question. Traditionally, it was assumed that growth that benefits elites will also reward the great majority, albeit to a lesser extent; now, Benjamin Schwartz argues, changes that are making upper-income Americans prosperous may actually be hurting something like 45 percent of their fellow citizens.[32] In fact, Robert Frank and Philip Cook make a persuasive case that the United States is becoming a "winner-take-all society," in which highly visible people toward the top of the heap win disproportionate rewards for marginal advantages: the best lawyers or anchor people or corporate executives or sports stars may be better than their rivals in the second tier, but they are not as much better as their salaries would suggest. At the top, the market is oligopolistic, with few sellers and many buyers, and competitive advantage turns on positions as much as abilities. The lure of the brass ring, moreover, is so great that Americans overestimate their chances of grabbing it, while more modest success and local celebrity seem not much better than defeat.[33]

At the same time, while technological change is unsettling old elites, it is also creating new ones. Power gravitates to those who can control or master new techniques, and the great majority, scrambling to catch up, acquire a level of skill only to find that it has already become obsolete.[34]

Clinton's Victory:
The Uncertain Community

The problem goes beyond the workplace. Economic and technological transformations demand adaptability and mobility, necessarily weakening commitments to place, to relationships, and to beliefs and values.[35] They encourage relativism and disengagement, undermining trust and loyalty across the board and generally eating up the "civic capital" of our institutions.[36] Growing numbers of Americans live in "common interest developments" specialized on the basis of age or class or—if only implicitly—ethnicity and culture, often walled and gated, essentially seceding from the public into a "culture of nonparticipation."[37] Families, destabilized and pressured, scramble for time, and more and more, children count as economic costs.[38] Meanwhile, the media intrude on and disrupt families and communities, shaping a "collective second identity" based on mass marketing's lowest common denominator.[39]

All of this results from the dynamics of the private sector; despite conservative complaints, government is a very minor player. The criticism of welfare has been critical for conservative politics, in fact, because it is one of the few cases in which it is possible to make a tolerable case that public policy bears a major responsibility for social demoralization.[40] The best conservative voices acknowledge the private sector's depredations: denouncing violence and sexuality in the media in the name of our "better nature," Bob Dole carefully exempted Republican contributors such as Arnold Schwarzenegger and Bruce Willis, but even Dole felt compelled to call attention to the damage done by irresponsible devotion to the bottom line.[41]

Especially where they are touched directly, the great majority of Americans expect government to patch or reweave such tears in the social fabric. They want government to regulate HMOs, for example, by banning "gag rules" or allowing longer hospital stays after childbirth, just as they insist that public authorities oversee the safety of air travel.[42] A significant number probably agree with Edwin Luttwak that the United States needs economic growth less than stability and work. And in less demanding and ambitious ways, very few of us don't look to government for some form of assistance or hope that it can guide change in a way that makes private life compatible with public principles.[43]

In recent years, however, we've become much less certain about what the standards are. Issues that were once handled locally, leaving room for cultural plurality, seem to demand national solutions, so that for some time Americans have been pulled toward a "culture war" over the nature of morality and the place of religion in public life.[44] There are plenty of people who doubt whether our institutions and our enfeebled civilities will be able to keep debate within the boundaries of democratic politics.[45] And as I have already indicated, a strong current opinion doubts that government has the power to make all that much difference, given the tide of globalization.[46]

In one sense, international politics was invisible in the campaign. In 1992, our first campaign after the end of the Cold War, George Bush still urged his foreign policy credentials, and Clinton's lack of them, as a major issue in the election, provoking Clinton to take hawkish positions, especially in relation to Bosnia, that he came to regret.[47] In 1996 there were criticisms, here and there, of Clinton's vacillations, but the dominant view seemed to agree with Lawrence Eagleburger's judgment, four years earlier, that the United States might be entering "a period of the absence of clear purpose" in foreign policy.[48] Clinton, in fact, had become increasingly sure-handed in foreign affairs.[49] Even his response to Iraq's intrusion into Kurdistan in September 1996 showed a nice calibration of the demands of domestic and international politics.[50] When Dole and Kemp criticized the president's ventures, in fact, they provoked William Kristol and Robert Kagan to charge that they were surrendering Reagan's legacy in favor of isolationism.[51] In fact, both Clinton and Dole are internationalists, free traders, and above all, pragmatists who are more inclined to adapt to events than to try to shape them according to some grand design.[52]

Globalization, foreign policy's strong presence in the campaign, was consequently a delicate problem for both candidates, since for millions of Americans, it has come to symbolize the loss of self-government to "uncontrollable forces ... with their daily mockery of domestic political agendas."[53] Of course, even more voters value the goods and opportunities that the world economy makes available, and attacks on globalization are somewhat unfair, since domestic technological change probably does more of the damage we complain of than foreign economic competition. Still, the intrusions of international economics are sensitive because they raise, so directly, questions about the value of citizenship, the meaning of nationality, and the reality of the common good.

In the world most of us grew up in, foreign policy, though sometimes a matter for bitter controversy, moderated the tension between the free market and political democracy. It wasn't always that way: early in American history, foreign policy was a major line of partisan and sectional division, partly because, in a society that was still fairly egalitarian, class issues bothered us less and democracy and capitalism seemed more easily compatible.[54] But industrialism, creating a new hierarchy, threatened civic equality, and a major argument for reform—for moderating capitalism in the interest of political community—relied on the need for strength and solidarity in foreign policy, as well as against the specter of socialism. With the Soviet Union as a foe, the two dangers merged, strengthening the hand of politics in its contest with economics.[55] It contributed to the rise of what Alexei Bayer calls "capitalist" as opposed to "market" ideology, an essentially corporatist doctrine centered on an implicit "contract" between management and labor.[56] Modern corporations, it was said, had restored the political relation between classes that had been—or so Marx and Engels argued—dissolved by the market.[57] As American economic dominance weakened, however, management began to find the contract onerous, particularly when victory in the Cold War reduced both the risk of overseas investment and the claim of American business to government protection.[58] In the contemporary global economy, businesses can plead their inability to protect the jobs and benefits of workers—a persuasive argument, apparently, and one that obviously softens any conflict between classes—at the same time that capital is freed from its always problematic relation to country.[59] That the highly publicized success stories of the international economy are so often authoritarian polities with market economies does not increase confidence about the political future.

American worries along this line help explain the impact of the Indonesian fund-raising scandal that hurt the Democrats in the last days of the campaign.[60] Plenty of observers professed not to see what the fuss was about: realistically, foreign money and influence aren't any worse than their domestic counterparts, particularly if, as in a number of prominent cases, the domestic money comes from companies controlled by foreign nationals.[61] But the voters who were troubled displayed, if perhaps only inarticulately, a more refined appreciation for the formal and legal boundaries of political community.

Nationalist sentiment regarding issues like trade and immigration was never far below the surface, full-throated and more than a little pathological in fringe groups fearful of a "New World Order" and only a little more respectable in Pat Buchanan's oratory, but in a quieter way, touching many hearts.[62] Illegal aliens and immigrants generally were a convenient target for worries, and many Republicans were tempted by the success of Proposition 187 in California.[63] Electorally, these flirtations backfired: Hispanic Americans appear to have been offended, and they were not alone, especially since a group of bemused Republicans in the House proposed repealing birthright citizenship for the children of illegal aliens, running against generations of civics classes that have inculcated the lesson that in America—unlike less enlightened nations—citizenship comes from the soil, not by blood.[64]

Still, even the overpunitive critics of immigration have a point. In our increasingly two-tiered politics, the bond of citizenship is growing thin.[65] Elites, more apt to be cosmopolitan than ever, are tied to place only lightly; most people are less ambiguously national and more dependent on the country. Millions among those less advantaged were attracted by the argument that our obligations to our fellow citizens come first and would have responded to Burke's famous argument that a political community is no "partnership . . . in a trade of pepper and coffee, calico or tobacco, or some other such low concern, to be taken up for a little temporary interest and to be dissolved at the fancy of the parties."[66] In a blundering way, the critics of immigration, and of the Democrats' Asian fund raising, were pointing to the principle that politics is entitled to primacy over economics. The majority of Americans would probably settle for a wider margin of security.

Virtually all of us are feeling at least somewhat baffled and considerably overwhelmed: our experience is an ever-closer match to the "paranoid position," and in 1996 the sense of being surrounded by shadowy, disordering powers took a giant step toward the mainstream.[67] Forty-eight percent of Americans, *Newsweek* reported, believe in UFOs, and similar numbers are convinced that the government is covering up the evidence; 29 percent believe that the government is in contact with aliens.[68]

In many ways, the mood of the electorate is captured by the hit television series *The X-Files,* in which part of the government is engaged in a conspiracy to conceal the presence of paranormal and extraterrestrial beings among us, but the hero and heroine are *also* government agents. Government, in this story line, is flawed and not always benign, but it is to some degree responsive and certainly our only means of combating the dark forces around us. And the movie *Independence Day,* a smash at the box office, spoke to its mass audience's desire for government to take control, even at great, apocalyptic cost.[69]

For similar reasons, the Oklahoma City bombing played a central role in the drama of 1996. In one sense, it was just another, more terrible evidence of our vulnerability and our exposure to terrorist violence, like the attack on the World Trade Center, but there was a politically crucial difference. Americans had become accustomed to associating political disorders with foreigners (especially Arabs) and with the left. But the turbulence of the 1960s—frequently presented as a bad example in Newt Gingrich's speeches—is decades away, and although there were undergrounds, the left we remember was desperately public.[70] Even the Unabomber, that lonely, antitechnological reminder of 1960's violence, was caught because of the manifesto he insisted on publishing. In 1996, however, Americans were forced to confront disorder from the right, in the burning of African American churches across the South as well as in Oklahoma City.[71] Moreover, rightist terror—secret, apparently respectable, and technologically adroit —proved to epitomize our more paranoid fears.[72]

Most important, the militias and the extremist right were linked to savage attacks on the government by the political right. Freshman Representative Steve Stockman accused Janet Reno of "premeditated murder" in the 1993 attack on the Branch Davidian compound at Waco and spoke of a "gestapo mentality" in government; his colleague, Helen Chenoweth, was comparably extreme; the NRA referred to government agents as "jackbooted thugs" wearing Nazi uniforms—prompting President Bush to resign from the organization; even Newt Gingrich opposed the administration's antiterrorism bill, referring to a "genuine fear of the federal government." And on talk radio, of course, there was much worse.[73]

Conservatives recognized their exposure. When Clinton denounced antigovernment rhetoric, suggesting, sensibly enough, that "words have consequences," the shrewdest among them, like Bill Kristol, more or less agreed.[74] Most Republicans, however, turned civil libertarian, denouncing the president's remarks as repressive, and their response indicated, as Dan

Morgan wrote, a sense that the conservative movement had been "subliminally tainted."[75]

The Oklahoma City disaster greatly raised Clinton's standing and, as Morgan observed, "put a human face on bureaucrats, and revealed a kinder, gentler federal government, with a day-care center on the ground floor."[76] Suspicion of government didn't go away; some 11 million Americans, if the polls are right, regard government as an "enemy," and 40 percent express milder distrust.[77] But right-wing terror reminded most Americans how much they depend on government and need to trust it: as Tom Esker, a youngish Californian, told Richard Morin, "I'm not afraid the feds will blow up our cities."[78] And that sentiment, pretty much, framed the election of 1996.

Republican Alternatives, Democratic Responses

Republicans didn't get it, at least until very late in the day. Bob Dole was the calculated choice of party leaders who knew and discounted his weaknesses. They assumed, back when the campaign began to take shape, that Clinton was a dead duck; in 1993, it was common to say that the president had contracted "Quayle syndrome," and in early 1995, Richard Morin reported, while calling into question, the Washington belief that Clinton's defeat was a sure thing.[79] The Republicans, on this view, didn't need a candidate to win an election, but to avoid losing one, and just as predicted, Bob Dole proved to be a candidate minimally acceptable to all elements of the Republican coalition, and one who could, helped by a front-loaded primary schedule, avoid a prolonged, embittering contest for the nomination.

The problem, of course, was that Republicans misread the mood of the country and the verdict of 1994.[80] The midterm election did show a marked distrust of government and a conservative tilt that shifted the terms of political debate decisively to the right.[81] And it is easy to understand how the exhilaration of victory encouraged Republicans to overreach, especially since so many political scientists saw a political transformation in the 1994 returns.[82] Yet even at the time, it was easy to see ambiguities; the 1994 election did not mark a "chapter" in our politics, Ross Baker observed; it was "somewhere between a page and a paragraph."[83]

Newt Gingrich and his allies, however, seemingly caught up in a sense of destiny, carried the idea of a constitutional revolution beyond the relative moderation of 1994's Contract with America.[84] In their version of ideological politics, social conservatism got little more than lip service: Gingrich, a "values-based libertarian," put his emphasis on dismantling the government, hoping to undo the legacy of the 1960s, if not the New Deal.[85] The new Republicans, Russell Baker wrote, are "full of ideas, and so young they can't remember they are ideas that have already failed."[86]

The goal of starving the government led Republicans to question programs, like the Earned Income Tax Credit, aimed to help the working poor, exactly the sort of policy that conservatives might be expected to support. Similarly, the Republican majority proved unwilling to spend money on "second chance homes," an effort to deal with illegitimacy and family instability, and Cardinal O'Connor was not alone in worrying that niggardliness about welfare might press the poor to have abortions.[87] In all of this, Republicans seemed to miss the point that a large part of popular disenchantment with welfare was concerned, not with the cost, but with the cultural and moral impact of public assistance, and plenty of voters who had marched to the Republican drum in 1994 had no desire to turn cutting costs into an excuse for hurting the poor.[88]

The Republican militants in Congress, convinced they were riding the wave of the future, were led to the belief that "shutting down the government," in their budgetary conflict with the president, would be regarded as an acceptable demonstration of moral conviction and strength of purpose, and that the president would eventually "blink."[89] They were wrong, of course: Republican intransigence was seen as just this side of nutty, and the shutdown was another reminder, for Americans, of the ways in which government is a convenience or a necessity.[90] In all probability, Republicans kept their majorities only by a "switch in time" to modest cooperation in the interest of "productive government."[91]

In fact, the voters who tipped the balance in 1994 did not vote *for* the Republicans so much as *against* Clinton and the Democratic "old gang" in Congress.[92] Having inspired high expectations, Bill Clinton began his presidency with a series of miscalculations, waverings, and botched appointments; his legislative victories, like the deficit reduction plan, were not the stuff to make hearts sing; the anticrime bill barely survived; welfare reform, which could have been both a humane new direction and a political triumph, never really got started; and the Clinton health plan, announced with ruffles and flourishes, died with barely a whisper.[93]

It wasn't entirely Clinton's fault. He was bound to fall short of his supporters' hopes, given the polyglot nature of his coalition and the increasing limits on the contemporary presidency.[94] But Clinton so insistently took center stage that he made himself a lightning rod, a fact that helps account for the disproportionate criticism he received from the press.[95] In any event, Clinton came to seem weak and inept, and what direction he had appeared to follow elite liberalism, though often in a bungling way—NAFTA, gays in the military, the insistence on a woman for attorney general, the hasty and later withdrawn nomination of Lani Guinier. Meanwhile, in Congress, the baronial Democrats moved with ponderous indifference.[96] In November 1994 the voters punished Clinton and his party for offering ineffective government, not because they opposed government per se.[97]

Clinton, of course, bent with the wind. The 1994 results confirmed his disposition toward a "third way" presidency, an "unabashedly mongrel politics" that leans toward "poaching on the territory" of the other party.[98] In general, the president conceded the relatively abstract and widely popular themes that Gingrich had helped make the Republicans' stock-in-trade—a balanced budget, smaller government, devolution to the states, and "ending welfare as we know it"—while taking visible, relatively conservative positions on social issues, abortion excepted, from support for school uniforms to opposition to gay marriage.[99] Increasingly seen as a moderate, Clinton shifted the debate from ideology to practice, into areas—Medicare, Medicaid, Social Security, education, and the environment—where the public's "operational liberalism" is demonstrated and long-standing, and where the Democrats' reputation as the party of government helps, since it makes their promise to protect such programs more credible.[100]

With Clinton staking out a claim to the center, what interest the campaign might have held disappeared with General Powell's decision not to seek the Republican nomination. As Juan Williams had guessed he would, Clinton ran as a mildly liberal Reagan, reasserting the optimistic themes of the Republicans' 1984 proclamation of "morning in America."[101] The last suspense ended when the president signed the welfare reform bill, outraging people on the left but taking away Bob Dole's best hope for a talking point.[102] In fact, having signed the bill, Clinton could tell critics that its very harshness made his reelection more necessary, to "fix" the law or to keep it from getting worse, turning his apostasy into a commendation.[103]

Bob Dole, haunted by gaffes and a rhetoric so graceless that even the sober-sided New York Times was moved to mockery, suffered from what Russell Baker called a "charisma chasm."[104] His campaign was a series of improvisations masking as themes. It began inside the Senate, where Dole hoped to pass legislation that would establish him as a man of action, but Dole found himself outgeneraled and caught up in the Senate's routine.[105] His resignation from the Senate won a few headlines, but it cost him influence with his colleagues, and it didn't change Dole's image, three and a half decades in the making, as a Washington insider.[106] Finally, in desperation, Dole surrendered to the supply side, proposing a tax cut he once scorned, winning brief cheers from libertarians like William Safire, but damaging his own credibility, "whittling himself down to Clinton's size" in his evident opportunism.[107] Nothing worked. The "bump" from the contrived Republican convention was slight and brief; the presidential debates were unmemorable, except for Dole's conspicuous avoidance of the conservative social agenda; even his best rhetoric—"a bridge to the past"— wound up allowing Clinton to present himself as a man of vision, capable of building a "bridge to the future."[108]

For too many voters, the campaign must have been another argument against democratic politics. Clinton and Dole—and Ross Perot, for that matter—contributed, agreeing that the difficulties of Medicare would be better handled by a bipartisan commission, off the political stage. Neither party, moreover, had much to say about the public's concern for secure and socially adequate work. In 1993 Hobart Rowen noted that Clinton had "no apparent answer to the jobs problem," and things weren't much different in 1996.[109] The administration mostly contented itself with accentuating the positives, complemented with appeals to Clinton's "growth agenda" and references to the obligation of business to avoid unnecessary downsizing.[110]

Republicans had even less to say. On the campaign trail, Dole tended to sidle around the issue of jobs—which had surprised him, after all, back in New Hampshire—and even Pat Buchanan, fulminating, had no program beyond protectionism.[111] For familiar ideological reasons, Republicans weren't willing to offer government as an ally. Gingrich, a technophile, is inclined to treat economic dislocations as a phase, and the Republican-dominated Joint Economic Committee of Congress declared that there is "no positive basis for criticizing any degree of market-driven inequality."[112]

In fact, Republican opposition to an increase in the minimum wage made it easier for Clinton to present himself as a friend of labor.[113] Enough Republicans eventually broke ranks to let the bill pass, but it did Dole no good, although it probably saved some Republican seats.

The Republicans' boldest initiative was Dole's tax plan, but even conservative experts, chastened by experience, had become skeptical, and respondents were apt to tell pollsters that the tax cut, even if passed, would bust the budget or have to be paid for in other ways. And they also frequently remarked that, apart from the promise of "growth," Dole's scheme said nothing about work at all.[114]

The Democrats' advantage, in other words, was largely negative, no long-term answer for the party, especially since Republicans will be able to take advantage of America's abiding individualism and distrust of public authority.[115] Both parties, however, have reason to be at least attentive to the widespread desire to *direct* change, rather than merely endure it. Failure to address the mounting level of anxiety, continuing to drain support for democratic institutions, encourages citizens to look elsewhere, and that searching will not always be directed to private faiths and lives.[116] The electorate, Kevin Phillips wrote, is "almost out of patience," and rebuilding trust in public life deserves to rank first on any political agenda.[117]

It is not a challenge for which Bill Clinton is ideally suited. In 1996 the president was lucky. Even his early failures provided a basis for the belief that Clinton was "growing" into his job, just as the criticism of his wife allowed him to seem chivalrous in her defense, reversing the pattern of 1992, when Mrs. Clinton had been called on to support her husband.[118]

Clinton's virtues of shrewdness and adaptability also mark his limits: no lion, he is at best a somewhat pious fox, not disposed to practice or ask for heroism and inclined to let fundamental issues slide.[119] His very imperfections combine with his deference to the decencies of faith, family, and country in a way that suggests Reagan grown clever—"a flawed man," Richard Ford calls him, "for a flawed time."[120]

It is not altogether surprising that the continuing doubts about Clinton's character made so little difference in 1996. Most voters discounted Whitewater as politically motivated and incomprehensible, and Rob Reiner's film, *The American President,* was virtually a pro-Clinton tract on the question of private conduct.[121] "I trust the hard way," Bob Dole said when resigning from the Senate, but most Americans don't: they belong to a world of suburbs, malls, and credit cards, not the "old railroad towns" to which Dole referred, and they suspect that the old virtues, too exacting for comfort even in their private lives, may be unsuited to contemporary politics. In recent elections, more or less able rogues have bested rivals with sterling character: Nixon beat Humphrey and McGovern, just as Clinton bested Dole.[122]

Our need for effective government is decisive. In a world full of perils and possibilities, Americans have adopted an essentially Machiavellian idea of political virtue: what matters in a leader is the ability to get results.[123] On that test, most Americans this year gave Clinton passing grades. "I think he can run the country," an Arizona Republican told Dan Balz and David Broder, "but he's going to lie to us doing it."[124]

Americans will have to hope that Clinton has high statecraft in his repertoire. The bridge America really needs, in the nearest possible future, is one linking its citizens with their government.

Politics and the American Future

A big part of the problem is inherent in the nature of the regime. In the framing of our institutions, distance between government and people was designed; the unique quality of American constitutionalism, Madison wrote, lies in the "total exclusion of the people in their collective capacity" from any share in rule.[125] And at the time, Antifederalists warned that the Constitution's politics—"intricate and perplexed," Cato said, "and too mysterious for you to understand"—were weighted to the advantage of elites. Effective national action called, even then, for large-scale organization, and Melancton Smith observed that "the great easily form associations; the poor and middling class form them with difficulty."[126]

For much of our history, this aspect of American government was checked by a politics—and a press—rooted in locality, the kind of "retail," face-to-face encounter that personalizes public life, conveys dignity, and encourages participation.[127] That sort of politics has been waning for some time now; our lives are shaped by forces that, constitutionally and in practice, can be dealt with only by federal power, if at all. In Washington in 1996, devolution was in fashion, but states and localities remained financially dependent, whatever discretion they gained in dealing with policy; willing to hand over responsibility, Congress was less eager, and probably not able, to transfer power. The local press has long been eclipsed by the electronic media, and the political parties, increasingly, are centralized, fund-raising bureaucracies, not federations of precincts and wards.[128]

In 1996 money was politically omnipresent, and very few voters did not at least sense that mass politics, while democratic in form, is more and more oligarchic in content. Money virtually defined our political choices. The Republican primary schedule put a premium on early fund raising, and Bob Dole, staggered in the first contests, needed only to survive until the first big round of primaries overtaxed his rivals' financial ability to compete effectively.[129] Bill Clinton was even better off, so well funded that, despite his liabilities, he discouraged challengers altogether, becoming the first Democrat nominated without substantial opposition since FDR in 1944. Moreover, the escalating cost of effective political participation discourages people from becoming active in civic life and tends to make even successful elected officials, weary of incessant fund raising, think better of the attractions of private life.[130] And obviously, greater dependence on money makes it more difficult to champion the interests of working- and middle-class Americans.[131]

There was enough unhappiness about the role of money in 1996 that some kind of campaign reform is likely to pass Congress, though how effective such legislation will be is open to question, and not only because congressional incumbents stand to benefit from the current system. A serious approach to the problem requires taking on the Supreme Court's decision, in *Buckley* v. *Valeo* (1976), that contributions of money are speech entitled to the protection of the First Amendment.[132] That ruling, Elizabeth Drew comments, is "wrong-headed, not to say bone-headed": among other things, donating money is a form of expression, but it isn't speech, since it doesn't give reasons or submit to questions.[133] The purpose of the First Amendment is to protect democratic deliberation, not to turn the public forum into private property.[134] Bill Bradley is right: we should be doing whatever it takes to get *Buckley* v. *Valeo* off the books, even if it proves necessary to amend the Constitution.[135]

Of course, the question of money and democratic speech inevitably involves the media, since the visual media add a special political problem. Robert Putnam's recent findings suggest that television, more than any other factor, works to erode our social capital.[136] Nor is this surprising: speech tends to unite the hearer and the heard, where sight isolates, separating the viewer from the seen.[137]

The technicians who shape the media, in politics no less than other programming, see audiences as consumers, desirous but essentially passive, and the logic of their craft aims to give the people what they want and no more—"stirring up emotions," Walter Goodman writes, "and shutting down minds"—following the tendency of the marketplace toward the lowest, and private, common denominator.[138]

In their professional capacity, political media technicians fear democratic deliberation, and with reason. Controversy, debate, dividing the yeas and nays is always risky, and in primaries and conventions has been associated with defeat at the polls; technicians have a natural preference for controlled, quasi-totalitarian spectacles.[139] In 1992 the Republicans let right-wingers, most notably Pat Buchanan, dominate the camera. This year, eager to avoid that mistake, they so tightly scripted their convention that Buchanan's delegates were not even allowed to vote for him.[140] And the Democratic convention was at least as thoroughly managed.

The difficulty, of course, is that this for-media version of politics is not very entertaining. As consumers, the audience knows and can find better shows; as citizens, most people realize that the real show is offstage.[141] If they miss the point, the news media will tell them: sensing the mass public's resentment and distrust, the news media have made attacks on authority a way of life.[142] And by covering elections as races, to the near-exclusion of any treatment of issues, the news media imply that what is said in public only matters as an indication of strategy.[143] Challenged about this or that enormity, the media justify themselves by reference to the duty to inform citizens, but—as the president might say—that dog won't hunt. The mass public displays a startling degree of civic illiteracy, seemingly unaffected by higher levels of education: in one *Washington Post* survey, two-thirds of the respondents couldn't identify their representative in the House; 54 percent knew neither senator; and a considerable majority believed that foreign aid costs more than Medicare.[144]

Disenchanted and muddled, citizens resent their estrangement from politics, but in expressing that sentiment, they are too apt to "shout opinions into the wind, then hang up," and they could benefit from greater exposure to the art of democratic controversy.[145] Steve Forbes was right when he urged his party not to shy away from open debate: "It's like making sausage. It's not nice to behold ... but it's absolutely necessary in a democracy."[146] As Forbes went on to say, discontent will find a voice, through demagogues if not in civil argument. "I don't know where they are going," Howard Baker said of the voters in 1994, "and I don't think they know either. But what frightens me is that, if we do not address their feelings, they may develop a tendency to savage our institutions."[147]

The political parties haven't found the answer. Ross Perot has worn out his welcome and people hate to waste their votes, but an awful lot of Americans are thinking kind thoughts about third parties. At a time of increasing partisanship among elected officials, voters are finding it harder to identify with the parties' broad coalitions, and their loyalties have become more ambiguous, where they still exist at all.[148]

The Republicans suffer a widely advertised internal division between basically probusiness, often libertarian champions of private liberty and social conservatives, especially the religious right, who expect government to uphold traditional values.[149] At the level of principle, the contradiction is basic, and since the ending of the Cold War removed that commonality, increasingly visible.[150] Ronald Reagan was able to give the Republicans the atmosphere of a joyous crusade, but Reagan—who still had the anticommunist drum to beat—had a special magic.[151]

Bob Dole didn't come close. He made every effort to conciliate social conservatives early in the campaign, but his pragmatism was never a secret, and in building conservative support, he relied heavily on Ralph Reed's willingness to compromise in the interest of victory.[152] It was no surprise, consequently, that by convention time, Dole had virtually abandoned social conservatism.[153] He even largely ignored the carefully crafted challenge to partial-birth abortions, although the president's veto of the ban on that procedure put Democrats at odds with a strategically important body of opin-ion.[154] Dole preferred to rely on his tax plan, borrowing one of Reagan's parlor tricks, but even if he persuaded himself to believe it, Dole lacked the sleight-of-hand to pull it off.

In the end, having swallowed their pride and followed Reed and Dole in order to win, social conservatives were forced to endure a humiliating combination of neglect and defeat. Moderate Republicans, of course, have been arguing that the party needs to move to the center, cultivating women voters and practicing "inclusion." Social conservatives read a different les-son. They conclude that, all things being equal, Republicans cannot defeat Democrats in an election that turns on economics and government pro-grams. They believe it is possible to score points on such issues, but they ar-gue for the need to *define* campaigns in terms of social and moral issues, speaking to the public's concern for civil order.

Despite some defeats, the right will be stronger in Congress and at local levels. The growing Republican strength in the South and among reli-gious conservatives, in a year when other groups hesitated or fell away, in-dicates a "subnational" realignment that is likely to strengthen the voice of social conservatives in Republican councils. It is a sign of the times that the Republican state platform in Iowa accused the 4-H movement of leaning to-ward socialism.[155]

Looking toward the election of 2000, "mainstream" Republicans will hope, almost desperately, for a Powell candidacy, since the general may have enough personal magnetism to overcome opposition to his moderation. A "New Deal kid" with traditional values, Powell is no opponent of govern-ment, and as a candidate, he might—as Theodore Roosevelt did a century ago—pull dialogue in the direction of civic engagement. All that is high speculation; what's certain is that social conservatives, and the concern for civil order, are not about to go away.

Not that the Democrats are in better shape. The electorate didn't like Newt Gingrich, but as the congressional results suggested, it didn't trust the Democrats to run the country.[156] Clinton did well among younger voters and Hispanics, and he scored gains among Catholics, but Democratic can-didates for the House showed little or no improvement with these voters, and, with Catholics, may even have lost ground.[157] As a party, the Demo-crats were still associated with liberalism, and that doctrine doesn't sell.[158] Republican attack ads that waved the "L-word" like a bloody shirt were not successful, but Democrats, including the president, generally tried to put distance between themselves and liberal ideology.[159]

For thirty years or so, liberalism has promoted a greatly expanded government *responsibility* for economic and social life; at the same time, it has defended a panoply of liberties, rights, and entitlements, especially for favored constituencies, that create immunities from politics, reducing government's *authority*.[160] Obviously, those cross-purposes amount to a long-term prescription for frustration and failure. Contemporary Democratic politics is effectively postliberal, but so far, the party has not developed an alternative. In 1996 Democrats managed a relatively harmonic front, but post-Clinton, it is hard not to expect a battle for the party's soul.[161]

So-called new Democrats or neoliberals are inclined to emphasize the limits on government. Broadly "postmaterialist," they defend the individual rights associated with social liberalism and they concern themselves with "quality of life" issues like education and the environment, but—although they emphasize the importance of economic prosperity—they tend to regard unions as relics and show little interest in economic equality.[162] Their position, Harvey Mansfield remarks, is "less caring than liberalism and less judgmental than conservatism," a stance that, to critics, looks like well-mannered indifference.[163] "Old Democrats," by contrast, are more typically working class and more likely to be partisans of equality. They preserve the New Deal's attempt to make government the ally of families, and they are apt to care about decency and civic order more than the niceties of individual rights.[164]

Bill Clinton, characteristically, has gone both ways, although the Republican majorities on Capitol Hill may push him in a new Democratic direction. For the Democratic Party, however, 1996 may indicate a different path. The party of most Americans at the lower end of the income scale, it will necessarily practice a kind of class politics, especially given the mood of the voters and their debt to labor's contributions in the election.[165] As the unions understood, however, American political culture makes it necessary to speak to class concerns without employing class rhetoric, speaking to Americans as a people in terms of the common good.[166]

That subtler politics of class helps explain why race was so invisible in the campaign. Just as it's hard not to see class frictions—particularly those associated with the rise of the black middle class—in the mounting hostility to affirmative action, evident in the California initiative in 1996, it is also true that addressing our common vulnerabilities in terms of widely shared civic values has at least the possibility of muting the politics of race.[167] In any case, when President Clinton took his usual step to the center, agreeing that affirmative action should be "mended," but denying that it should be scrapped, his concession to the prevailing wind was largely understood and accepted by African American voters. And it is at least a straw in that wind that the five African American incumbents in the South, redistricted out of safe, majority-minority districts by court order, all won reelection. Incumbency helped, of course, but those results at least weaken the case for reverse gerrymandering and suggest that, for enough voters to make the difference, policy preferences can override race.[168]

In the same way, the welfare reform bill can open a new chapter. Passing the bill changed the terms of debate: there will be less talk about "welfare chiselers" and, grim though it is, more evidence of desperate families and suffering children. In the short term, there will be no "fixing" the bill, but Democrats can and should be arguing for compulsory national service and a role for the government as an employer of last resort. The old welfare system always slighted the fact that citizens have a duty and a right to contribute to national life, and defending that moral imperative could realize some of the very unfulfilled promise of Clinton's New Covenant.[169]

But the Democrats' most fundamental problem is one that also transcends party. In the anxieties of the contemporary middle class, E.J. Dionne sees an analogy to the old Progressive movement and the promise of a new one.[170] There is, as Dionne contends, still much to admire in the Progressive support for a government actively using scientific administration and political power in the service of civic duty and community.[171] But the Progressives never solved the problem of accountability, and their innovations—like the direct primary and the initiative—did at least as much harm as good. Any new Progressive movement must begin there, aiming to revitalize politics as a condition of policy, limiting the role of money, opening the media to serious democratic deliberation, and encouraging the development of party organizations that are local, closer to citizens, and better able to provide them with a public voice.

As if that were not challenge enough, the administrative state can be held accountable only on the basis of some standard or measure. Liberals and libertarians sometimes speak as if politics could be morally neutral, indifferent to first things, and Democrats, inclined to generosity, have often been disposed to agree. But ultimately, all policy—even a generous and tolerant one—rests on a judgment; for all parties and all citizens, politics comes down to a question of right.[172] American democracy is not formless: it presumes the superiority of citizenship, government by the people, and the principle of equality that is the foundation of both. For democracy—and historically, for Democrats—cultures and individuals are not separate islands. Our diverse republic rests on equality's enduring challenge to things seen, in which human differences are only occasions for inquiry and wonder. Cultural "stories," treated with genuine respect, are arguments, efforts to understand what is true and best.[173] Our different perspectives are the starting points of a politics that, as Michael Sandel argues, is "more clamorous than consensual," at least in the first instance, but reduced to civility by a sense of our own limits and the respect due to equals.[174] The election of 1996 offers ample evidence of America's need for leaders and parties who can invigorate the contentious decencies of democratic self-government.

Notes

1. Garry Wills, "A Mandate to Get Along," *New York Times,* 7 November 1996, A33.

2. Frank Rich, "Blowing in the Wind," *New York Times,* 20 November 1994, E15.

3. Peter Baker, "An All-Time High for Ballot Box No-Shows," *Washington Post National Weekly,* 11–17 November 1996, 11.

4. Robin Toner, "In This Race, It's the Center against the Middle," *New York Times,* 17 March 1996, E3.

5. Albert O. Hirschman, *The Rhetoric of Reaction: Perversity, Futility, Jeopardy* (Cambridge: Harvard University Press, 1991); Thomas Byrne Edsall, "The GOP Gains Ground as Trust in Government Erodes," *Washington Post National Weekly,* 12–18 February 1996, 12. This analysis follows Tocqueville's discussion of individualism, *Democracy in America* (New York: Knopf, 1980), 2:99.

6. Peter L. Berger, *The Sacred Canopy: Elements of a Sociological Theory of Religion* (Garden City, N.Y.: Doubleday, 1967), 93–101.

7. Jean Bethke Elshtain, *Democracy on Trial* (New York: Basic Books, 1994).

8. William Graham Sumner, *What Social Classes Owe to Each Other* (1883) (Caldwell, Idaho: Caxton, 1978), 10. Of course, the "all" in Sumner's saying refers to orthodox social scientists, as opposed to promoters of "social quackery," 101.

9. Stephen Skowronek, "The Risks of 'Third-Way' Politics," *Society* 33 (September/October 1996): 32–36. With Cleveland, however, this policy had a hard, principled edge: in 1887, vetoing a bill to provide seed corn to devastated Texas farmers, Cleveland declared that "though the people should support the government, the government should not support the people." Veto Message, 16 February 1887, cited in Matthew Josephson, *The Politicos* (New York: Harcourt Brace, 1938), 391.

10. In fact, in his three presidential campaigns, Bryan never carried an industrial state.

11. William Jennings Bryan, "Speech Concluding Debate on the Chicago Platform," in *Late Nineteenth-Century American Liberalism,* ed. Louis Filler (In-

dianapolis: Bobbs-Merrill, 1967), 61; in place of the later "trickle-down," Bryan referred to the idea that elite prosperity will "leak through on those below."

12. As Louis W. Koenig observed, the transformation of the Democrats, and the party system, was confirmed by Bryan's tireless work, over the next two decades, in party caucuses and conventions. *Bryan: A Political Biography* (New York: Putnam's, 1971).

13. Henry Allen, "In a Manner of Speaking," *Washington Post National Weekly*, 10–16 June 1996, 11.

14. With the exception of Indiana and North Dakota, Clinton carried every state that went for McKinley in 1896.

15. David Broder, "Hanging Together," *Washington Post National Weekly*, 2–8 September 1996, 4.

16. R.W. Apple, "Economy Helps Again," *New York Times*, 6 November 1996, A1.

17. In February, Dole told a New Hampshire audience that he hadn't expected jobs and trade to be important issues (Howell Raines, "Struggle in the Snow," *New York Times*, 20 February 1996, A18), a comment as startling as his mid-campaign praise for the no-hitter pitched by Hideo Nomo of the *Brooklyn Dodgers*.

18. Greenstein's comment is taken from the *New York Times*, 10 November 1994, B5. On the economy in 1994, see Peter Passell, "Why Isn't a Better Economy Helping Clinton's Popularity?" *New York Times*, 3 November 1994, D2.

19. Clay Chandler and Richard Morin, "Two Sides of the Coin," *Washington Post National Weekly*, 4–10 November 1996, 9.

20. Harvey C. Mansfield Jr., "Change and Bill Clinton," *TLS*, 13 November 1992, 14–15; Robert E. Lane, *The Market Experience* (New York: Cambridge University Press, 1991).

21. Louis Uchitelle, "The Rise of the Losing Class," *New York Times*, 20 November 1994, E1. On postwar American optimism, see James Patterson, *Great Expectations: The United States, 1945–1974* (New York: Oxford University Press, 1996).

22. Richard Morin, "A Nation Split Down the Middle," *Washington Post National Weekly*, 24–30 July 1995, 37; Richard Morin and Mario Brossard, "A Gamble That Isn't Paying Off," *Washington Post National Weekly*, 3–9 June 1996, 37.

23. Louis Uchitelle, "It's a Slow Growth Economy, Stupid," *New York Times*, 17 March 1996, E1.

24. *New York Times*, 3 August 1996, 8.

25. The *New York Times'* series "The Downsizing of America" began on 3 March 1996. On the general point, see Edwin Luttwak, "America's Insecurity Blanket," *Washington Post National Weekly*, 5–12 December 1994, 23.

26. *New York Times*, 19 August 1996, D2.

27. Louis Uchitelle, "A New Era of Ups and Downs," *New York Times*, 15 August 1996, 1; Hobart Rowen, "Our Own Worst Enemy," *Washington Post Na-*

tional Weekly, 26 September–2 October 1994, 10; the 1996 improvement is reported in the *New York Times,* 5 October 1996, A1.

28. E.J. Dionne Jr., *They Only Look Dead: Why Progressives Will Dominate the Next Political Era* (New York: Simon and Schuster), 1996; Louis Uchitelle, "A Top Economist Switches His View on Productivity," *New York Times,* 8 May 1996, D2; William Julius Wilson, *When Work Disappears: The World of the New Urban Poor* (New York: Knopf, 1996).

29. Richard Morin and John M. Berry, "Economic Anxieties," *Washington Post National Weekly,* 4–10 November 1996, 6–7; Kerth Bradsher, "Gap in Wealth in U.S. Called Widest in West," *New York Times,* 17 April 1995, A1; Steven A. Holmes, "Income Disparity between Poorest and Richest Rises," *New York Times,* 20 June 1996, A1.

30. Russell Baker, "Let's Get Sore," *New York Times,* 18 November 1995, 21.

31. Peter Passell, "Economic Scene," *New York Times,* 29 March 1996, D2; Kerth Bradsher, "America's Opportunity Gap," *New York Times,* 4 June 1995, E4; Chandler and Morin, "Two Sides of the Coin."

32. Benjamin Schwartz, "American Inequality: Its History and Scary Future," *New York Times,* 19 December 1995, A25.

33. Robert H. Frank and Philip J. Cook, *The Winner-Take-All Society* (New York: Martin Kessler/Free Press, 1995); see also Derek C. Bok, *The Cost of Talent: How Executives and Professionals Are Paid and How It Affects America* (New York: Free Press, 1993).

34. Jacques Ellul, *The Technological Society* (New York: Vintage, 1964), 208–18; Steve Lohr, "Reluctant Conscripts in the March of Technology," *New York Times,* 17 September 1995, E16; technological change also creates a mystique around new, high-performance products, which come to be valued beyond their utility. Robert Post, *High Performance* (Baltimore: Johns Hopkins University Press, 1996).

35. Daniel Bell, *The Cultural Contradictions of Capitalism* (New York: Basic Books, 1984); Joshua Meyerowitz, *No Sense of Place* (New York: Oxford University Press, 1985). For a very concrete example, see Sara Rimer, "A Hometown Feels Less Like Home," *New York Times,* 6 March 1996, A1.

36. Robert Putnam, "The Strange Disappearance of Civic America," *American Prospect* 24 (Winter 1996): 34–48; Henry Allen, "Ha! So Much for Loyalty," *Washington Post National Weekly,* 4–10 March 1996, 11; Tara L. White and Elaine Washington, "Youth: Changing Beliefs and Behavior," in *The State of the Americans: This Generation and the Next,* ed. Urie Bronfenbrenner (New York: Free Press, 1996), 1–28.

37. Evan McKenzie, *Privatopia: Homeowner Associations and the Rise of Residential Private Government* (New Haven: Yale University Press, 1994).

38. Lester Thurow, "Companies Merge: Families Break Up," *New York Times,* 3 September 1995, E11.

39. Todd Gitlin, *The Twilight of Common Dreams: Why America Is*

Wracked by Culture Wars (New York: H. Holt, 1995); Frank Rich, "Jenny Jones' Victory," *New York Times,* 23 March 1995, A25.

40. Robert Putnam, "Tuning In, Tuning Out: The Strange Disappearance of Social Capital in America," *PS* 28 (1995): 671; Steve Scott, "Defining Family Values," *California Journal* 27 (August 1996): 8–12.

41. E.J. Dionne Jr., "Dole v. Hollywood," *Washington Post National Weekly,* 12–18 June 1996, 29.

42. Robert Kuttner, "Free Market, Bad Medicine," *Washington Post National Weekly,* 29 July–4 August 1996, 5, and "The Case for Regulation," *Washington Post National Weekly,* 18–24 December 1995, 5.

43. Luttwak, "America's Insecurity Blanket"; Robert Reich, "Drowning in the Second Wave," *New York Times,* 2 April 1995, E15.

44. James Davison Hunter, *Culture Wars: The Struggle to Define America* (New York: Basic Books, 1991); Theodore J. Lowi, *The End of the Republican Era* (Norman: University of Oklahoma Press, 1995).

45. E.J. Dionne Jr., "A Matter of Respect," *Washington Post National Weekly,* 4–10 September 1995, 24; Eric M. Uslaner, *The Decline of Comity in Congress* (Ann Arbor: University of Michigan Press, 1994).

46. Richard Flacks, "Reflections on Strategy in a Dark Time," *Boston Review,* December/January 1996, 25; Michael Sandel, "America's Search for a New Public Philosophy," *Atlantic,* March 1996, 57, 72.

47. *New York Times,* 10 August 1992, A9.

48. Thomas L. Friedman, "Rethinking Foreign Affairs," *New York Times,* 7 February 1992, A7.

49. Thomas W. Lippman and Ann Devroy, "Matching Policy to Rhetoric," *Washington Post National Weekly,* 18–24 September 1995, 6–7.

50. R.W. Apple, "What's Bad for Hussein Seems Good for Clinton," *New York Times,* 5 September 1996, A11.

51. William Kristol and Robert Kagan, "The New Isolationist?" *New York Times,* 14 October 1996, A17.

52. Roger Cohen, "Global Forces Batter Politics," *New York Times,* 17 November 1996, E1.

53. Ibid.

54. Jürgen Habermas, *The Structural Transformation of the Public Sphere: An Inquiry into a Category of Bourgeois Society,* trans. Thomas Burger (Cambridge: MIT Press, 1991).

55. E.H. Carr, *The Soviet Impact on the Western World* (New York: Macmillan, 1949).

56. Alexei Bayer, "Beneficial Capitalism, R.I.P.," *New York Times,* 16 June 1996, F13.

57. Adolf Berle, *The Twentieth Century Capitalist Revolution* (New York: Harcourt Brace, 1954); Karl Marx and Friedrich Engels, *The Communist Manifesto,* trans. Samuel Moore (Baltimore: Penguin, 1967).

58. Peter Passell, "Life's Hard? Blame the Market," *New York Times,* 8 May

1994, E3; Steve Lohr, "Big Business in Turmoil," *New York Times,* 28 January 1993, A1; A.H. Rosenthal, "American Class Struggle," *New York Times,* 21 March 1995, A21; Flacks, "Reflections on Strategy," 26.

59. Uchitelle, "The Rise of the Losing Class."

60. Apple, "Economy Helps Again."

61. Russell Baker, "Yellow Peril's Return," *New York Times,* 7 December 1996, 23.

62. Thomas L. Friedman, "Buchanan for President," *New York Times,* 24 December 1995, E9.

63. Marc B. Haefele, "California Shipwreck," *Boston Review,* April/May 1995, 26–27.

64. Robert Pear, "Citizenship Proposal Faces Obstacle in Constitution," *New York Times,* 7 August 1996, A13.

65. Ronald Steel, "Internationalism Reconsidered," *Washington Post National Weekly,* 12–18 June 1995, 23.

66. *Works of the Rt. Hon. Edmund Burke* (Boston: Little, Brown, 1884), 3:359.

67. Michael Paul Rogin, "JFK: The Movie," *American Historical Review* 97 (1992) 502–5; Peter Applebome, "An Unlikely Legacy of the '60s: The Violent Right," *New York Times,* 7 May 1995, 1.

68. *Newsweek,* 8 July 1996, 50.

69. Frank McConnell, "Expecting Visitors?" *Commonweal,* 22 November 1996, 21–22; David Ansen, "Earth, You Have a Problem: Kaboooom!" *Newsweek,* 8 July 1996, 51.

70. Paul Berman, "Clinton Does Battle with Chicago '68," *New York Times,* 25 August 1996, E13; E.J. Dionne Jr., "Why the 60's Still Won't Go Away," *San Francisco Chronicle,* 27 August 1996, A19; Carol Muske Dukes, "When 'The System' Worked," *New York Times,* 30 May 1995, A17.

71. Although the Centennial Park bombing during the Olympics remains unexplained, the idea that it was connected to rightist fears of World Order is more plausible than most. *New York Times,* 28 July 1996, E12.

72. Dukes, "When 'The System' Worked."

73. *New York Times,* 9 May 1995, A18, and 11 May 1995, A1; Fox Butterfield, "Terror in Oklahoma: The Gun Lobby," *New York Times,* 8 May 1995, A17.

74. Todd Purdom, "Shifting Debate to the Political Climate, Clinton Condemns 'Promoters of Paranoia,'" *New York Times,* 25 April 1995, A19; *New York Times,* "Combustible Rhetoric," 27 April 1995, A24.

75. Dan Morgan, "A Revolution Derailed," *Washington Post National Weekly,* 28 October–3 November 1996, 21.

76. Ibid.

77. Richard Morin, "Not So Fast on Those Budget Cuts," *Washington Post National Weekly,* 22–28 May 1995, 37.

78. Ibid.

79. Ann Devroy and Ruth Marcus, "The Clutch Seems to Be Slipping," *Washington Post National Weekly*, 14–20 June 1993, 12; Richard Morin, "A Not-So-Bad Midterm Grade," *Washington Post National Weekly*, 20–26 February 1995, 37.

80. R.W. Apple, "The Selling of a Used President Gets Easier," *New York Times*, 2 April 1995, E1.

81. Richard Morin, "The Message from the Voters: Less Is More," *Washington Post National Weekly*, 21–27 November 1994, 8.

82. *New York Times*, 4 September 1995, 8.

83. Baker is quoted in Richard Berke, "Epic Realigments Often Aren't," *New York Times*, 1 January 1995, E3; E.J. Dionne Jr., "A Shift, Not a Mandate," *Washington Post National Weekly*, 28 November–4 December 1994, 28.

84. Adam Clymer, "Politics and the Dead Arts of Compromise," *New York Times*, 22 October 1995, E1.

85. The description of Gingrich comes from an admirer, Jeffrey Eisenach, explaining the Speaker's opposition to a proposed anti-smut rule for the Internet, which Dole favored. (Edmund L. Andrews, "Gingrich Opposes Smut Rule for Internet," *New York Times*, 22 June 1995, A20.) On the direction of Republican policy, see David Broder, "Is Gingrich a Democratic Mole?" *Washington Post National Weekly*, 3–9 April 1995, 4; and Robin Toner, "Coming Home from the Revolution," *New York Times*, 10 November 1996, E1.

86. Russell Baker, "Time for the Pain," *New York Times*, 13 May 1995, 19.

87. David Broder, "So Much for Fairness," *Washington Post National Weekly*, 2–8 October 1995, 4; Robert J. Samuelson, "And Principles," *Washington Post National Weekly*, 2–8 October 1995, 5; E.J. Dionne Jr., "Moynihan's Complaint," *Washington Post National Weekly*, 7–13 August 1995, 28. For O'Connor's comments, see *New York Times*, 5 March 1995, 24.

88. Richard Morin, "Fed Up with Welfare," *Washington Post National Weekly*, 29 April–5 May 1996, 37; Richard L. Berke, "Poll Finds Public Doubts Key Parts of GOP Agenda," *New York Times*, 28 February 1995, A21.

89. Adam Clymer, "A Big Risk for GOP," *New York Times*, 11 November 1995, 10; in a remarkably unfortunate image, one Republican operative, Bill McInturff, called Clinton a "hostage" to "terrorist" Republicans. Katharine Q. Seelye, "Wouldn't Mother Have Been Proud?" *New York Times*, 18 June 1995, E5.

90. Kuttner, "Case for Regulation"; Richard Morin, "A Shutdown with Few Winners, Many Losers," *Washington Post National Weekly*, 20–26 November 1995, 37.

91. Helen Dewar and Eric Planin, "Choosing Pragmatism over Partisanship," *Washington Post National Weekly*, 12–18 August 1996, 12.

92. Dionne, "A Shift, Not a Mandate"; Alfred Tuchfarber and Eric Rademacher, "The Republican Tidal Wave of 1994," *PS* 28 (1995): 689–96. Notably, there was no increase in the percentage of voters calling themselves Republicans. (Richard Berke, "Asked to Place Blame, Americans in Surveys Chose, All of the

Above," *New York Times,* 10 November 1994, B1.)

93. John Hart, "President Clinton and the Politics of Symbolism," *Political Science Quarterly* 110 (1995): 398; Adam Clymer, "Americans Have High Hopes for Clinton, Poll Finds," *New York Times,* 19 January 1993, A13; Robert DiClerico, "Assessing Context and Character," *Society,* September/October 1996, 29–31.

94. Adam Clymer, "The Hidden Antagonist of Clinton's Health Care Plan," *New York Times,* 19 June 1994, E1; David Broder, "A Presidential Seal of Disapproval," *Washington Post National Weekly,* 12–18 September 1994, 14; Charles O. Jones, "The Separated System," *Society,* September/October 1994, 18–24.

95. Howard Kurtz, "Over Easy on the Opposition," *Washington Post National Weekly,* 12–18 September 1994, 24.

96. Steven D. Stark, "Populist Revolt," *Providence Phoenix,* 11 November 1994, 12; Morin, "Message from the Voters."

97. Dionne, *They Only Look Dead;* William Raspberry detected a mandate to "fix" a government that wasn't working. "It Doesn't Work," *Washington Post National Weekly,* 28 November–4 December 1994, 28.

98. Stephen Skowronek, "The Risks of 'Third-Way' Politics," 32–36; E.J. Dionne Jr., "Clinton Swipes the GOP's Lyrics," *Washington Post National Weekly,* 29 July–6 August 1996, 22.

99. Walter Dean Burnham, "The 1996 Elections: Drift or Mandate?" *American Prospect,* July/August 1996, 43–49; Dionne, "Clinton Swipes the GOP's Lyrics."

100. Byron E. Shafer and William J.M. Claggett, *The Two Majorities: The Issue Context of Modern American Politics* (Baltimore: Johns Hopkins University Press, 1995).

101. Juan Williams, " 'Morning in America': The Sequel," *Washington Post National Weekly,* 20–26 November 1995, 23.

102. Mickey Kaus, "The Revival of Liberalism," *New York Times,* 9 August 1996, A27; Richard L. Berke, "Fulfilling a 1992 Promise, Capturing a 1996 Issue," *New York Times,* 1 August 1996, A25.

103. *New York Times,* 19 August 1996, B7.

104. Russell Baker, "The Charisma Chasm," *New York Times,* 23 April 1996, A23; Garry Wills, "One Sings, the Other Doesn't," *New York Times,* 14 May 1996, A23; *New York Times,* 11 March 1996, A16.

105. Adam Nagourney, "Dole Meets a Setback," *New York Times,* 18 April 1996, A1.

106. R.W. Apple, "Going 'Outside': Bold May Be Perilous," *New York Times,* 16 May 1996, A1; Morin and Brossard, "A Gamble That Isn't Paying Off—Yet;" Eric Schmitt, "GOP Seems Ready to Drop Political Fight," *New York Times,* 18 September 1996, B6.

107. Richard Cohen, "Not as Low as Yeltsin—Yet," *Washington Post National Weekly,* 17–23 June 1996, 28; Blane Harden, "The Changing Value of Bob Dole's 'Word,' " *Washington Post National Weekly,* 4–10 November 1996, 12.

Dole's resistance to fiscal demagoguery had led Harvey Mansfield to make him the example of "responsible conservatism." *America's Constitutional Soul* (Baltimore: Johns Hopkins University Press, 1991), 79–80.

108. On Dole's "bridge" image, see Russell Baker, "Surely He Is Spoofing," *New York Times,* 20 August 1996, A19.

109. Hobart Rowen, "The Job Ahead," *Washington Post National Weekly,* 6–12 December 1993, 5; Elizabeth Kolbert and Adam Clymer, "The Politics of Layoffs: In Search of a Message," *New York Times,* 8 March 1996, A1; Richard Goodwin, "Has Anybody Seen the Democratic Party?" *New York Times Magazine,* 25 August 1996, 33–36.

110. Louis Uchitelle, "President's Theme: Layoffs Fall and Wages Rise," *New York Times,* 27 July 1996, 8; *New York Times,* 5 March 1996, A19.

111. David Sanger, "Dole's Tax Message Heard, Not Heeded in Midwest City," *New York Times,* 18 September 1996, A1; Kolbert and Clymer, "Politics of Layoffs," A22.

112. Bradsher, "America's Opportunity Gap."

113. Helen Dewar and David Broder, "Giving Democrats a Cents of Unity," *Washington Post National Weekly,* 29 April–5 May 1996, 14.

114. Alan Blinder, "The Republican Riverboat Gamble," *New York Times,* 20 August 1996, A19; David Sanger, "Dole's Tax Message"; Steven Weisman, "The Return of Voodoo Politics," *New York Times,* 23 August 1996, A26.

115. Ruy Teixeira, "A Democratic Revival," *Boston Review,* October/November 1995, 36.

116. Goodwin, "Has Anybody Seen the Democratic Party?"; Joel Garreau, "Candidates Take Note," *Washington Post National Weekly,* 10–16 August 1992, 25.

117. Kevin Phillips, "The Voters Are Already Tapping Their Feet," *Washington Post National Weekly,* 21–27 November 1994, 23.

118. Alison Mitchell, "Clinton, in Midwest, Takes Page from Reagan's 'Morning in America,'" *New York Times,* 18 September 1996, A18; Todd Purdom, "Advisers See Bright Side in Criticism of First Lady," *New York Times,* 25 August 1996, 1.

119. David Maraniss, "Bill Clinton, Born to Run," *Washington Post National Weekly,* 20–26 June 1992, 6–7.

120. Richard Ford, "The Master of Ambiguity," *New York Times,* 17 October 1996, A17.

121. Richard Cohen, "Character Issue Fatigue," *Washington Post National Weekly,* 4–10 November 1996, 28.

122. See my essay "Losing— the Hard Way," *In These Times,* 10 June 1996, 22ff.

123. Harvey C. Mansfield Jr., *Machiavelli's Virtue* (Chicago: University of Chicago Press, 1996).

124. Dan Balz and David Broder, "The Clinton Republicans," *Washington Post National Weekly,* 14–20 October 1996, 11.

125. *The Federalist*, No. 63.

126. Herbert J. Storing, cd., *The Complete Anti-Federalist* (Chicago: University of Chicago Press, 1981), 2:111, 6:158.

127. Lowi, *End of the Republican Era;* Steven J. Rosenstone and John Mark Hansen, *Mobilization, Participation and Democracy in America* (New York: Macmillan, 1993), 218.

128. Kenneth N. Weine, "Campaigns without Human Faces," *Washington Post National Weekly*, 4–10 November 1996, 24; the privileged status of "soft money," of course, makes matters worse. Elizabeth Drew, "The 'Reform' That Corrupted the System," *Washington Post National Weekly*, 11–17 November 1996, 34.

129. Dan Balz, "In Control of His Own Fate," *Washington Post National Weekly*, 25–31 December 1995, 14; David Broder, "Not in Front of the Voters," *Washington Post National Weekly*, 14–20 October 1996, 10; *New York Times*, 6 March 1996, A1.

130. Henry E. Brady, Sidney Verba, and Kay Lehman Schlozman, "Beyond SES: A Resource Model of Political Participation," *American Political Science Review* 89 (1995): 271–94; James L. Hyland, *Democratic Theory: The Philosophical Foundations* (Manchester: Manchester University Press, 1995), 254, 264; Michael Wines, "Bradley's Exit Is Not Just the Democrats' Problem," *New York Times*, 20 August 1995, E1.

131. Thomas Byrne Edsall, *The New Politics of Inequality* (New York: Norton, 1984); Darrell M. West and Richard Francis, "Electronic Advocacy: Interest Groups and Public Policy Making," *PS* 29 (1996): 25–29; David Samuels, "Presidential Shrimp," *Harpers*, March 1996, 47.

132. 424 U.S. 1 (1976).

133. Drew, "The 'Reform' That Corrupted the System."

134. Cass R. Sunstein, *Democracy and the Problem of Free Speech* (New York: Free Press, 1993); John Rawls, *Political Liberalism* (Cambridge: Harvard University Press, 1993), 362–63.

135. Bill Bradley, "Congress Won't Act. Will You?" *New York Times*, 11 November 1996, A15.

136. Putnam, "Tuning In, Tuning Out," 677–81; Samuel Popkin, *The Reasoning Voter* (Chicago: University of Chicago Press, 1991), 226–31.

137. Walter Ong, *Orality and Literacy: The Technologizing of the Word* (London: Methuen, 1982).

138. Walter Goodman, "What's Bad for Politics Is Good for Television," *New York Times*, 27 November 1994, 33.

139. Michael Beschloss, "Let's Have Conventions with Cliffhangers," *New York Times*, 11 August 1996, E13; James Bennet, "GOP Readies a Made-for-TV Convention," *New York Times*, 8 August 1996, A1.

140. R.W. Apple, "Fleeing the Ghost of 1992," *New York Times*, 13 August 1996, A1.

141. Frank Rich, "San Diego Unplugged," *New York Times*, 17 August

1996, 19; Richard Sandomir, "With So Little to Report, There's Little to Watch," *New York Times,* 16 August 1996, A28; Christopher Reeve's appearance at the Democratic convention inspired a mild dissent from the rule. E.J. Dionne Jr., "Non-Pols Deliver the Message," *San Francisco Chronicle,* 28 August 1996, A19.

142. Thomas Patterson, "Bad News, Period," *PS* 29 (1996): 17–20.

143. Thomas Patterson, *Out of Order* (New York: Knopf, 1993); Richard Morin, "Keeping Watch on the Pollsters," *Washington Post National Weekly,* 18–24 November 1996, 37.

144. Richard Morin, "Tuned Out, Turned Off," *Washington Post National Weekly,* 5–11 February 1996, 6–8.

145. Dukes, "When 'The System' Worked"; Bill Moyers, "Old News and the New Civil War," *New York Times,* 22 March 1992, E15; Robert Entman, *Democracy without Citizens: The Media and the Decay of American Democracy* (New York: Oxford University Press, 1989).

146. *New York Times,* 13 March 1996, B7.

147. *New York Times,* 10 November 1994, B4.

148. Burnham, "The 1996 Elections," 45, 49; Lowi, *End of the Republican Era;* David Broder, "Is the Party Over?" *Washington Post National Weekly,* 19–25 August 1996, 21–22.

149. E.J. Dionne Jr., *Why Americans Hate Politics* (New York: Simon and Schuster, 1991).

150. Robert J. Samuelson, "Mixed Messages," *Washington Post National Weekly,* 19–25 August 1996, 5; David Rosenbaum, "Republicans Like Both Previews and Reruns," *New York Times,* 11 November 1994, E1.

151. Lisa Schiffren points out the shortcomings of a post-Reagan GOP, but without acknowledging how difficult it would be to replace Reagan himself. "Nixon's GOP Will Always Be a Loser," *New York Times,* 9 November 1996, 23.

152. For example, see *New York Times,* 19 December 1995, A20.

153. *New York Times,* 13 August 1996, A16, and 15 August 1996, A1.

154. Advocates of abortion rights, the *Times* reported, were notably "subdued" in voting to sustain Clinton's veto. *New York Times,* 27 September 1996, A20. On late-campaign relations between Dole and social conservatives, see Gustav Niebuhr, "Dole Gets Christian Coalition's Trust and Prodding," *New York Times,* 16 September 1996, A1.

155. Dan Balz, "For the Republicans, Was It Half Empty or Half Full?" *Washington Post National Weekly,* 18–24 November 1996, 11; the Iowa state platform is reported in the Rutgers *Daily Targum,* 8 October 1996, 7. On the concept of "subnational realignment," see Peter F. Nardulli, "The Concept of Critical Realignment, Electoral Behavior, and Political Change," *American Political Science Review* 89 (1995): 10–22.

156. David Broder, "Power to Both Parties," *Washington Post National Weekly,* 11–17 November 1996, 7–9.

157. Thomas Byrne Edsall, "But the Democrats Don't Seem to Get It Either," *Washington Post National Weekly,* 18–24 November 1996, 11.

158. Tuchfarber and Rademacher, "Republican Tidal Wave of 1994."

159. James Bennet, "Liberal Use of 'Extremist' Is the Winning Strategy," *New York Times,* 7 November 1996, B1. In the 6 October presidential debate, President Clinton stopped just short of directly disclaiming liberalism—he disdained "labels"—but he clearly thought the term no advantage, as in his comment regarding reductions in Medicare, "calling it conservative won't make it right." *New York Times,* 7 October 1996, B10.

160. William G. Mayer, *The Divided Democrats* (Boulder: Westview, 1996); Thomas Byrne Edsall, "The Revolt of the Discontented," *Washington Post National Weekly,* 21–27 November 1994, 28; Joseph M. Schwartz, *The Permanence of the Political: A Democratic Critique of the Radical Impulse to Transcend Politics* (Princeton: Princeton University Press, 1995).

161. Thomas Byrne Edsall and Dan Balz, "United They Stand—For Now," *Washington Post National Weekly,* 2–8 September 1996, 10–11.

162. For example, see Mickey Kaus, *The End of Equality* (New York: Basic Books, 1992).

163. Mansfield, "Change and Bill Clinton."

164. Dionne, *They Only Look Dead.* This persuasion is anything but monolithic. For two very different voices, see Michael Lind, *Up from Conservatism* (New York: Free Press, 1996); and Joshua Cohen and Joel Rogers, "After Liberalism?" *Boston Review,* April/May 1995, 20–23.

165. Michael Kazin, "The Workers' Party?" *New York Times,* 19 October 1995, A21; Goodwin, "Has Anybody Seen the Democratic Party?"; Robert Kuttner, "Will Clinton Pay His Union Dues?" *Washington Post National Weekly,* 18–24 November 1996, 5.

166. Edsall and Balz, "United They Stand—For Now," 11; E.J. Dionne Jr., "Work, Kids, and Families," *Washington Post National Weekly,* 30 September–6 October 1996, 29.

167. William Raspberry, "Less Heat, More Light," *Washington Post National Weekly,* 22–28 May 1995, 29; Wilson, *When Work Disappears;* Sam Roberts, "The Greening of America's Black Middle Class," *New York Times,* 18 June 1995, E1; Jennifer Hochschild, *Facing Up to the American Dream: Race, Class, and the Soul of a Nation* (Princeton: Princeton University Press, 1995).

168. Kevin Sack, "Victory of 5 Redistricted Blacks Recasts Gerrymandering Dispute," *New York Times,* 23 November 1996, 1; Charles Cameron, David Epstein, and Sharyn O'Halloran, "Do Majority-Minority Districts Maximize Substantive Black Representation in Congress?" *American Political Science Review* 90 (1996): 794–812.

169. Kaus, "Revival of Liberalism"; Peter Passell, "Economic Scene," *New York Times,* 8 August 1996, D2; E.J. Dionne Jr., "In the Wake of a Bogus Bill," *Washington Post National Weekly,* 12–18 August 1996, 26.

170. Dionne, *They Only Look Dead.* Dionne is not alone; witness Michael Lind's reference to a "new nationalism," with its echoes of TR: *The Next American Nation: The New Nationalism and the Fourth American Revolution* (New

York: Free Press, 1995).

171. Eldon J. Eisenach, *The Lost Promise of Progressivism* (Lawrence: University Press of Kansas, 1994).

172. See Philip Selznick's review of Rawls's *Political Liberalism* in *Society,* September/October 1994, 93; Hadley Arkes, *First Things: An Inquiry into the First Principles of Morals and Justice* (Princeton: Princeton University Press, 1986).

173. As Todd Gitlin observes, "postmodern" theory actually illustrates this principle because it characteristically "privileges" accounts from the victim's point of view, claims universality for the doctrine that all theories are only "standpoints," and hopes to *overcome* the cultural identities it often treats as impenetrable monads: "Where We're Coming From: Blinded Identities," *The Good Society* 6 (1996): 24–27; see also Ronald Beiner, *What's the Matter with Liberalism* (Berkeley: University of California Press, 1992.

174. Sandel, "The Search for a New Public Philosophy," 70.

APPENDIX

Second Inaugural Address

PRESIDENT WILLIAM JEFFERSON CLINTON

My fellow citizens,

At this last presidential inauguration of the twentieth century, let us lift our eyes toward the challenges that await us in the next century. It is our great good fortune that time and chance have put us not only at the edge of a new century, in a new millennium, but on the edge of a bright new prospect in human affairs—a moment that will define our course, and our character, for decades to come. We must keep our old democracy forever young. Guided by the ancient vision of a promised land, let us set our sights upon a land of new promise.

The promise of America was born in the eighteenth century out of the bold conviction that we are all created equal. It was extended and preserved in the nineteenth century, when our nation spread across the continent, saved the union, and abolished the awful scourge of slavery.

Then, in turmoil and triumph, that promise exploded onto the world stage to make this the American Century.

And what a century it has been. America became the world's mightiest industrial power; saved the world from tyranny in two world wars and a long cold war; and time and again, reached out across the globe to millions who, like us, longed for the blessings of liberty.

Along the way, Americans produced a great middle class and security in old age; built unrivaled centers of learning and opened public schools to all; split the atom and explored the heavens; invented the computer and the microchip; and deepened the wellspring of justice by making a revolution in civil rights for African Americans and all minorities, and extending the circle of citizenship, opportunity, and dignity to women.

Now, for the third time, a new century is upon us, and another time to choose. We began the nineteenth century with a choice, to spread our nation from coast to coast. We began the twentieth century with a choice, to harness the Industrial Revolution to our values of free enterprise, conservation, and human decency. Those choices made all the difference. At the dawn of the twenty-first century a free people must now choose to shape the forces of the Information Age and the global society, to unleash the limitless potential of all our people, and, yes, to form a more perfect union.

When last we gathered, our march to this new future seemed less certain than it does today. We vowed then to set a clear course to renew our nation.

In these four years, we have been touched by tragedy, exhilarated by challenge, strengthened by achievement. America stands alone as the world's indispensable nation. Once again, our economy is the strongest on Earth. Once again, we are building stronger families, thriving communities, better educational opportunities, a cleaner environment. Problems that once seemed destined to deepen now bend to our efforts: our streets are safer and record numbers of our fellow citizens have moved from welfare to work.

And once again, we have resolved for our time a great debate over the role of government. Today we can declare: Government is not the problem, and government is not the solution. We—the American people—we are the solution. Our founders understood that well and gave us a democracy strong enough to endure for centuries, flexible enough to face our common challenges and advance our common dreams in each new day.

As times change, so government must change. We need a new government for a new century—humble enough not to try to solve all our problems for us, but strong enough to give us the tools to solve our problems for ourselves; a government that is smaller, lives within its means, and does more with less. Yet where it can stand up for our values and interests in the world, and where it can give Americans the power to make a real difference in their everyday lives, government should do more, not less. The preeminent mission of our new government is to give all Americans an opportunity—not a guarantee, but a real opportunity—to build better lives.

Beyond that, my fellow citizens, the future is up to us. Our founders taught us that the preservation of our liberty and our union depends upon responsible citizenship. And we need a new sense of responsibility for a new century. There is work to do, work that government alone cannot do: teaching children to read; hiring people off welfare rolls; coming out from behind locked doors and shuttered windows to help reclaim our streets from drugs and gangs and crime; taking time out of our own lives to serve others.

Each and every one of us, in our own way, must assume personal responsibility—not only for ourselves and our families, but for our neighbors and our nation. Our greatest responsibility is to embrace a new spirit of community for a new century. For any one of us to succeed, we must succeed as one America.

The challenge of our past remains the challenge of our future—will we be one nation, one people, with one common destiny, or not? Will we all come together, or come apart?

The divide of race has been America's constant curse. And each new wave of immigrants gives new targets to old prejudices. Prejudice and contempt, cloaked in the pretense of religious or political conviction are no different. These forces have nearly destroyed our nation in the past. They plague us still. They fuel the fanaticism of terror. And they torment the lives of millions in fractured nations all around the world.

These obsessions cripple both those who hate and, of course, those who are hated, robbing both of what they might become. We cannot, we will not, succumb to the dark impulses that lurk in the far regions of the soul everywhere. We shall overcome them. And we shall replace them with the generous spirit of a people who feel at home with one another.

Our rich texture of racial, religious, and political diversity will be a Godsend in the twenty-first century. Great rewards will come to those who can live together, learn together, work together, forge new ties that bind together.

As this new era approaches we can already see its broad outlines. Ten years ago, the Internet was the mystical province of physicists; today, it is a commonplace encyclopedia for millions of schoolchildren. Scientists now are decoding the blueprint of human life. Cures for our most feared illnesses seem close at hand.

The world is no longer divided into two hostile camps. Instead, now we are building bonds with nations that once were our adversaries. Growing connections of commerce and culture give us a chance to lift the fortunes and spirits of people the world over. And for the very first time in all of history, more people on this planet live under democracy than dictatorship.

My fellow Americans, as we look back at this remarkable century, we may ask, can we hope not just to follow, but even to surpass the achievements of the twentieth century in America and to avoid the awful bloodshed that stained its legacy? To that question, every American here and every American in our land today must answer a resounding "Yes."

This is the heart of our task. With a new vision of government, a new sense of responsibility, a new spirit of community, we will sustain America's journey. The promise we sought in a new land we will find again in a land of new promise.

In this new land, education will be every citizen's most prized possession. Our schools will have the highest standards in the world, igniting the spark of possibility in the eyes of every girl and every boy. And the doors of higher education will be open to all. The knowledge and power of the Information Age will be within reach not just of the few, but of every classroom, every library, every child. Parents and children will have time not only to work, but to read and play together. And the plans they make at their kitchen table will be those of a better home, a better job, the certain chance to go to college.

Our streets will echo again with the laughter of our children, because no one will try to shoot them or sell them drugs anymore. Everyone who can work, will work, with today's permanent under class part of tomorrow's growing middle class. New miracles of medicine at last will reach not only those who can claim care now, but the children and hardworking families too long denied.

We will stand mighty for peace and freedom, and maintain a strong defense against terror and destruction. Our children will sleep free from the threat of nuclear, chemical, or biological weapons. Ports and airports, farms and factories will thrive with trade and innovation and ideas. And the world's greatest democracy will lead a whole world of democracies.

Our land of new promise will be a nation that meets its obligations—a nation that balances its budget, but never loses the balance of its values. A nation where our grandparents have secure retirement and health care, and their grandchildren know we have made the reforms necessary to sustain those benefits for their time. A nation that fortifies the world's most productive economy even as it protects the great natural bounty of our water, air, and majestic land.

And in this land of new promise, we will have reformed our politics so that the voice of the people will always speak louder than the din of narrow interests—regaining the participation and deserving the trust of all Americans.

Fellow citizens, let us build that America, a nation ever moving forward toward realizing the full potential of all its citizens. Prosperity and power—yes, they are important, and we must maintain them. But let us never forget: The greatest progress we have made, and the greatest progress we have yet to make, is in the human heart. In the end, all the world's wealth and a thousand armies are no match for the strength and decency of the human spirit.

Thirty-four years ago, the man whose life we celebrate today spoke to us down there, at the other end of this Mall, in words that moved the conscience of a nation. Like a prophet of old, he told of his dream that one day America would rise up and treat all its citizens as equals before the law and in the heart. Martin Luther King's dream was the American Dream. His quest is our quest: the ceaseless striving to live out our true creed. Our history has been built on such dreams and labors. And by our dreams and labors we will redeem the promise of America in the twenty-first century.

To that effort I pledge all my strength and every power of my office. I ask the members of Congress here to join in that pledge. The American people returned to office a President of one party and a Congress of another. Surely, they did not do this to advance the politics of petty bickering and extreme partisanship they plainly deplore. No, they call on us instead to be repairers of the breach, and to move on with America's mission.

America demands and deserves big things from us—and nothing big ever came from being small. Let us remember the timeless wisdom of Cardinal Bernardin, when facing the end of his own life. He said: "It is wrong to waste the precious gift of time, on acrimony and division."

Fellow citizens, we must not waste the precious gift of this time. For all of us are on that same journey of our lives, and our journey, too, will come to an end. But the journey of our America must go on.

And so, my fellow Americans, we must be strong, for there is much to dare. The demands of our time are great and they are different. Let us meet them with faith and courage, with patience and a grateful and happy heart. Let us shape the hope of this day into the noblest chapter in our history. Yes, let us build our bridge. A bridge wide enough and strong enough for every American to cross over to a blessed land of new promise.

May those generations whose faces we cannot yet see, whose names we may never know, say of us here that we led our beloved land into a new century with the American Dream alive for all her children; with the American promise of a more perfect union a reality for all her people; with America's bright flame of freedom spreading throughout all the world.

From the height of this place and the summit of this century, let us go forth. May God strengthen our hands for the good work ahead—and always, always bless our America.

THE SECOND CLINTON ADMINISTRATION
(* = INCUMBENT)

Position Name	Age	Residence	Occupation	Previous experience	Education
PRESIDENT *William J. Clinton	50	Arkansas	Lawyer	Governor of Arkansas	A.B., Georgetown; Rhodes Scholar, Oxford; J.D., Yale
VICE-PRESIDENT *Albert A. Gore Jr.	48	Tennessee	Journalist	U.S. Senator, U.S. Representative	A.B., Harvard
SECRETARY OF STATE Madeleine Korbel Albright	59	Maryland	Political scientist	Ambassador to United Nations	A.B., Wellesley; M.A., Ph.D., Columbia
SECRETARY OF TREASURY *Robert E. Rubin	58	New York	Investment banker	Chair, National Economic Council	A.B., Harvard; LL.B., Yale
SECRETARY OF DEFENSE William S. Cohen	56	Maine	Lawyer, novelist	U.S. Senator, U.S. Representative	A.B., Bowdoin; J.D., Boston University
ATTORNEY-GENERAL *Janet Reno	58	Florida	Lawyer	State Attorney, Miami, Florida	A.B., Cornell; J.D., Harvard
SECRETARY OF THE INTERIOR *Bruce Babbitt	58	Arizona	Lawyer	Governor of Arizona	B.S, Notre Dame; M. Phil., Newcastle; J.D., Harvard

Position / Name	Age	State	Profession	Role	Education
SECRETARY OF AGRICULTURE *Daniel R. Glickman	52	Kansas	Lawyer	U.S. Representative	A.B., Michigan; J.D., George Washington
SECRETARY OF COMMERCE William M. Daley	48	Illinois	Lawyer, banker	CEO, Amalgamated Bank of Chicago	A.B., Loyola; LL.B., John Marshall Law School
SECRETARY OF LABOR Alexis M. Herman	49	Alabama	Employment manager	Director, Women's Bureau; Director, White House Office of Public Liaison	A.B., Xavier
SECRETARY OF HEALTH AND HUMAN SERVICES *Donna E. Shalala	55	Wisconsin	Political scientist	Chancellor, U. of Wisconsin	A.B., Western College for Women; Ph.D., Syracuse
SECRETARY OF HOUSING AND URBAN DEVELOPMENT Andrew M. Cuomo	39	New York	Lawyer	Assistant Secretary; Chair, New York City Committee on the Homeless	A.B., Fordham; J.D., Albany
SECRETARY OF TRANSPORTATION Rodney E. Slater	41	Arkansas	Lawyer	Federal Highway Administrator; Chair, Arkansas State Highway Commission	B.S., Eastern Michigan; J.D., Arkansas

Continued . . .

THE SECOND CLINTON ADMINISTRATION — *Continued*

Position Name	Age	Residence	Occupation	Previous experience	Education
SECRETARY OF EDUCATION *Richard W. Riley	63	South Carolina	Lawyer	Governor of South Carolina	A.B., Furman; J.D., University of South Carolina
SECRETARY OF ENERGY Frederico F. Peña	49	Colorado	Lawyer	Secretary of Transportation; Mayor, Denver	A.B., LL.B., University of Texas, Austin
SECRETARY OF VETERANS AFFAIRS *Jesse Brown	52	District of Columbia	Administrator	Director, Disabled American Veterans	Chicago City College
WHITE HOUSE CHIEF OF STAFF Erskine Bowles	51	North Carolina	Banker	Small Business Administrator; Deputy Chief of Staff	A.B., North Carolina; M.B.A., Columbia
DIRECTOR OF THE BUDGET *Franklin D. Raines	48	Washington, D.C.	Banker	Deputy Director of Budget; Vice-Chair, Federal National Mortgage Association (FNMA)	A.B., J.D., Harvard

Position / Name	Age	State	Profession	Prior Position	Education
DIRECTOR OF CENTRAL INTELLIGENCE W. Anthony Lake	57	Massachusetts	Political scientist	National Security Adviser	B.A, Harvard; Ph.D., Princeton
AMBASSADOR TO THE UNITED NATIONS William B. Richardson	49	New Mexico	Politics, diplomacy	U.S. Representative	A.B., Tufts; M.A., Fletcher School
NATIONAL SECURITY ADVISER Samuel R. Berger	51	Washington, D.C.	Lawyer	Deputy National Security Adviser	A.B., Cornell; J.D., Harvard
CHAIR, NATIONAL ECONOMIC COUNCIL Gene Sperling	37	Massachusetts	Public policy administration	Deputy Director	A.B, Minnesota; J.D., Yale
ADMINISTRATOR, E.P.A. *Carol M. Browner	41	Florida	Lawyer	Florida Secretary of Environment	A.B., J.D., University of Florida
U.S. TRADE REPRESENTATIVE Charlene Barshefsky	47	Illinois	Lawyer	Deputy Representative	A.B., Wisconsin; J.D., Catholic University

Index